THE WINDS OF YOUR HEART

Where these words come from makes all the difference in the world. Do they come from my head? No. They come from my heart. And that is what you're really after.

—Emahó

THE WINDS OF YOUR HEART

Emahó

Sequoyah Publishing
Pacific Grove, California

Published by
Sequoyah Publishing
P. O. Box 814
Pacific Grove, California 93950

Copyright © 2005 by Emahó
All rights reserved. No part of this book may be reproduced or utilized in any form or by any means, electronic or mechanical, including photocopying, recording, or by any information storage and retrieval system, without permission in writing from the publisher.

Editor: Marianne Riedman, Ph.D.
Designer: The Woods Publishing Group

First Edition
1 2 3 4 5 6 7 8 9 10

Publisher's Cataloging-in-Publication Data
Emahó.
The winds of your heart / by Emahó. — 1st ed.
p. cm.
LCCN: 2005924258
1. Spiritual life. 2. Self-realization—Religious aspects.
3. Conduct of life. I. Title.
BL624.E467 2005 204 QBI05-200098

ISBN 0-9648600-2-3

For information on Emahó, please visit his website:
www.emaho.ws

Photo Credits: Jöerg Müller
(www.aarauposters.com)

To order CDs of Emahó's workshops,
contact Ingrid Kwirant (kwirant@snafu.de)

To the people of Europe who have come to my workshops over the years, for they have taught me far more than I have taught them.

Acknowledgements

I wish to thank to the following individuals for their help and support: Crystal Accola, Tine Bender, Nicholas Bolton, Michael and Andrea Buchanan, Gaba Dornier, Marge Evans, Sasha Govorova, Dee Haner, Torsten Hausamann, Lori Hendricks, Stefan and Verena Hespeler, Annette Hoctor, Ed Jarvis, Alison Jones, Helena Karger, Jill Kirkpatrick, Ingrid Kwirant, Peter and Jing-Yng Chen Lienhard, Jayne Mitchell, Doris Müller, Jöerg and Margaret Müller, Joe Parente, Ron and Jane Rieck, Marie-Claude Rives, Evelyn Hürlimann Rohr, Myra Schläpfer, Linda Sivertsen, Alan Vitous, Sara Wilbourne, Kathleen Wise, and Linda Wood. My sincerest thanks especially goes to Martin Bossart, Amanda Kochhar, and Rainer Wiest, who have made my workshops in Europe possible. Finally, I wish to express my deepest gratitude to all the current European workshop coordinators: Martine Chartrain, Rose Comyn, Marisa Fornillo, Andreas Gehring, Irène Heidelberger, Dieter Hoelken, Eva Hofinger, Heidi Hostettler, Patricia Mitchell, Marianne Moser, Bernard Pedrono, Leslie Robertson, Annette Schaefer-Seidel, Bettina Schroeter, and Sabine and Wolfgang Vollmar.

What is most important to remember is to get your heart activated, because then it becomes a transmitter, sending out radar signals to life. There is no greater antenna out there than your own heart. There is no greater telephone system than what you have in your own heart.

—Emahó

Editor's Note

These chapters were created from transcriptions of Emahó's lectures in Europe and America, as well as from material he prepared specifically for this book, the first in a series, which represents but a small sample of Emahó's substantial body of work.

Table of Contents

1. Glass Houses 1
2. Getting Connected 23
3. Prayer 59
4. The Living Sacraments 87
5. The Petrol Station 117
6. Find Something to Love 137
7. Hurt and Disappointment 151
8. Forgiveness 175
9. What Lasts Forever? 191
10. The Preciousness of Life 217
11. Becoming a Better Sailor 243

CHAPTER 1

GLASS HOUSES

Do you think you have your little secrets? Do you think you can hide behind a tree? Life sees you.

I'd like to tell you a story about something that happened to me long ago, which began to open up worlds I never knew existed, realities I never could have fathomed. This story, along with the other stories and reflections on life that I offer in this simple book, is very personal to me, and I share it with you from my heart, in the hope that it will begin to open up new worlds for you, too.

Going back twenty or thirty years, I didn't have any beliefs in an afterlife or anything of a spiritual nature. I thought all this was simply a figment of one's imagination. I had no faith in any realities other than those I had been taught by my teachers, my parents, or my community. Do you know those men who are extremely logical, even reasonable to the point of being a little neurotic? Well, I was one of them.

I also had a hard time believing in the existence of anything I could not see, hear, or touch. If I could see it and understand it, all right. If not, it didn't exist. As a result, I always made things hard on myself, because I was constantly demanding proof of what was unseen and unknown to my mind. Sometimes my stubbornness paid off. I knew it was healthy to question and doubt, at least until my naiveness subsided and I had the wisdom to see on my own. But the stubbornness also gave me heartache that I didn't quite understand at the time. It created great distance with my feelings, and even prevented me from reading the books of certain philosophers and teachers who could have helped me and opened up my world much more.

During this time in my life — despite my stubbornness, my skeptical mind, and all my doubts — I was going through an internal process of waking up from ordinary existence, you could say, which was showing me that there was far more to life than I knew. I hadn't asked for this process to take place, yet it was happening, whether I liked it or not. There was nothing I could do to stop it. And this process was happening very quickly and intensely.

To make a long story short, it left me confused, anxious, and wondering if what was happening to me was real or if I was making it up. "Is there goodness in it?" I wondered. I didn't really know. I didn't have much discretion at the time. So I was constantly searching for answers, trying to make sense of it all. "What is life?" "Who am I?" "What's happening to me?"

What especially confused me was this: I knew who I was — as a citizen, as a young man living in society. I was a typical, average American man with good self-esteem. And at the time, I didn't see how it could be in my destiny to have the kind of wisdom I was beginning to develop. It was as though the mailman had delivered this package to the wrong house. There was no doubt in my mind — wrong house! But I had already opened up the package.

All the teachers I met were also baffled when they came across me, because they couldn't understand why I had this "gift," as they put it, which was coming through so strongly and seemed to be touching the hearts of many other people who came into contact with me. But they all felt that the transformation that was taking place within me, although unusual, was very good.

Still, a number of people who knew me didn't think it made sense that this gift should have come to me. "It can't be good," they said. "Why you? There's nothing different about you. You're ordinary." Yet other people were supporting me. "This process is real," they told me. "I don't know how it came about, but it is happening and it's good."

So there was a big debate going on, and I was at the center of it. As a result, I became confused. I didn't know who to believe. And it put a tremendous amount of doubt into my mind about what was happening to me.

"Who in the world can I trust?" I asked myself. "There has to be a way to find out if this process is good or not." Because I felt that I couldn't completely trust myself at that time, as well as most of the people around me, I decided to point my eyes to the East, to established teachers that Westerners call "gurus." After all the research I'd done, I had found that these holy men and women had a great deal of authority through the lineages they embodied. I knew they would have an understanding of this unusual process that was happening to me.

So I said to life from my heart: "All right. I will only trust gurus from India to tell me the truth — nobody else. If this process is real and if it's good, I want validation from people I know I can rely on. If you give me seven gurus from India, and they all acknowledge me, then you've got me. If you don't give me seven, if you only give me six — forget it. But give me seven and I'll walk with you."

Ordinarily, I never would have put myself in a position to seek out any kind of guru. I didn't like to do that sort of thing. It just didn't interest me. And I definitely knew I didn't want to follow any guru or spiritual teacher. What I was really doing was testing life.

I knew life couldn't meet my challenge — or so I thought: "It's going to take fifteen or twenty years to give me seven gurus, maybe even the rest of my life. So I've got my life back. I'm free!" Yet I also knew that if this was a sincere and true process, life would go to extraordinary lengths to meet my request, because it would help bring peace to my mind, and peace is a necessary element to bring in and hold wisdom when it comes. And I realized that whatever process was transforming me from within worked in conjunction with my personality, my thoughts, and my feelings. You could say that it needed me. And I still had my free will.

To some degree, I could delay the process for as long as I wished. I could create detours—small detours or very long, arduous detours.

Some of my close friends realized that I was going through a very difficult process, and they were always trying to help me in any way they could. One of my friends knew a Sikh guru from India called Yogi Bhajan, who lived in Española, New Mexico.

"You have to go see this teacher," she said. "I know he can help you. And he's giving a retreat soon." From what I knew of this guru, he was a good man, and I also thought he might be able to help me. A number of my friends wanted to see this teacher, too, so we packed up two cars and took off to New Mexico, which was a two-day drive from Santa Cruz, California, where we were all living. This was in 1985.

When we arrived at Yogi Bhajan's ashram in New Mexico, we registered for the retreat and began to settle in. We found ourselves among about five hundred of his students who were all wearing white robes and turbans, although most of them were Americans. Only about thirty of us were dressed in plain Western clothes, so we stood out. We felt a little like outsiders.

I decided to wait a few days before approaching the guru, even though I wasn't sure exactly how I would go about asking for confirmation from him. I could tell that Yogi Bhajan was someone who could see well. I knew I could trust him. As the retreat progressed, we all felt that he had touched our hearts and helped us a great deal. Although I was happy to be attending this retreat and receiving the blessings and teachings, I knew I couldn't be a Sikh. That just wasn't me.

After we had been there for four or five days, I said to life, "Okay, this is the day I want acknowledgement from the guru. Let's see if he will tell me whether this process is real and valid."

After Yogi Bhajan finished teaching in the afternoon, he would walk out the back door of the large tent where everyone gathered and head toward his house, which was about two or three hundred meters away.

He always walked along the same path, and each day there would be crowds of people lined up all along the path to get his blessings. Not wanting to be intrusive, I hung back. I didn't want to bother him or insist that he give me an answer. So I stood about a hundred feet back from the path and waited for him to come out of the tent. It seemed impossible that the guru would go so far out of his way to acknowledge me. I'd never seen him do that before with anyone.

"All right life, here it is," I thought. "I want confirmation about this process. If he acknowledges me, then I will believe." After a few moments, Yogi Bhajan appeared and began to walk along the path. Part of me wanted him to continue walking, and yet at the same time I was hoping that he would at least look at me and give me a smile.

Suddenly Yogi Bhajan stopped, looked over at me, and walked all the way over to where I was standing. When he reached me he took my hands in his, looked into my eyes and smiled.

"Everything is going to be all right," he reassured me. "You're doing a good job. You're doing a *very* good job. Don't worry. *Everything will be all right.*" Then he rubbed my head and gave me a blessing, smiled at me once more, and walked away. I was stunned. Yet I also found myself feeling happy and relieved.

Yogi Bhajan was the first guru I encountered. It took a while, but within about seven or eight months, I met a number of other gurus from India — one after the other — and within two years, I had been approached by all seven. And in every case, I didn't seek out the gurus. The right set of circumstances just happened to come about to put me in their path. All of the gurus told me the same thing: "Everything will be all right. You're doing a good job. Don't worry. It's *all right*. You're doing a good job. It's all right."

Yogi Bhajan's acknowledgement affected me a great deal, but it was still hard for me to take it in. After two or three more gurus acknowledged me, I began to feel reassured, but even then, my mind still had some reservations. "Maybe I'll believe," I thought. "Maybe." But after I came across all seven, I finally let go of my doubts. Over the next several years, as the process of awakening continued to develop within me, and life kept speaking to me in ways that were so very personal, I found that I was able to let go and trust life even more.

The Barrio

Just because we have a thick skull doesn't mean that life doesn't see. Life hears every thought. Life knows every feeling. Everything is observed.

There is more to the story than I've told you so far. Something I'll never forget happened on the way to see Yogi Bhajan, something that affected me for years, and this is perhaps the most significant part of the story. On the trip to New Mexico, we decided to drive down the coast to Los Angeles and then head east to the desert. Los Angeles is a very big place with lots of confusing freeways, and as we were driving through the city, our two cars became separated. Then we got lost.

In our frustration, we decided to take the next exit to get our bearings, and we happened to find ourselves in a part of Los Angeles known as the "barrio." The barrio is a very poor section of the city where a lot of Latinos live together. Many are Mexicans who crossed the border illegally. Tens of thousands were living in this small area. I had never seen the barrio before, but I'd heard about it.

As we were cruising through the streets of the barrio, looking for a gas station, everyone in the car became very quiet. It looked like the aftermath of a war. Everything was destroyed. Trash was everywhere. Broken glass and beer cans littered the ground. It was shocking. All the houses and buildings were falling apart. Windows were hanging off their hinges. The walls were dirty. People were walking around with no care or respect whatsoever. We drove past block after block like this.

It reminded me of certain areas in Mexico that I'd visited. But to see this in America was appalling.

As I witnessed this devastation, I found myself passing judgment on these Mexicans. I was very hard on them for destroying their community here in America. My anger wasn't directed at the Mexican people themselves, but at their mentality. It troubled me that they could bring their poverty and "no care" attitude into America, where it was growing and beginning to destroy the country.

At this time my heart was starting to open and the theme was: *don't judge — understand*. So I could feel this dichotomy working within me. I knew it wasn't right to judge these people — not the way I was doing it. Yet I couldn't seem to stop it. I felt justified. "But they deserve it. Look what they're doing to America. To themselves. Shame on them!" And here I was, on my way to see this wonderful, enlightened holy man not only to find out about this process that was consuming my life, but also to learn about goodness and love, compassion, and opening the heart — except that now I had this excess baggage in my pocket.

Finally we made our way out of Los Angeles. We never did find the other car, but we knew where to meet up in New Mexico, so we decided to head east and continue on with our trip. Late that night we checked into a motel in Arizona. If you've ever been to Arizona or New Mexico, you'll see just one motel, like this one, and not much else for hundreds of miles. We were surrounded by nothing but desert, lizards, and coyotes.

Being summertime, it was extremely hot. After being stuck in a car full of people who had been talking nonstop all day, I was tired and needed a break from everybody. So I decided to get out of my room, go for a walk out in the desert, and just be with the stars for a while. I walked far enough away so that nobody would see me. I didn't want to talk to *anybody* or hear anybody's voice. I just wanted to cool off and rest my mind. So I sat alone in the darkness for a few moments, airing myself out and trying to relax.

Suddenly I noticed a man, obviously somewhat drunk, walking out of the motel. It looked like he'd had a few beers. By the way he was positioning himself, I could see that he was looking for someone to talk to in this desert.

"Oh god, I *hope* he doesn't see me," I said to myself. But even though I was way out there in the dark, he spotted me. And headed right toward me.

"You look like a nice guy to talk to," he said. "Let's talk." I didn't say anything. He didn't ask my name or where I was from, he just started talking. He happened to be a geologist who worked for one of the petroleum companies. I could see that he was an educated man in his late fifties or early sixties, quite a bit taller than I was. Nice man.

After a few minutes, he starting telling me about his adventures in World War II. He had fought in Japan, as my father had, so I began to get a little more interested. His war stories were good. Still, I didn't say much. I just listened.

All of a sudden, something odd began to happen to this man. His staggering stopped and the drunkenness completely left his mind and body. He stood up very straight and looked down at me. It even seemed as though he grew an inch or two. The expression on his face completely changed, becoming very serious. His eyes dilated and started to grow with intensity. Looking right into my eyes, he said, "Emahó, even people in the barrio have a heart." As he said this, he moved his head down very close to mine and glared at me sternly.

Then just as abruptly as this presence had come in, it suddenly left him and he went back into his drunken state and continued his war stories. I realized that this man did not know what he had done.

I was shocked. This was not supposed to happen. My mother never told me anything about this. I never read about this in a book. I never even thought about the possibility. But it happened. I was so confused. Angry. Frustrated. And scared down to my bones, because of the implications of what had just taken place. It showed me that I was always being watched. Always. I couldn't hide in the closet. I couldn't hide in the basement. I could not conceal my thoughts and feelings from life. This I did not like one bit. All my most private moments. All my ideas. All my wishes. All my dreams. Exposed. Thrown on the table for life to see. I didn't want to believe it. My pride and ego sank all the way down to the bottom of my feet. It felt as though I were stripped naked.

What bothered me wasn't that I had just witnessed proof that there's more to life than what I knew. It wasn't the reprimand about my judgments in the barrio. I didn't care about that. What I cared about was that someone or something could see inside my head, reading all my thoughts. I had no privacy. None. That's what I minded.

It was a different matter when I asked life for validation from the gurus, because I put the challenge out there intentionally. I thought I could be selective about what I chose to broadcast out to life and what I chose to hide. But it looked like that wasn't the case.

"My god," I realized. "I'm an open book! My mind, my thinking, my personal secrets: all reside within a glass house. And it's not just me. We are all glass houses." Just because we have a thick skull doesn't mean that life doesn't see. Life hears every thought. Life knows every feeling. Everything is observed. We just kind of pretend we aren't seen. Yet there's no fooling anybody, really. It is very much like this: if you've ever been a parent, you know when your children are lying. It's obvious. But the children think you don't know.

We are open broadcasting stations. But it is much more profound than just words going out. Our pictures and stories are emanating out of us by the moment. Do you think you have your little secrets? Do you think you can hide behind a tree? Life sees you.

I had no idea what "life" was at the time. But I knew there was something far bigger going on here than I could comprehend. "I mean, is life that big?" I wondered. "Is life really that alive? Do angels actually exist, and do they really hear our innermost feelings?"

It took at least two years for me to work through this experience until I could acknowledge it with no fear or anxiety, because the reality was so harsh and so profound. It was very hard on my personality. For many months after this happened, I was furious. It felt as though my life had been stolen from me.

"Whatever's inside this skull is my business," I said to life. "You're only supposed to hear it if I speak it. You're only supposed to see it if I demonstrate it. You've violated my personal rights." I even went through a stage of rebellion: "I don't care. Watch me be nasty."

After stomping around for a while, I found that it wasn't doing me any good whatsoever. Once I stopped having pity for myself, I realized that there was nothing I could do about the phenomenon of the glass house. So even though I didn't like it, I came to terms with the situation: that's just the way it is. I became very careful with my feelings and thoughts. And I began to think about this predicament: "If we all live in glass houses, and if life is actually alive, maybe there's some good in it." So I decided to find out what this was all about.

When I reflected back on my experience in the desert, as well as with Yogi Bhajan, I realized that it opened up and exposed three unique and separate dimensions. One was the dimension of my innermost thoughts and feelings. The second was the external world I live in — the drunken man standing before me, talking, who suddenly completely changed before my eyes, and the gurus who went out of their way to speak to me and reassure me with the same words. The third was the existence of something invisible and unknown that is always in touch with the first two dimensions: my internal world and my external world. So a third dimension was revealed that was not just of spirit, but an environment that encompasses all of life. Later on, I discovered that it is this third dimension that one can develop a relationship with by means of contemplation, understanding, honesty, and simply speaking to life from one's heart. This relationship in turn will affect the first two dimensions.

For a while, I was still confused. "If you see and hear everything, then where were you when I was lost? Where were you when I didn't have that map? Where were you when I was crying? When I needed you?" It took a number of years for me to realize that life is always there. Always. We are all loved *so much*. But what is in our minds? Where do we turn our attention? To this third dimension? To the goodness of life? Or to our dramas, our heartaches, and our belief that nothing is there, that life is nothing special? Yet life is a miracle. But most of us cannot see the miracle, the aliveness, of ordinary life.

In time, I began to look at life differently. I saw that there is so much more to life than I could perceive with my eyes or understand with my mind. And this is where faith came in for me. I realized that life was alive, with an intelligence that was incomprehensible. I found myself wondering what it would be like to see through the eyes of life instead of only through my own eyes. And I came to understand that life itself was something I could have a personal relationship with — as personal as the relationship with my children, my friends, my lover — and that no matter how alone I felt, how lost or confused I was, I could always turn to life for help.

Our Flags

What message do you want to broadcast out to life with your flags?
What kind of people do you want to attract? This is up to you.

If we are glass houses to life, does that mean we are also glass houses to each other? *Yes.* The true nature of human beings is that we all see and hear one another on the various subtle levels. We *really* do. It's truly amazing. In essence, we are so psychic it's unbelievable, although some of us see and sense better than others. Within the subtle realities, thoughts and feelings are always traveling from one person to the other, like tiny missiles being launched, and those who have developed their inner seeing can actually observe this. Yet for most of us, this kind of seeing hasn't

THE WINDS OF YOUR HEART

seeped up to a conscious level. We rely on our eyes and ears, for this is how we have been taught to perceive. As a result, we practically play dumb when, in reality, we know who someone is inside. We can tell what is taking place beneath the nice suit or fancy dress. We cannot really hide from each other. But we pretend we can. A predicament.

All human beings have a vast antenna to hear not just the voices coming through people's mouths, but also to hear their minds. We can hear silent feelings and emotions. And this isn't intuition. We have senses that can immediately detect if a person walking through the door wants something. Sometimes we can tell if a person is a crook. Sometimes we can tell if a person is someone we want to marry. We hear this subtle language. It's just that most people don't pay attention to it.

It is one's silence that really speaks. That's what I pay attention to when I'm talking with people. It's not what you say, but what the inner part of you is saying. Any good friend or good teacher will pay attention to that as well. Mothers do it easily. Fathers have a more difficult time hearing the silent language of their children. But mothers naturally know what their children are saying. It is the same with you and life.

In essence, human beings are like ships at sea, each flying a different set of flags. What flag were you born under? Your nationality is only *one* of your flags. What other flags were you born under? Your mother, your father, your grandma and grandpa. After reaching a certain age, maybe you've acquired a flag of hurt or disappointment. We each have a lot of different flags on our ships at sea.

For instance, there's a common flag that we are all very used to — the flag of attraction. We've seen the magic of it. Someone could be clear across a room and...zoom! We zero in on her. Or him. And no one else notices the flag of attraction but that particular person. Then sometimes we look away and pretend we didn't see it. Or we start to feel shy.

Why do these particular flags suddenly become so apparent? Because there is an emotional charge in them. They're full of life.

Whether the person who's waving the flag is nicely dressed or not, the charge is still there.

These flags are quite real to the inner mind. Subconsciously we *see* them inside. Yet people try to hide with all kinds of strategies: suits, make-up, nice hair styles, smiles. Think back to a time in your past when you walked into a particular situation and something inside you said: "You'd better not..." But the suit and tie were so nice. You bought the outer appearance. You saw the flag, yet you did it anyway. And I know that practically everyone has experienced times like these.

In business, in the workplace, flags are constantly affecting everyone. What kind of flags do you have up when a customer comes in? What kind of flags do you have up, as an employee? When you have a gripe, a complaint, a particular state of mind that is inappropriate in some way, even if you're trying to hide it as well as you can, the flag is still there because the emotional charge is activating it.

When you're carrying around inappropriate attitudes, inappropriate feelings toward life or certain people, they can build up into a particular "personality" to the point that it becomes a neurosis—a flag of skull and crossbones. When you raise that flag, everybody sees it on your face. Then let's say that you walk into a job interview and ask, "Can I have a job?" What do you think will happen?

There are many people who will turn their ship in the opposite direction and sail away from you when they see a flag of skull and crossbones. And then you'll find yourself wondering, "Why doesn't anybody want to talk to me?" On the other hand, some ships will gravitate toward you. There are people who, for whatever reasons, love to get beaten up and victimized, and they will come to get abused by you. Other people will come and try to save you. Sometimes *they* get beaten up too! Still others will come to challenge you. And guess what? The flags on their ships are bigger. And they have bigger guns. Then you'll say, "What on earth did I do to deserve this?" Well, *you* put up the flag. You designed it. It's really that simple.

What message do you want to broadcast out to life with your flags? What kind of people do you want to attract? You can attract any kind of a person you want. You can attract those who do nothing but harm. You can attract those who do nothing but good. This is up to you. We all have this ability inside.

Are you looking for protection, surrounding yourself with walls? Either you'll find yourself alone or approached by those who are curious: "What are you hiding?" It's like those wonderful old European castles with thick rock walls: the bigger the wall, the more someone wants to see what's inside. Life is a living process, very much alive. There are a lot of eyes looking around to see what it is that they can take. To see what it is that you're hiding. To see what it is that you have. Many, many eyes.

When we feel we have to protect ourselves from other people, we carry this flag of protection in our faces, in our eyes. It becomes part of us. We can also hold fear in our eyes. Sadness, hope, happiness, a dreamy mind — it can all be read in our eyes. And when we say, "This is *my right* to feel this way, I have good reasons to protect myself, I have good reasons to feel sad," what kind of people are going to come into our lives?

"Come on, love me. I really do want it. Honest, I do. I really want to be loved. Hey, everybody, I'm really a nice guy. I'm wonderful! Come on."

These flags are this obvious to our subconscious. They are *this* obvious to life. And then we ask for help from life: "Open me up! Teach me! Open my heart! Please help me. Just show me what it is that I do not see." Yet how can life help us with flags that say otherwise, flags we've raised of our own free will? How can we receive from life with our flags of protection? What about the aspects of ourselves that don't want help? That don't want to change? This is why simple honesty, again, is so important to have. We don't have to rip all our flags away — just acknowledging that they exist is all we need to do. Life will do the rest.

Let's take another common flag: the flag of judgment. When it comes to judgments, like those I made in the barrio, whether you look into someone's eyes or watch that person from a distance, if you think to yourself, "You look terrible," or you judge that person in any way, do you really think you got away with it? *Not at all.* In essence, you actually "shot" the person. You put their name on a target, shot them in the head, and said, "What do you think of that?" Pow. Pow. We're shooting each other all day long. Pow. Pow. Pow. "Whoa, I had a hell of a day today. Rough day." The implications of our thoughts are immense. This doesn't mean you shouldn't make use of good, common-sense discretion when it comes to seeing what is inappropriate in other people, in society, in teachers. That's healthy. But that is different from judgment.

Believe me, human beings are so sophisticated internally with high-tech radar that we sense when someone judges us. Many people have this attitude: "Show me your good side, but not your dark side, because I will crush it. I will accuse it. I won't like you anymore. I will not forgive you. I don't have the courage or the time or the effort even to understand you. So I will set up my flags accordingly." When this happens, we'll read these flags subtly inside the subconscious. And we will make sure that these particular people see only our good side. It's a very fine-tuned process.

When in your mind and heart, you stop judging all human beings, you will find people coming up to you and practically giving you a confession, telling you things that they would never tell another person, because they can trust you. They see your flag of nonjudgment. Again, you're a glass house. I'm a glass house. There's no hiding in this world. Nobody gets away with anything.

In looking back on my life, I used to have what I considered to be a great deal of bad luck. I grew up with quite a few problems. I thought maybe I was born under a bad sign. But when I realized I was a glass house, and that many of my troubles came about as a result of my inner flags, my life began to make more and more sense. No wonder I was getting into trouble. No wonder I was having hard times with other people. With myself. So I decided to see if I could change my "luck."

I started asking myself, "What do I want? What kind of people do I want to attract? What is good for me? What flags do I want to project?" And I was as honest as possible. When something happened to me, I didn't say, "Hey, I didn't put up that flag!" I acknowledged my flags. What helped me tremendously was not only learning to recognize the flags I had raised, but those other people had raised as well. And I didn't take myself so seriously. I learned to laugh at my flags. I was kinder to myself.

I realized that all I had to do was look behind me for the last five or ten years, and my future for the next five or ten years would be pretty much the same. But I knew I could change it little by little every day. And I found out that my future did change. It took time, but I stopped getting into so much trouble. My luck got better. My misfortunes subsided. And this can happen for you, too, as the world begins to respond to you differently.

Hide-and-Seek

Once we stop the hiding, it stops the drama. But when we hide, it creates gaps in our mind. It constructs walls and valleys between ourselves and life. It feeds the subconscious.

Many people, when they hear the story of the barrio, would look at it as fascinating, or they might think, "I wish something like that could happen to me." But none of us can truly know what it means unless it actually happens to us personally and we *realize* that our innermost thoughts are broadcast out. This is because throughout our lives, we've become so accustomed to quietly, secretly, unknowingly but knowingly believing that no one can hear our thoughts and feelings unless we speak them. We look at our inner mind as a safe with a combination that nobody else has but us. So we play hide-and-seek with ourselves. We play hide-and-seek with the external forces of life. And we continue to pretend, not realizing that we're glass houses. As long as we think we can hide, it's easy to deny, easy to forget, easy to play our games of hide-and-seek.

Do you know how the subconscious mind came into existence? Remember the game we played as very young children? We would put our hands over our eyes and say, "You can't see me. You can't see me." Then it turned into: "Oh, you can't tell whether I am lying or not. You can't hear my deepest secrets. I have a secret, and you don't know." This is how we still think, for it was reinforced by the adult world as we grew up. We were never taught anything different. So from a very young age, we begin to lie and twist our words externally. In time this transfers inside, and soon we start to twist the words, thoughts, and pictures in our inner world. Then what happens? This habit turns in on us, and before long we're keeping secrets from our own selves. Then we start saying to ourselves, "I have a secret." "No, you don't." "Yes, I do." And this is how the subconscious develops.

Here's another way to look at it. Young children watch their parents very carefully. They know their parents well. They know when the parents are lying. They know when the parents are playing games. They see it easily. When the kids see that the parents continue to play the game, they quickly learn how to play the game, too. Yet they know they're playing the game. The parents don't.

But in time, what happens? When the children continue to play the game, after so many years they fall asleep in it. The game becomes natural. And then lying becomes natural. Fantasies become natural. Ulterior motives become natural. Complacency takes root, in time working itself into the very nature of that little one's mind, so that the dishonesty is now too difficult to see. The conscience is also pushed farther and farther back until it becomes a distant voice. The gap between the subconscious and conscious mind widens even further.

So everybody plays this game of the subconscious and the conscious. We see but we don't see. We understand but we do not want to understand too much. We'd better not understand it. We can't believe it. But it happened. How can it be so?

You see, once we stop the hiding, it stops the drama. But when we hide, it creates gaps in our mind. It constructs walls and valleys between ourselves and life. It feeds the subconscious. This is something so simple, yet it has such a profound impact on the human psyche that billions of people are trapped in this predicament, not realizing the damage it causes to their lives.

What to do about this predicament? First, realize it exists. One of the best ways to realize we cannot hide is by watching movies. Let's say you're watching a scene in a movie in which a man is in a room all by himself and he takes money out of someone's wallet. "Ah, I got away with it," he thinks, as he walks out the door. But as a witness, you know that's not the case: "I see you." As you go through other films and find the scenes in which the actor is all alone, yet observed by you, you'll get the gist of the glass house, and a lot of familiarities will start to come through. You'll remember those times when it felt like something was witnessing you, although you were all by yourself. It is like a camera, recording exactly what is taking place without judgment, but it's you watching yourself. Now, what if the actor in the movie were to look your way and realize that you were present, or at least wonder what else was out there? What if his sincerity began to arise and he acknowledged what he had done — to you or to whatever might be listening? This is how one starts to connect with life.

What else can you do about the habit of hiding — from yourself and from life? All that is buried and hidden away deep within your subconscious: let it rise to the surface. It's offering the honesty of who you are that's important, not stripping yourself of all aspects of your personality.

When I realized I couldn't hide, I decided that I might as well show it. So I started to pull every thought and feeling, every flag — no matter how distorted — into my eyes. I didn't say one word to anybody, but like a big road sign along the highway, I put it out there and offered it up to life: "Look, this is me. This is how I am. This is how I think. This is what I've done. Here it is." When I went to see a teacher, I walked in with pockets full: this is me. And this was how I began to speak to life, all day long.

But I did this with goodness behind it, with respect for the people around me. I tried to be as kind as possible, as appropriate as I could. I was also careful to keep hope alive in my eyes for others, especially the children, to see. I held the understanding that everyone else lives in their own predicament, just like me. Without fighting with myself or struggling to change, I simply put my cards on the table as well as I could. I was able to look at the good and the bad, the strengths and the weaknesses within myself. The inappropriate thoughts. The little ulterior motives. My pictures, my hurt, my stories, my misunderstandings, my fears — I let them all rise up like smoke, not claiming or judging them, for I knew I was not these things. Those flags, subpersonalities, or neuroses I could not perceive, although I knew they must be there, I simply acknowledged. I knew that my blindness was part of the predicament. And I realized there was nothing spiritual, mystical, or mysterious about this process whatsoever. So I became straighter with myself as I cleaned up my mind. I couldn't do that before because I could hide.

Centuries ago, in the basements of their castles, the French kings and queens built a secret dungeon in the ground called an "oubliette." When a servant did something wrong or the royalty didn't like him anymore, they would take the servant and drop him into this dungeon through a trap door at the top. The meaning of an oubliette is "to be forgotten in." And this is what happened: the servant was forgotten. Problem gone. The attitude was, "He's out of sight. It's over. New servant." We do the same thing with ourselves. Whether it's guilt, shame, or something we cannot face, we bury it in our oubliette.

Most people are so unfamiliar with the vast subcultures within their own minds. Most people are not friends with themselves. They don't like certain aspects of themselves, or they think they've done too many bad things, so they keep all this locked away in various rooms within their subconscious. "No, I don't want you to see this. Let's put it over here in this pocket. No, I don't want you to see that. Let's put that over there in this other pocket. Oh, *this* one I'm going to hide over here. I don't want my mother-in-law to see that!" We're always on guard, trying to hold all this back. As a result, what's left in our eyes? A front. And we get used to this front. "Oh, it worked. There's no reaction. The person doesn't see." And so we start to adopt a new way of displaying ourselves.

That's why everything you have done that you're ashamed of, let it come out and paint it on your eyes. But never speak of it, unless you're in the presence of a trusted friend or therapist. And remember that most people are not good therapists. Don't tell people about your neuroses or expose everything you've done wrong. That's dangerous. I find that so many people will talk to practically anybody about their problems. But every human being you speak with has a particular influence and will radiate something on to you. Every time you reveal your feelings or open up your heart just a little bit, your wounds and vulnerabilities are also opening up. If the person you're confiding in has a mind that is not healthy or sane to some degree, you're in trouble. If that person is confused and passes on just one confused word in a comment to you, and you take it in, it can take months or years for you to unlock it. Be very careful who you talk to.

But always be honest with yourself, even though it may hurt. Don't hide something or force it to go back. That's what creates the subconscious. Then pretty soon you've got another world back there to contend with. Everything suppressed beneath the surface must come out, "breathe," and live externally before it can dissipate. By holding the reality of what has happened in the past, this creates the alchemy to make the medicine to transcend your hurt and neuroses. Yet this process isn't just to get out all the shame. It is also to see the beauty, the art that you have created inside — the architecture, the buildings, the vast cities. All the wonderful dreams and hopes. Very simply put, it is to know thyself.

Do you know what this whole game of a spiritual process is, once you break it down? It is really nothing but being consciously *aware* to the point that you no longer have a subconscious. Once more, it comes down to simple honesty. What it is to awaken? It is when the subconscious and the conscious become one mind.

When you talk to a friend or go to therapy and get a little counseling, sometimes all of a sudden you'll say, "My god, why didn't I see that before?" There it was. Good therapy is supposed to relax your filters — whatever is in the way of seeing what is — enough to allow you to dive down into that subconscious so you can pull those pictures out, pull those feelings out, pull that underground city out into the conscious world and become familiar with it.

It's that *simple*. But it takes an awful lot of courage to do this, because what are you going to do with all your causes, your gripes, your hurt? With the people you don't like, with the world you protect yourself from? Bring down the flags. "But, wait a minute, they were so nice!"

To expose your subconscious and bring it into the conscious mind isn't easy, but a most wonderful way to start is this: have faith in life. Have faith in humanity. Start putting faith into your neighbors, into your community, into other human beings, *regardless* of what has happened or what they have done. Have faith because the predicament is really much bigger than most people can perceive.

And learn to respect and befriend your mind. You see, we are also a glass house to our mind. When we are being honest with ourselves, when we aren't playing games, our mind sees this. Our mind knows when something is real and when it's not. It knows when we're talking to life with honesty and when we're not. It knows when we are genuinely in prayer and when we're not. Our mind sees all this, without judgment, but it doesn't say anything. It just knows: "Playing games again. Playing hide-and-seek again." But if the mind sees that we are truly sincere, whether we are in prayer, asking for forgiveness, or talking with a friend, it takes notice. And a whole new development, a whole new course, a whole new way of being starts to unfold, because now we have a very good friend to help us — our mind. And in time, we begin to see what mind is. We begin to understand that we are not our mind at all. We have just identified with it because we have no other reference points. And we start to realize that it is honesty of self that always unlocks the doors within.

We've all learned to cope on the surface — with our words, our thoughts, our feelings, our sensations. And as we glide along through life, we're successful to some degree. But what gives us more depth is to have a continuous relationship with our innermost thoughts and feelings. Our mind and heart need to be in constant union with each other. To do this is a big job. It's not easy to have a personal, in-depth, relationship with oneself.

But to have a personal relationship with life, we must have this relationship with the subtle world — the subtle feelings and thoughts within our own mind and heart. Where are our words coming from? Are we consciously aware of our feelings and thoughts and where they are emanating from? This is the relationship. Most of us try to develop a relationship externally, yet that's not easy to do when we are hiding inside, dishonest with ourselves, or protecting ourselves from life. First we have to establish this relationship within ourselves. Then we can do it with life.

Again, most of us have been living in ignorance, thinking that just because we don't speak out our thoughts, no one can hear. And so we start to chase our tail inside. We become trapped — by our own thoughts, our mind, our misunderstandings. We believe that, "No one else exists but those *I* see in a physical way." It's easy to think, as I once did: "There's really no help, no one listens to me, there's no life out there, nothing in existence beyond what I can see or touch. There's nothing to connect with, no one to reach out to." But there is. And that's what the rest of this book is about.

CHAPTER 2

GETTING CONNECTED

*The true relationship is just between you and life itself.
Who else knows you better than life?*

Among all these teachings, it is one of my strongest wishes that the relationship between you and life itself becomes a living matter, a living function, a living reality. The true relationship is just between you and life and no one else. Remember that. Each person is unique. No one can speak to life in the way that you can. Life is *very, very* personal — as personal as a daughter to her mother, as a son to his father. In this world or in spirit, it's that personal. You could say that life itself is really your lover. It is your best friend. It is your parents.

We are children of life. Why? Because we have been born and we are alive. If we are children of life, we have parents, so to speak, who are always helping us. Many of us can sense this. Some would call these parents "God," but I call them "life," for it is far too big for me to understand, and I have too much respect to name it. You will see that I speak of "life" in many different contexts, but when I am referring to the Creator in any way, you'll sense a reverence behind the word.

When we start to turn our eyes, our intent, our mind, and our heart into the direction of whatever has given us life, what happens? When a child starts looking at his or her mother and father, *then* the parents can help their child. The child receives feedback. When any child asks *from the heart*, the parent comes. What happens when we are sincerely looking into the eyes of our mother or father? We're appealing. We're appealing for help, for a word, for understanding. When we are sincere and honest, as a child, what do we receive from our parents? This is when life cannot deny us.

But if a child pays no attention to the parents and refuses to look them in the eyes, what happens in the relationship? A separation develops, not from the parent's point of view but from the child's point of view. The child starts to feel alone and empty inside. When the child will not look into the parents' eyes, the parents cannot help their child. When the child does not wish to talk to the parents, when the child says "no," the parents cannot do much about it other than let the child live out his or her life. Those of you who are mothers and fathers know that when a little one doesn't want to do something, there's *nothing* you can do. No god can do anything. No angel can do anything. Nobody can do anything, until the little one says, "yes." That's how it is.

As children of life, it doesn't matter what we have done or what dilemma we find ourselves caught in — as long as we are honest with it. That is what matters. When we become dishonest with ourselves, how can life help us? It is the honesty of our predicament that we can offer up to life. Then life can help. We do not have to go through our so-called "karma" or live out all our mistakes. Our obstacles, our conflicts, our suffering: we can offer it all up to life.

Life is patience. Life is like any parents who watch their children grow and go through experiences, trip and skin their knees. The parents do what they can and help when it's needed, but all they can really do is wait and watch. Life has given us, as children, individual wills to do as we wish, to think as we wish, to be as we wish. This is our gift.

Behind all the shadows of this world is the goodness of life. It is impossible for life to be bad. As children we can be bad, but life is nothing but goodness. Nature does what nature does, but life is goodness itself. What we do as children is up to us. Life will do its best to accommodate our feelings, our thoughts, and our wishes, because life loves us very, very much.

Look around — who gives us light? Who gives us air? Who has given us this earth to stand on? Who has given us our intelligence? There must be goodness in whoever put the children here, in whoever is smart

Getting Connected

enough to keep our hearts beating, to give us another day. It is up to us to seek out this goodness of life, if we wish. Into which direction do we look most of the day? Do we turn our eyes toward people's weaknesses, or do we try to understand their predicament and the strong gravitational pull that affects all of us so much? Do our eyes turn to people's inconsistencies and what they do wrong, or do we see other human beings on the streets going through another day and doing the best they can? Do we seek out the shadows or the beauty of this world?

Remember that there is not a human being who is not loved by life, no matter what he or she has done. That person is also a child of life. It is just that sometimes the predicament and the ignorance can be a little too strong in this world. *You were created out of love, and no matter how terrible a person you are when you leave this planet, you will be carried in love.*

Little by little, if we let our mind and heart mature enough to turn toward life, our loneliness will start to disappear. In the desert, we will begin to see life. We will see opportunities. The separation we will understand. When we turn our eyes to the Mother and Father of life, how we can feel the wind behind our back, the support beneath our feet, the joy in our eyes, and the spirit in our blood. It is then that our mind and heart will settle, and we'll find an intelligence that was always around the corner, a wisdom that was always there, a knowingness that was always present but had somehow escaped.

Creating a Communication Link with Life

You are never alone. You never were. You were always heard, always cradled, always understood.

Life—the creator of the individual—is *so* extraordinary that a direct communication between you and life is always accessible. This connection is like the "hot line" that used to exist between the United States and Russia. There was a special phone, with one exclusive line that no one else could tap into, that connected the leaders of each country. It was direct. When one of them picked up this phone, he knew who was going to be at the other end of the line. It is the same with you and your Creator: no one can tap into this phone, not even someone who loves you with his or her whole mind and heart. It is a unique gift to each individual. And the communication between you and your Creator is no one else's business but your own.

What is the proof that you have access to this "phone number?" The proof is that you were born. You are alive. You are a child of life. That's all the proof you need. It doesn't matter how "bad" you think you are — everyone has the ability to talk with life. How do you tap into this communication link with life? What is the phone number? If you ask from your heart, you will know how to dial up life. *Ask.* When the *sincerity* is there, guidance is available. This doesn't necessarily mean that any of your physical circumstances will change. It depends. But life will hear you.

What is life? As we keep studying our universe and breaking it down with our sciences, we are beginning to see the blueprint of what is behind the air, the trees, the sky, the water, the light, the stars — which reveals to us, more and more, the intelligence, beauty and mystery of life. But even though we have become more intelligent and know a lot about our world, do we really know what life is? We know how to send a rocket up into space. We know how to remove someone's heart and transplant it into another person. We have watched ourselves grow from children to adults — having experiences, learning at school, developing a profession, depositing money into our bank accounts, and putting petrol into our cars. But what is life itself?

Life is not a thing. Life is not a hope. Life is not an object or a label. Life is not a concept. Life is a knowingness. It cannot be separate from us. Life is so personal. It wraps around our very faces and enfolds our every thought. It supports our feet and keeps the blood moving through our bodies. It nourishes our smiles, our hopes, our dreams.

What I'm saying is that *life is alive.* It is in the air, the ground, the waters, the clouds. It is in all of us. Do you know that fire is alive, just as we are alive? The air is not just a word or a thing, it is a force — a living force. The life in the air and the water sustains your life. When you respect these basic elements that most of us hardly ever think about, their life force comes out and speaks to you with very loud "words." They touch you like someone caressing your cheeks. They kiss you like someone embracing you with tenderness. They talk to you like someone speaking with the softness of the heart. They move your emotions, like someone's kindness that has touched your feelings. When you connect with these elements, a relationship is established. A communication link is created. Now you are not just a citizen of Germany, Switzerland, or the United States. You are a human being living on this planet, which in itself is very much alive.

Once this communication link is established, no philosophy can bend you. No one else's words can confuse you. You can go into any country, any time, any place, and be at ease with what is in your heart and mind. You don't have to belong to any clubs because, very simply, you know you are of life.

So learn how to connect very quietly, and establish this link with your whole heart and mind. How you communicate and speak and feel is up to you. That is why I say that the most sacred prayer is from your own heart. Speak to life simply and in your own language, the way you naturally talk. Just speak as you would talk to your best friend. Speak what is inside your heart. Be straight and honest with yourself. As you speak to life, you will find that where there is reality, energy will follow. And that is the wind behind your back. That is what helps to create the movement in your life, removes your obstacles, or creates obstacles for your own good.

But remember that sometimes it takes time for someone to answer the phone or return your call. You have to learn to be patient. But never give up on life, and if you do, find your trust again. When your heart is cold and your mind is stiff, have faith. Do not give up. If you get knocked down ten times a day, remember that what matters is how you stand back up, not how many times you get knocked down. Hold that faith.

When you learn to communicate with life, it is like a confession. You are exposing yourself to life. It is not necessary to expose yourself to another human being. You don't have to be accountable to another person. People are too preoccupied with their own problems. It is not always appropriate to show others your neuroses, your hurt, or your pain. They are too busy with their own hurt and pain. Is it right to confuse them even more?

Even though all people are busy with their own lives, you can always turn to life itself for help. Who has more time than life? Who knows you better than life? Who truly knows your thoughts? Who knows what you have gone through better than that which has given you life? Who understands why your heart beats and resonates the way it does other than life itself? You could call it a communion, an understanding, a relationship. You can share your words, your touches, and your stories with friends and loved ones. But no human being can know you as life can.

I cannot give you life. Your neighbors cannot. Your children cannot. Your mother and father cannot in the sense that I mean here. I did not put the heart into your chest, life did. I did not give you a body, life did. I did not put the grandmothers and grandfathers into this world, life did.

Whoever put this heart in my chest and started it beating, this is who I talk to, whether or not I can see who did this. "I do not know what your name is. I do not know what you look like or where you come from. But I see small fragments of you, life, because I can see other people. I can see their goodness. I can see their homes. I can see the sky. I can see the sun. I listen to the laughter." This is how I speak to life.

Getting Connected

In speaking to life, we speak to all the people who have lived before us. In establishing a communion and a relationship with life, we can ask for help and guidance with whatever project we wish to do. Despite all that has happened to us, we still live in the grace of life. Our neighbors, our families, our sons, our daughters, and the people who have lived before us — all live in the grace of life. So take the time to create a relationship and communicate with whatever this is that encompasses everyone and everything within its grace.

Like all parents who wish that their children grow up to be independent, life also wishes this for each of us. The Mother and Father of life wait for their children to grow up, leave home, and live their lives as they wish, but with as much wisdom, respect, and kindness as possible. For your teachers will eventually pass away, your neighbors are busy, your mother and father and your brothers and sisters all have their own lives to live. Even the angels are busy. But whether you are asleep, working at your job, or walking into the desert, you are always living in the grace of life. Whether you know it or not, you cannot escape from it.

When you realize this, you know that you can stand on your own. Even if the entire community rejects you or your mother and father disinherit you, you know to whom you belong. You know that as you belong on this earth, you belong in this solar system, you belong in this galaxy, you belong in this universe, you belong in this life. It is then that you will never feel lonely or isolated, for you are never alone. You never were. You were always heard, always cradled, always understood.

YOU WERE ALWAYS WITH ME

Human beings.
Nothing to beware.
I was always at your side.
Night and day.
Even in your dreams.
In a shadow or two.
Even when you were hungry, too.
I was there when your moments were quiet.
I was there when you were tearing so.
I never left you.

I was not just on your right or on your left.
And not in a pocket or two.
Did you find me in your heart?
But where is your heart?
Did you find me in your mind?
But where in your mind, and what did you find?
Did you find me in your dreams?

I was always there.
You were always looking at my face,
but you never saw me.
You could not recognize me,
for you were looking right through me,
reaching for that pencil,
reaching for that phone,
reaching for that apple.

For I understand.
Too busy.
Too hungry.
Too many dreams.
It's all right.
For there is another day, another time.
Something will cross your path.
Another sound.
Another picture.
Another experience.
What will it take?

I have never left you.
You just could not see my face,
for you were looking right through me.
But you were always with me.

Are You Speaking From Your Heart?

It's not how evolved you are, it's how sincere you are.

How do you know if you are speaking from your heart? It is not easy to tell. Nor is it easy to explain. Most of us think we are speaking from our heart just because we are crying, sad, or wishful — but are we really? Most of the time, no, we aren't. It's very difficult to get into this space.

What does it mean to speak from one's heart? Watch the children, for they can show us. When we see a child who is naturally speaking from the heart, we know it immediately. The innocence, the tone of voice, the mannerisms reveal it easily.

Certain movies can also help us to understand what it means to come from one's heart. In these films, various situations and predicaments build up to a point where the character is suddenly forced to speak from a different place, deep down inside. Often it's a time when the person is finally being honest with himself or herself. When this happens, many people in the audience feel tears starting to come, because they can sense how the character has been touched. The sincerity has finally emerged, and this is when one is speaking from one's heart. It doesn't happen throughout the entire movie. It might last for only a few moments — as it is in life. All it takes is but a moment to activate one's heart.

For example, there is a scene in the movie *Braveheart* when the future king of Scotland, Robert the Bruce, is walking through the battlefield by himself after an especially bloody battle between the English and the Scots. The young lord had been persuaded by his father to betray William Wallace, who was fighting to win freedom for Scotland. So Robert the Bruce, disguised by a full-face helmet, fought with the English against the Scots.

Later, as he was surveying the aftermath of the battle, Robert the Bruce witnessed all his countrymen who had been killed or injured because of his deceit. He saw the women who were crying over their dead husbands and the children who had lost their fathers. And it finally touched him. Before this point, although you could see that this man was heartful, his heart was never truly touched. A lot of people had to be killed to force the young lord into his heart. It took a great deal of anguish and remorse for the moment to arise when he could genuinely speak from his heart. "I will never be on the wrong side again," he later vowed to his father.

Yet we usually avoid those times that can activate our heart. We run the other way, because it can be quite hard on us to reach this stage, when our ulterior motives and subconscious games are revealed. The truer nature of our mind and our intentions is exposed. This is when honesty, as well as a certain amount of humility, comes in. Unfortunately, the majority of human beings do not have the honesty, the humility, or the understanding to tell if they are speaking from their heart, and they will usually claim that they are, when in reality they are not at all.

You see, it's not how evolved you are, it's how sincere you are. We've all heard stories about someone who was drunk all the time or someone who did many terrible things in the past, and then suddenly a holy person or teacher took this person in as a student. Why? Because these individuals became honest and sincere with their situation. They finally spoke from their heart.

Generally it takes extreme measures and tremendous contrast for this to happen. But most of us don't have this in our lives. Everything's too smooth. Our lives work. We're well protected on many levels. So it's hard for us to know how tempered we are inside and how we would act when we are pushed to the edge, yet these are usually the times that finally force us to be honest about ourselves and our lives. It's difficult for us to walk into the situations that finally activate our sincerity to the point that we find ourselves speaking not just from our mind, but from our heart.

If you are speaking from your mind, that's all right — just know it. The mind is a wonderful tool. Use it when you speak to your mechanic about your car. Use it when you speak to the government about your taxes.

But speak to your Creator from within your own heart. When your subtle fields start to vibrate, when your heart radiates out, your voice becomes extremely loud, even though your lips may not move. And that is the real voice—the silent voice. Once you find this voice, I can tell you this: you will *never, ever* be lost or confused again.

Grace

The purpose of grace is to ease the predicament of existence.

It is not easy to change one's course in life. Envision a ripe apple hanging from a tree. When the time comes for the apple to drop and it leaves the branch, the apple is going to fall toward that one particular spot on the earth. In this lifetime, we are like the apple in the tree. Because we are who we are, to change our destiny is as difficult for us as it is for that apple to change its course while being pulled to earth by the force of gravity. It is destined to land on the ground in a certain place.

Ah, but grace can come in. The sky hears our prayer, our voice. The wind hears it. A helping hand, a big gust of wind can come to move us, to shift that apple, to create a whole different way of life. Because life is alive, when one speaks from one's heart, as much as possible life helps. But the wind needs to catch us at the right time.

When grace does not come to help you, not even a little breeze, and you know you have landed in that one spot, do not feel despair. Instead, feel happy that the gust of wind comes and helps another. Feel grateful that you are able to witness grace, for you can see it is alive out there in the world and that it does work. Even though it didn't work for you, it worked for someone else. That in itself is what will give you hope. Your prayers will become stronger, because you know it is just a matter of time before grace comes to you, too. When you place enough faith, hope, and understanding on the other side of the balance scale, something will happen.

THE WINDS OF YOUR HEART

The purpose of grace is to ease the predicament of existence. Grace comes in because the predicament does get heavy and at times we need fresh air. Grace exists because of nature, because of complacency, because the sleep is strong. Grace exists because there is a striving inside the spirit to wake up, to realize how precious life is, to get a different point of view about life. Grace exists to give us encouragement when we need it. Sometimes we need that friend to come around. We need those special moments. Grace is when someone comes out of nowhere in the desert and gives us water. But that doesn't always happen. That's life. We need to make this all right and come to terms with it. But grace is wonderful when it does happen. And if you have been touched by grace, you are connected.

When you are confused, when you do not understand, when you find yourself struggling through hard times, just know that grace is there. Grace never leaves. It only seems to be gone. It's just that sometimes we have a hard time picking up our hands to receive it — to receive it just because we were born, just because we are alive. Actually, it is during the times when we are not feeling good about ourselves that we need to reach out our hands and ask for help. Real courage is when we are feeling this way and yet we can still ask. Real strength is when we watch our hands open up, and feel the vulnerability touching our heart and mind. I used to think that there were people who were blessed and people who were not blessed. But I found that no matter what the circumstances, all people are blessed and grace can reveal itself to anyone.

So contemplate the nature of grace, the predicament, the apple falling, time and destiny, and the reality that centuries have passed and will continue to pass. To transcend the mind, you can only do so much. And this is where grace comes in. This is also where the heart comes in. My hope is to get you to that point in time where the wind can come and push you at the right moment so that you land in a better spot.

No matter how many days we live, no matter how much we try to clean up our personality inside, you could say we are bound by time, bound by destiny, bound by ourselves. But by raising and changing our intent, this in itself changes the time, changes the course of destiny, changes the alchemy of what we are bound by — and attracts grace. To have grace walk next to us, to have grace walk behind us, to have grace walk in front of us — how that would change our lives. What else draws grace? The feeling for life. The passion, the belief in the goodness of life. Life listens and it waits. You see, it is a matter of getting *you* connected.

What Connects You?

All of us are wired to broadcast and receive. What do you want to broadcast?

Do you know how important it is to have connections in any society? Connections can help you get a better job. They can lead you into a wonderful relationship. They can open doors to all sorts of opportunities for you. We know that connections make a difference. It is the same in spirit. There are some "discarnate spirits," as some people call them, who are completely lost. They have few connections and few friends. You could say that they are bound by the chains of fate and destiny, and yet their fate can be changed. The fate of poverty is not necessary. The fate of ignorance is not necessary. People don't have a good fate for no reason. People don't have a good life for no reason, and people don't have a bad life for no reason. There is a reason, and part of it has to do with the ability to activate your heart and establish these "connections."

Then what connects you? It is not an introduction. It is not a card. It is not a phone call. It is when your heart is radiating like a radio wave, broadcasting out a certain frequency with pictures and words. We know that the various species on earth are particularly sensitive to a certain range of sounds and frequencies. Similarly, the various benevolent spirits are especially attuned to particular frequencies when they are radiated by the human heart. When there is enough caring and softness in your heart, you are self-generating, emitting these waves of various frequencies. This is what establishes connections. You are one big antenna. You are also a radar signal, a radio station. All of us are wired to broadcast and receive. What do you want to broadcast?

There are many benevolent spirits, divine beings, and personal "friends" of all kinds that exist out there. When you happen to be broadcasting a certain signal from the heart, one, two, or perhaps many will come running to you so quickly, *if* they hear you, to help and provide guidance. Not all beings are adaptable to all people. It takes a certain "chemical mix." But your prayer, your calling, has to be heard if it is sincere and transmitted loudly enough.

Who helps you depends on the circumstances. There are those beings who have a unique gift, so that the nature of your situation happens to fall within their "professional field." They can even gather together others who have specific abilities and form a kind of team to provide help. It is like physicians who have become specialists in their field of interest. Some specialize in bones, while others focus on internal organs or the brain. By doing so, they become experts who can help their patients even more. In fact, what makes each of us so unique is that we naturally become specialists with our personality and our point of view. We can each create many different shapes and designs out of the same clay so that it becomes our own reflection.

It is the same with the benevolent beings, who are also, one could say, specialists. Not all can work with every dimension. Some are highly specialized and function within only one dimension. Others are extremely benevolent, and they are able to work within a large, multidimensional area. There are those who are nothing but love. Others are not. Some live in the water, and some exist in the sky or underneath the earth. Some may even be a neighbor or two who have come to help you just for that one day, that one moment — hoping to catch you at the right time and place. And some you will never touch or feel. But somehow you can inhale what's in their lungs — a breath of their own life.

Some benevolent beings, you could say, are masters of the seas of destiny who work to alter fate, which is a very difficult thing to do. They ferry people from one shore to the next, so to speak, under many different circumstances. Sometimes they can ferry you to more of your destiny, clearing out a lot of the rubble, inconsequential matters, and obstacles. The young lord in the movie *Braveheart*, which I mentioned earlier, was ferried across from his mind to his heart. He could have done this by himself, or one of these unseen helpers could have helped him to transcend. But to connect with these benevolent beings, your heart has to radiate that certain frequency. You have to be in a particular space. It is like meeting your lover eye to eye. Your eyes lock together. Without effort, your feet naturally seem to pick themselves up and carry you over.

Sometimes people ask me what such a benevolent being is like. How does a bug or a dog look at us — humans who build strange things that fly in the sky and talk with pencils and paper? These creatures also have thoughts and feelings. They wonder and contemplate. Their brains are not as big. Survival is much stronger. But they have a life, too. To them, we are like gods. Yet as they cannot really perceive us for who we are, we cannot perceive these benevolent beings. But I can tell you this. If you ever get the chance to see the face of such a benevolent being, and you were to look along the cheek, you would see infinity within a centimeter. As you kept looking farther and farther across the cheek, you would continue to perceive infinity upon infinity that just never seems to stop.

You can look at it this way. We know that there are human beings who stand out above the crowd. They have a greater vision. They're strong leaders. It is the same in nature, in the universe, in the heavens, in all of life: there are certain individuals who always seem to stand out, who are looked up to by others. This has nothing to do with a hierarchy. It is just that they have more channels, more resources, more connections. There is a uniqueness about them. Some spirited beings have more common sense, more wisdom. They have more light, more forgiveness, more compassion.

And like good neighbors anywhere, these benevolent beings understand the neighborhood. When somebody needs help, they see it. Maybe it's an elderly lady who is too sick to leave her house, or someone whose car battery went dead. In any community, there are always those who seem to stand out, who are always ready to lend a hand. This is how you can think of these unseen helpers.

One beautiful aspect of most traditions is that they tell us we are not alone. It is true. We are *definitely* not alone. Wonderful help is available for us. But many of us think, "I don't see anybody, there's nobody around, so I'm just speaking to myself." But that isn't necessarily the case. Remember that we are glass houses. "Then why don't I feel it? Why don't I sense it? Why isn't it happening?"

Maybe when the help is there, we simply do not have the eyes to see it or the sensitivity to feel it. Maybe we receive guidance in our dreams at night, but we don't realize it. Maybe we can't receive the help, in part, because we're too busy shielding ourselves from opportunities, without even being aware of what we're doing. Maybe we're a little too defensive. "I have to protect myself from the world, from all those nasty people. It's a terrible world out there." Maybe because of history, because of how our great-great-grandparents had to live in a world where survival was much more difficult, we're still protecting ourselves, too, on some level. Yet this can make it difficult for us to allow the help to come.

This is where the heart comes in. The heart opens up doors. There is no judgment within the heart, it just allows. But most of us are ruled by our wonderful, influential minds. The mind has all kinds of sensible and rational reasons why to protect itself. "Oh, that's because you *deserve* to be kept out. I've been hurt by life, I'm not going to let you back in any more. I can't trust you now." If you lose faith in one human being, you lose faith in life. If you get hurt and hold onto that hurt and don't forgive, you have no forgiveness for life. This is because all creatures within the "chicken coop" live under the same sun and breathe the same air. We are all brothers and sisters. There is no escape from one another.

When we have ill wishes and ill intent for others, we have ill intent for life itself. This is one of the things that keeps the help away.

To let life come a *little bit* closer, to feel a little bit more takes a lot of courage. Why? If we live under the pain and confusion of any kind of contraction for so long, when we let in a little light it is going to hurt. But if we simply hold this understanding, along with an intent to let life in, it helps create the necessary change.

Here is something else to contemplate. As Westerners, we grow up with a lot of independence. We are independent thinkers. Like a child who says, "I can do it, let me do it," this is healthy. But this habit can make it hard for us to ask for help. It is not unhealthy to want to do things for ourselves, but if we have just a featherweight of arrogance associated with an attitude of "I can do it on my own," the help goes away. With any form of arrogance, self-importance, or pride, we will find ourselves on our own.

I use the word "power" very little, because many people abuse this word. But our arrogance can be so immense that we do have the power to not want help or seek help from anybody or anything. And that's one of the great misfortunes for so many human beings. The element of arrogance actually creates a certain kind of chemical reaction that separates us from the help, much like oil and water cannot mix with one another. We can easily develop distance between spirit or whatever assistance we have because the arrogance creates a bubble or a shield around us. A mirror-like substance forms on the edge of our aura — the personal, spirited field around us — so that when we look out, our mind reflects back upon itself. It's like looking into a mirror. Our view isn't clear like it is when we look through glass, so we become blind. That's what makes arrogance and inappropriate pride so deadly: we become encased in a house of mirrors.

A friend of mine told me about a workshop she attended in which all the participants wore blindfolds so they couldn't see for an entire day. The idea was to get a sense of how a blind person lives. What affected her the most was the realization of how dependent she was on the people who could see to help her. When we don't realize our predicament, there is nothing others can do to help. If the blind person doesn't ask for help, nothing can happen. If we do not ask for help — realizing that we, too, are blind in many respects — no help will come.

There are a couple of old traditions in which people put their entire body, mind, and spirit into the hands of what they call God. They just give up everything. Surrender all. Most Westerners cannot do this. It is not in our make up. However, as Westerners what we can do is to be honest about our predicament. "I know I cannot see. There is something I do not understand and cannot comprehend. Yet I know that there has to be someone or something out there that can sense my call for help." When such a call is spoken from the heart, this is what attracts help. What is most important is to get help drawn to you. A friend — a good friend — really does help. Good connections really do help.

Using Anger to Call for Help

Prayer is developing the courage to point your anger up or down.

In addition to the radiation of your heart, you can actually use strong emotions, such as anger, despair, grief, frustration, extreme joy, or love, and transform them into a call for help. Love is like a volcano. Anger is also like a volcano. Let's take anger as an example. There is a way to channel the energy of anger so that it's expressed correctly and works for you and not against you. Why not take advantage of those times when you are angry?

There is a difference between as appropriate anger and inappropriate anger. Appropriate anger is when you find yourself thrown into the predicament of life and you become angry because the predicament is heavy. Inappropriate anger involves "shooting" anger at another human being. Obviously that is not good. The person who is "shot" will get devastated. It's very much like getting hit by a bullet and having to recuperate. You can argue and you can discuss, but when you start to direct anger at others, you'll get it back. If you continue to shoot people with your anger and ill wishes, all you are doing is taking off your shoes and throwing them into your future to trip over.

Actually, we're constantly shooting people with our thoughts. It's a very natural thing to do. This is how we communicate, back and forth. But when you have a harmful motive behind your thoughts, you're in trouble. And so is the other person. Be careful with your thoughts. They fly as easily as bullets fired from a gun. When it comes to anger, you can feel frustration, disappointment, disgust, or dislike, but don't shoot another human being. Don't punish people or act out of spite or revenge. And especially do not wish harm or ill intent on another out of anger.

Instead of shooting your anger into others, with all your courage and strength, point that "gun" down into the earth or up into the sky and turn it toward the predicament of life itself. This is how one can transcend the energy of anger and make it appropriate. Instead of shooting anger at a person, you are using your intent to create a massive radar signal, a great booster rocket that is going to shoot your feelings and thoughts out into the cosmos of life, with a goodness of intent. The message is, "Listen, I have a problem. I am caught in a predicament." You are using your anger to reach someone somewhere who will listen to you and come to help. You have transformed the anger. And because of this your life will change.

To leave this gravitational field takes great energy and tremendous strength. When you use the energy of anger to call out and a benevolent being hears you, it knows what your intent is. It can see and feel what you are trying to say. It's in the message. It is in the light. The story is right there. That being can see how you did not turn your anger or frustration on a human being, you turned it toward the predicament. "Okay! I come."

Even if you are furious with someone, because of your love, your care, your understanding, you are not shooting anger at that person. You're holding it back. You could be expressing anger, but you are doing this without spite, hatred, or ill wishes. Instead, you are holding your intent: it's the predicament, the spirited human being in nature. To do this takes a lot of courage.

Now you are drawing in and holding what can be called an "astronaut's perspective." If you don't have this perspective, where is the energy of your anger going to go? It has to go somewhere. Where are you going to shoot it? The most logical place is at someone else.

With the astronaut's perspective, although an eruption is taking place, inside you are holding a little ray of light. That tiny ray of hope amongst all the darkness is all you need. That little bit of intent is going to make a big difference. It's like mixing a few drops of one chemical into a glass of other chemicals; that's enough to create a transformation. When anger is appropriate it is not destructive. It transforms. It changes. It's a tremendous communicator.

Someone once asked me if directing the forces of anger into the earth could be harmful to the planet. No. Among other things, that is what the earth is for. It knows how to filter those energies. It does it all the time. If we put out carbon dioxide, the earth will clean it. Yet if we put too much pollution in one spot, we know what will happen. That is where common sense comes in, and in this case, it is up to us to take care of the environment. But when we channel our anger into the earth, it is something like washing dishes; the dirty water simply goes back into the ground without hurting the earth.

Do you know why most people cannot pray effectively or do not seem to experience much grace in their lives? It is because they cannot reach out far enough. They don't have enough energy to reach benevolent spirits, benevolent help, benevolent human beings who will hear their calls and come to help. It is as though they are stranded in the middle of a desert and nobody can hear them. But when we have enough energy, our calls go out and draw attention. That's what an understanding of energy does. And that's what anger can do. It's a powerful force.

Anger and other strong emotions are a commodity. Use them. Profit from them. They are great message carriers. But you must prepare yourself first. If you do not prepare, you will always find yourself reacting to the anger, asleep in the process. So get ready when it's a good day and nobody's pressing your buttons. Then when the anger comes, instead of pointing it at a human being, use your will and point it down into the earth or up toward the heavens, with your message and your intent inside: "I need help. Someone, please help me with this." In the beginning you may forget and get caught up in the anger, but don't be too hard on yourself and try to do better next time.

When you turn the face of anger into the predicament itself and not into what we call our righteous causes and rationalizations, that in itself becomes the prayer. Prayer is developing the courage to point your anger up or down. It's a most amazing feeling when you do. It is like sending out an especially compelling letter. We know the difference when we receive a letter written by someone who is genuinely sincere and asking for help, as opposed to a letter that says, "I need help, send fifty dollars to this address." That is just junk mail. A lot of junk mail goes out. There is junk mail everywhere in all the realms. Do you think we're the only ones bothered by it? All spirits are busy. But no one can resist a sincere message and a genuine, heartfelt plea for help, if they hear it. No one can.

The Firefly and the Zoologist
Life naturally heads toward the light that is bright.

Besides using emotions such as anger, how can we catch life's attention? First, we need to ask ourselves, "How does life see us? How does it interact with us?" Is it another being with very big eyes, observing us through a telescope? No. Is it a god in another dimension who is constantly watching our every movement? No. Is it an angel perpetually at our sides, guiding us? No, although angels can help us at times. You could say that angels are busy, gods are busy, nature is busy, all beings in all realms are busy, so it takes something out of the ordinary to catch their attention.

Imagine that human beings are fireflies and life is a zoologist who has a great passion for animals and insects and tries to assist them as much as possible. You can think of the zoologist as the angels, the benevolent beings, the awakened ones, the wind, or nature. The zoologist has the wisdom of all the sciences.

One night the zoologist is walking through the forest. She has been walking along this same path for tens of thousands of years. There's no moon out, but she knows the way in the dark. Like all of life, she is very busy as she observes the millions of forest creatures and takes notes.

After a while the zoologist comes across a field of fireflies. As she scans them, she sees that nothing seems out of the ordinary. But all of a sudden she notices one firefly that is twice as bright as the others. Most fireflies produce a similar kind of light that gives off a soft glow at night. But when a firefly sincerely asks for help, it throws out a much brighter light. In essence, this is what attracts life, which naturally heads toward the light that is bright.

"That's interesting," the zoologist thinks, as she walks over and searches for the firefly that shines so brightly. The zoologist knows what the firefly is asking for. She knows its heart. She knows its intent. And so she takes the little firefly in and helps it as much as she can.

You could say that the firefly and the zoologist live in different dimensions. As an insect, the firefly cannot really see or comprehend the zoologist. But the zoologist can see the firefly. She understands its predicament. And she knows that there is something unusual taking place that caught her attention, whether it is a chemical reaction between the two of them, a personal affinity for that particular firefly, a certain radiation of its heart that touched her, or just a chance encounter. Something created an attraction.

That is what sincere prayer does. It eventually attracts. Very few prayers are answered, not only because life is always busy, but because so many prayers are not genuinely spoken from the heart with enough brightness to attract attention. To attract help, it takes not only good timing, but a brilliant light that is broadcast as often as possible. Even still, the light must catch the zoologist at the right time of the night, she must have the time even to turn her head to see the firefly, and finally, she must go out of her way to head toward the light and do what she can to help. That's the nature of life.

So even if you're shining brightly on a given day, it doesn't necessarily mean that you are attracting any help whatsoever, although your chances of being noticed are much better. It's funny — people think that just because they're human, when they need help there will be *a line* of spirits waiting to help them. They assume that just because they're asking for assistance or thinking of spirit, a response will come at a moment's notice.

But as it is in this world, so it is in the other worlds: we're all very busy within our own worlds. Whether one is living on the streets, running a company, chasing down deer for dinner, or running away from lions — all species, all beings are extremely involved in their own lives. Naturally, in spirit there is a different kind of busyness. The angels aren't out there grocery shopping and doing errands!

Think of it this way. Can you imagine what it would be like if one human being speaks, asking for help, and all the spirits in all the known universes hear that person? Then imagine that six billion people on earth are speaking and thinking and dreaming and wanting and wishing — all at the same time. What would that be like for all the spirits who cannot help but hear these never-ending thoughts and feelings and desires? It would practically drive them crazy. "Aggghhh! Stop it! Stop it!" They would be closing their doors, shutting their windows, and unplugging their phones. No wonder it doesn't work that way.

Even though all beings are immersed in their own lives, you could also say that life is always available to hear you. But the volume, the intensity, has to be there. The pleading has to be strong enough that it reaches out and really grabs someone's attention.

Imagine if you could actually see each of your thoughts in the form of pictures or words, and you counted every single one of the thoughts you had every day for a year. At the end of the year, as you are looking at your countless millions of thoughts, you ask yourself, "All right, which ones veered out toward the heavens to make contact? Which ones held enough caring to amplify the signal so that it projected out into space?" If you were to do this, you would find that almost all of your thoughts had very little, if any, projection qualities.

It takes a much more than just a thought, or even a simple wish or hope, to reach out and make contact. To turn the radio up louder, it takes not only intensity, but elements such as sincerity, desire, honesty, and understanding. It takes enough depth of heart in the calling. It takes a combination of the various feelings, thoughts, and experiences that happen in a given life. Sometimes it takes a strong will, intent, or passion. Sometimes it takes innocence. Sometimes it takes pain or hurt. Sometimes it takes guilt. It could be some aspect of suffering, joy, tragedy, an enlightened thought or experience, or necessity that produces the right blend of ingredients to create a prayer that will shine brightly enough and travel far enough to be noticed.

And the pharmacist, which is you, mixes it all together. One could say that the pharmacist is making dynamite. What is the dynamite? It is the sincerity, the intensity, the effort — whatever it takes to design an explosion that will create as many fireworks as possible. A little firecracker won't reach a mile high. It's going to take a good-sized amount of dynamite to propel your prayer, your call for help into the heavens far enough to attract attention. Yet this isn't an easy thing to do — the pharmacist definitely has to work at it.

Here is another way to look at this predicament. Envision a man who is so agoraphobic that he is afraid to leave his house. For years he has been locked up inside his home. To get that man to leave his house is going to take a tremendous amount of intensity, therapy, or an extremely compelling reason — either that or a fire! In a sense, we're somewhat agoraphobic with our own selves. To get us out of our conditioning, our comfortableness, our complacency, and our habits — it practically takes a fire, a blast of dynamite, or at least a mix of the right elements so that we can finally walk out the door. To speak with life, to connect with help, we have to get out of our house, so to speak, which isn't all that easy once we have become comfortable. But it can be done. It happens all the time.

Something else to consider is this: how naturally connected are you in life? There are all kinds of ways to be connected and to be heard. At one level, all people are always heard by life, just as everything and everyone within the bubble of nature is always heard, for everything is interconnected. That's the glass house. But at what level are you being heard? It depends on your depth of heart and the clarity of your mind. Those few human beings who are heard at a deeper level have a far greater depth of heart. They have a connection that is unique. They are not just connected to the eyes and ears of nature and evolution, but to the eyes and ears of another dimension of spirit. So we're all connected. But how connected are you? And to what dimension? And does this connection mean that you have the gift of true prayer?

Most people have a hard time finding the honesty within themselves to answer these questions objectively. In my workshops, I encounter a lot of people who think they have a natural connection with spirit and that all their prayers are heard. When they first start attending the lectures, they come to me and explain how connected they are. Yet I can see that isn't the case at all. After four or five years of attending workshops, these students finally begin to admit that they never had the gifts they thought they had. They realize that they never really knew how to pray, especially when it comes to third-stage prayer or divine prayer, which I explain in the next chapter.

It's very much like this. We know that some people who come into this world are born geniuses. Mozart. Einstein. Galileo. Why aren't you a genius? These prodigies somehow have connections that allow them to tap into channels of music, philosophy, physics, and so forth. Why don't you? It shows that not everybody can be a genius. Not everybody can be an inventor. Not everybody can have these kinds of connections. And to have a connection with God, that's pretty darn unique. Some prayers can head straight to God, but this is rare. Usually it takes an intermediary of some kind.

Throughout history we know that human beings walked the earth who were genuine saints. They were truly touched by God. But how many of them existed in comparison to the general population? Very few. So again, we see how rare it is to be connected in this way. Some people are naturally born with it. Most aren't.

Naturally, one's relationship to life, to one's God, is very personal. But what you really have to consider is this: is your heart bright enough? Or are you just speaking to the winds, just praying to yourself? Just because you feel like calling for help or praying at any given moment doesn't mean you can. It is much more difficult than that, as we are learning here. Just because you can cry, think good thoughts, recite a prayer, or feel good about humanity doesn't mean you have this deeper kind of connection at all. It just means you're a good human being.

Some human beings are more connected to life through their dream states, where they can access help more easily than in the physical world. Within dreams and other realms is where their strength lies, and their prayers reflect this. Most people, however, can pray only in their waking states. But when you can pray in both the waking and dream states, your prayers become extremely effective. So another avenue for prayers to come through, and one that few people may have considered, is by means of dream states, especially those dreams that have a strong sense of reality about them.

The essential point here is simply being honest as well as extremely practical when looking at the figures and facts: how many human beings are well connected? Most people don't like to look at the figures to see where they fit in, especially when it's not a pretty picture. But acknowledging the reality is what is most important. It's not whether you are connected or aren't connected — what matters is that you're honest with where you are in the overall picture. Then you have a good starting point.

And remember that even if you are not connected at this deeper level, and even if you do not have the gift of divine prayer, it is still possible to activate your heart and to develop connections with life in a way that is extremely personal. When you are sincere, when you are honest, it can happen. A living relationship with life itself is possible for everyone. Keep this hope alive, for it is a good hope to have.

Your Tribe

*When one prays, and one is not bound by time and space —
they hear. They come.*

Many people might be surprised to hear that not all spirits connect with all humans — it takes a certain frequency in common. People tend to have this idea that when you die, suddenly all the female spirits become like your mother. But most don't know who in the world you are. Many of us assume that in spirit, all is love. No, it's not so. The ones who can love you, the ones whose particular frequencies match your own, fall within a particular "family." To meet someone you genuinely connect with, whose frequencies resonate with yours and touch your heart, is very difficult — just as difficult as finding someone you can truly fall in love with. The odds are almost against you, although we know it happens.

It is something like this. When it comes to other human beings, we always seem to find ourselves thinking: "Oh, I like you. I like you just a little bit. I don't like you at all. I *love* you. I love you *a lot.*" We all do this and we're extremely good at it. It's especially natural for young children to respond in this way. Why? It is almost like a radio frequency emitted by others that we tune into. There is something else taking place that runs far deeper than what we see with our eyes when we look at someone, and this is why we instinctively feel a connection with certain individuals. It is no different in spirit.

If our prayers are strong enough to be heard, who hears them? Although some prayers are picked up by those benevolent spirits who hear our calling, most prayers generally head toward help within our "tribe," not just in this dimension, but in other dimensions, where our family, our old friends hear them. They head toward what is familiar.

All people have their roots, their own tribe. Those in your tribe are the ones you can truly speak to, no matter what your predicament. There is a kinship that reaches down to the very depths of your bones and the very vase of your heart. You could say it is a home of homes. When your heart beats out its signal, and when a friend is not confined by time and space, that friend can actually come to assist you personally. A friend from your own family — your real family. Not mine. Yours. Even on earth, if you are receptive enough, you can sense a signal from one of your tribe. Maybe you don't think you can hear it, but suddenly you may feel a compulsion to walk in a certain direction that leads you to the one who is calling out.

Most of us, because of how long we have existed, have so many good friends. There isn't a spirited human being who is not an adventurer, voyaging from life to life. For one who has been traveling for billions of years, it's hard not to pick up friends along the way. Can you imagine how many friends we really do love, besides those we love just in this one life? Sometimes we have never met these friends in the flesh, but they are still of our tribe. And when one prays, and one is not bound by time and space — they hear. They come.

This earth is a train station. It's a bus stop. An airport. All creatures come from every imaginable place. Some spirits come from so very far away. In this universe, there are many planets, many worlds in which to live.

Yet somehow we found ourselves here, ready to catch the next train someplace else. This is not our home. We are nothing but guests. Then where is our real home? It lies in the realm of the Uncaused Light of spirit. The life force of our spirit is Uncaused Light — living light with no cause behind it whatsoever. Every now and then, we slip into infinity where there is no time, and we can sense our home, where our spirit resides. Wherever your home is, you could say that this is where you'll find your tribe.

It is the fate of all spirits to go in many different directions on the adventure. Sometimes we forget about our home and fall asleep. We get lost in the journey. But until we start to speak to life and radiate out our feelings inside, no one in our tribe can know where we are. Then it's easy — too easy — to be lost.

Sincere prayer is very much like beating a drum. When you beat this drum, whether you have a small heart or a big heart, the vibration of your prayer goes out and travels a very long way. It can travel for light years. Eventually, that drumbeat reaches a particular spirited being who is somehow attuned to you. If there's a note in that vibration of seeking some form of help, it's read in the drumbeat. And help will come.

Sometimes it's a friend next door who comes to help. Sometimes the help comes from very far away. Sometimes the one who helps is a friend behind the doors of birth and death — a friend with a big heart and mind who has the right connections and better ways and means to assist you. But no matter how distant this help may be, first you have to start tapping out your own drumbeat, producing your own smoke signals. And like all radio signals, e-mails and SOS codes, eventually someone will receive your message.

When I left home, I realized that my father and mother could no longer walk at my side. Even my best friends, once they finished school, went off into separate directions. I found that I couldn't be with my teachers all the time. They'd just get tired of me. Or they'd move away. With every passing year, I seemed to find myself more and more on my own. The only thing that followed me was my shadow. Yet I found that even in my own shadow, there was far too much ignorance. I knew I needed help.

But like all human beings, I had a free will to decide whether or not to pick up the phone and call for help. And sometimes, even though I didn't pick up the phone, I hoped that somehow someone would get the message anyway and call me. Who knows, both my friends and I could be waiting and hoping that the other would call.

There is nothing like getting assistance. Once you know how to attract help, it's simply a matter of learning to receive. But if you don't want help, no problem. You see, all I did was to touch my own tribe. And I learned to stop pushing the help away, thinking that I could do it all by myself. I let my pride relax and allowed someone to help me, teach me, and re-educate my mind and heart. You could say I found an internal teacher. I realized that to have the doors open to alter destiny, it takes a tremendous amount of help. And this is what has taught me to be as humble as possible, to be in awe of life. I learned to appreciate the help, for I could not have done it alone. My hope is that you, too, can learn to relax the grip of your mind, so that someone from your own tribe can come and help you as well.

If you aren't sure about the existence of anything unseen or unknown, whether it's your tribe, benevolent spirits, or whatever encompasses all of life in its grace, don't worry. If you feel you don't know how to pray or send out your drumbeat, then please don't know. Continue not to know. One of the most beautiful attributes of all creatures is innocence. But when innocence pretends, one is in trouble. Know what you know, and know what you do not know. There's nothing wrong with not knowing. What matters is your innocence and your honesty. *That* is your communicator, your transmitter, sending out its signals to life. If you have your innocence, you have direct communication to what is above. If you lose the innocence, you cut the wire. You sever the line.

The adult world robs so many children of their innocence — rips it away and doesn't think twice. Yet deep down inside, we all still have our innocence. And when our pride is relaxed, our arrogance is not so strong, our anger is far away, and our criticisms and doubt have died down, very magically we look up by chance and catch a shooting star. And in that moment, we make a wish, like the wish of a child who still has the innocence. These are the kinds of wishes that reverberate throughout the universe, that keep love flowing through, that bring new light and new hope. These are the wishes that are so easily heard by our tribe. And when the wishes are made with such innocence and sincerity — whether they are to have a particular profession, a good friend, a future lover, or even to awaken from the predicament of existence that confines all human beings — eventually they can come true.

The Wish of a Goldfish in the Pond

There must be more to life than just my life in my small pond.

Sometimes I wonder what it is like to be a little goldfish in a pond. The goldfish's entire universe lies in that pond. But playing around the water, beyond the world of the goldfish, are human girls and boys. I wonder if the goldfish can truly realize what the minds of the human girls and boys are like. Can a goldfish comprehend the sun or even see it for what it is? Can a goldfish really know about the oxygen in the atmosphere of the world above its world?

No doubt, the goldfish feels some love, has a mind to make decisions, and experiences adventures and disappointments. It also gets sleepy and hungry. Life does not just reside in a human body. There is as much life in a spider, a tiny bug, a bird, or a goldfish. They all have their own kinds of thoughts and feelings, emotions and curiosity. But how can the goldfish truly understand the world of the human girl and boy, whose water is thinner and called "air?"

As a human being, I wonder what lungs I will need when I pass away. What air will I breathe then? When I look back upon my life, I will seem like that goldfish, and the very thin, light air I used to breathe will appear as thick as water in comparison to the atmosphere of spirit. I could not see the world above me, as the goldfish could not see the world beyond the pond where the girls and boys played. It was too much for my mind to comprehend.

What is it like beyond my world? Even though I'm like a goldfish and I am very small, I know that life can teach me to comprehend, see, feel, and hear like whatever that species is that does not need this water to breathe. I know that somehow this thick water I am breathing today will turn into a thinner and more subtle atmosphere. But I do not wish to wait until I pass away to breathe whatever that atmosphere is. It is my right as a living human being to breathe that atmosphere now, to change the thickness of this water, to see not only through the eyes of a "goldfish," but to be more than my life, more than my name, more than my dreams in my small pond.

The funny thing is, I will always live in a little pond, although when I understand the paradox of it all and the microcosm becomes the macrocosm, I will also live in the atmosphere beyond my pond. No matter how small or big our pond, whether we become an ocean or a universe, we will always be a "little pond" within the awesomeness of life. That is the beauty and grace of life. You see, in this goldfish story, we are taking the spiritual processes that have always been quite mysterious and looking at them very simply.

What is it that takes our mind and heart outside the atmosphere of the water and into the other atmosphere, where we can see that there is another way to live and another way to breathe? How can we tap into the perspective that exists through the mind of the human boy and girl walking and playing by the pond? What element is needed for the goldfish to realize that there is another atmosphere? An act of grace.

Suddenly the goldfish doesn't move anymore and stops searching through the grasses for little bugs to eat. The water is still. Even the sun seems to be still. *Immense* quietness surrounds the pond. A thought emerges out of the goldfish's tiny head: "Is this all there is? There must be more to life than just my life in my small pond." An entire lifetime has been compressed into a moment. It is not just curiosity about the other atmosphere; now the goldfish has touched its bones inside. The goldfish has touched its heart.

"Whoom!" Someone from another place and time will hear the goldfish and know how sincere the little fish is. Maybe it will be the young boy or girl who hears the goldfish, or maybe it will be a mother or a grandmother. Maybe it will be the old man walking by whose mind is immense in understanding compared to the tiny mind of the goldfish.

"What is this?" says the old man as he looks down and sees the goldfish. "Who speaks? Who dares to ask such a question? Who is so courageous?" An affinity has been established. A relationship has begun. A transference of consciousness has started to take place. The compassion of the old man is touched and he says, "I hope and wish that what I see and know, one day you will see and know."

For the little goldfish as well as ourselves, it takes help from others — not only from those living in the flesh, but also from those living above and those dwelling below, where the nature spirits reside. How difficult is it for a mother to deny the child that she loves? How difficult is it for a good friend to turn down another friend? Because you asked from your heart, they will give help.

When you sincerely speak something inside that is true to your heart and it cries out, there could be one or perhaps a hundred other beings out there that have an affinity, a vibration, a frequency that is tuned just for you. When you ask from your heart and that "radar" goes out, time cannot stop it. There are no walls that can hold it back. In essence, it is like a prayer. There are many Buddhas, many gods, many beings everywhere and they are all busy. But when they get hit with your prayer, and there is enough brightness and sincerity within that prayer, they know who is speaking. They know. They cannot reject you. They cannot say no. When a loved one comes to you and asks very sincerely from the heart, "Please, please help me," you cannot help but say, "Of course." This is true of all beings in all worlds.

There is no way I could be where I am today if it were not for the help I received. It took many friends. For my destiny was not to be teaching as I am, at all, and I had so many obstacles to overcome. Every day we find people helping others. During World War II, there were many individuals who went far beyond the call of duty to save other people from being murdered and persecuted by their enemies. They put their own lives in jeopardy. It happens everywhere. And whether you are a human being or an angel, when you help someone, that person may never recognize your help. But the point isn't that you get recognized. The point is that you helped. And this is how goodness is passed on, from one generation to the next.

When a friend is at your side and gets closer and closer to your life, they can change your fate and destiny, like a bulldozer cutting through the earth. It is not easy, even for your friends from above. Their lives aren't a bed of roses. For they pay a price, too, and they know it. When someone is dangerous, when someone is hateful, when someone is rude, you will pay a price to go and be that person's friend. But how much do you care about this human being? So it is for your friends from above.

What is most important to remember is to get your heart activated. Why? Because then it becomes a transmitter, sending out radar signals to life. An activated heart is a most amazing tool, yet it's not just a tool, it is a living process. It is the telephone to life with a direct connection. Even though all of life is busy, when you are genuinely speaking from your heart, grace can show up. No matter where you are in your little pond, someone will hear. Someone just for you.

You could say that I had enough faith and held it long enough until it broke my confusion and shattered my ignorance. I had enough faith that life is goodness, life is not suffering. I had enough faith that there has to be goodness behind all the shadows and all the terrible things that happen in this world. I had enough faith that life could hear the transmission of my heart and that grace could walk into my life. And that is what faith is for — to help us until we no longer need it. So remember the little goldfish and have faith.

HOPE AND FAITH

*Hope and faith are two amazing elements
that touch the human heart
and make the blood come alive.*

*When that door opens in your heart,
something instinctively speaks:
have faith that there is goodness behind it all.
Have hope that there is a little light,
even if the sky is dark,
or war is waging all around you,
or all you see is disappointment in this life.
Hold that hope deep down inside your heart,
that little lighthouse.*

*Even though it may be a tiny spark,
hold that little flame.
Do not let go of the hope.
Water the faith
that goodness has to be behind
all the shadows and all the misgivings
and all the war and all the terror.
It has to be above and below.
Do not ever give up.
And if you do, get back up.*

*Once hope and faith have done their job,
you do not need them anymore.
Then one day you'll be able to say,
"Thank you, you have helped to carry me so far.
So many miles you have walked with me.
A good job you have done.
You have sustained me through it all.
But now I do not need you anymore.
For now I know I am alive.
Now I see that the sun
is not just a word with three letters.
Now I see your light.
Now I see your mountains.
Now I see what the face of God is like.
You never left me.
I was never alone.
I simply did not understand."*

THE WINDS OF YOUR HEART

CHAPTER 3

PRAYER

Real prayer is not asking for something. One who knows divine prayer says, "I hold in my hand that this predicament exists, and I pray because there are no easy answers."

The Most Sacred Prayer

For thousands of years, generation after generation has tried to connect with life, to seek the spirit behind life, yet more than ninety-nine percent never made it. Why? Those few individuals who broke through knew instinctively how to pray from their heart. They did not pray from a book. They did not pray with someone else's words. They had reverence and respect for life, and when they prayed from their heart, they genuinely prayed.

One of the most important things I ask you to contemplate is that the most blessed prayer of all simply comes from your own heart, not from a holy book or from another human being. It does not come from your mother or father, your child, your wife, your neighbors, your priest, or your teacher. I used to think that a prayer was "Hail Mary, full of grace." But when I learned what it meant to pray from the heart, I realized that this was the most sacred prayer. Remember this.

If you were to realize this simple reality, what would it do to your life — to your every thought, to all your feelings, to all your stories? How would it affect your disappointments, your anger, and your unresolved conflict? Your happiness and joy? How would it affect the way you look at other people on the street, the people you do not understand or do not like? Would you see your town and your friends in the same way? Would you see the passing away of your relatives, the future of your children, and even the history of humanity in the same way? What doors would this realization unlock?

By simply realizing that the greatest prayer of all is the prayer from your own heart, you would have to rewrite the book of life in your mind. You would have to let go of your hurt. You would have to let go of your concepts. You would have to change. You would get back the life that you were given at your birth. And you would see that life is the result of your prayers, your dreams, your hopes—for what you want will eventually happen—just give it time.

Someone else's sacred prayer may have touched a lot of people. But when it is from your *own heart*, that is what starts the spark. That is what starts to connect the "telephone lines" to life out there. That is what starts to move situations and mountains. Just keep speaking from your own heart with as much honesty as you can. Lay your cards on the table, no matter what they show. Know that someone is listening.

This has nothing to do with religion. When you pray, you don't need a picture of a particular deity or the name of any god. You don't have to know any special prayers, words, or mantras. You don't need to know any fancy words—just be sincere with your words. It is "street talk," actually. Speak as you naturally speak, feel as only you can feel. You can even speak to yourself. Remember a time when you were attracted to that one person who you really wanted? Sometimes the one you liked eventually came around and began to like you, too. What made it work? Your focused attention. Your heart and your passion was in it. It was personal to you. This is what it takes to speak to life from your heart.

When you contemplate that the most sacred prayer of all is coming from your own heart, this is putting the value back into your own blood. Have faith in yourself. Don't let anyone fool you. There is no better medicine than the medicine of who you are, for your own medicine is unique, unlike anyone else's. All human beings are very good doctors unto themselves. Whoever created you has put together all the necessary ingredients for you to make your own medicine and to reconstruct your life. But please give yourself plenty of time. And someday life will speak to you—not in words, but life will speak and you will know.

Remember that your prayers are for no one else's ears to hear. They are between you and whoever created you. For life is so very personal. Most of us have to be at the doorstep of death before we can truly understand how personal life is. So keep it personal. You do not have to know all the words in the dictionary, for when you connect, your voice will speak loudly from your heart.

Please, realize this. Fight for your life. Get your life back. And learn to understand that there can be no prayer more sacred than that from your own heart. If there were just one thing I could teach you, it would be this.

The Three Stages of Prayer

Divine prayer is asking for help because a predicament exists, but from a greater sense of reality and a greater perspective that is uncommon to the common mind.

Prayer is something that touches all of our lives in one way or another. Yet there is much more to understanding the true spirit of prayer than most of us realize. In essence, three stages of prayer exist: first-stage or wishing prayer, second-stage or intervention prayer, and third-stage or divine prayer. Although prayer itself transcends the boundaries of any categories one can devise, looking at the nature of prayer in terms of these three stages can help us to understand prayer from a perspective that many of us may not have considered before.

The first stage of prayer encompasses ordinary wishes, hopes, desires, and thoughts. Wishes—good or bad—belong here. Naturally, people don't consider negative wishes to be a form of prayer. This is thought of as voodoo or black magic. But it still lies within the realm of wishing. Whether one wishes something for oneself or for someone else, one is still in the first stage of prayer. Typical wishes might include a desire for a relationship, a good job, a new home, or something more meaningful for humanity like freedom or peace, which can transform into the second or third stage of prayer, as I describe later on. So wishes are a form of prayer, but the essence of prayer itself is not wishes.

The second stage of prayer takes one out of the domain of ordinary life and into the realm of asking spirit for intervention. You might pray to spirit to change the course of your destiny. You might ask to be safe from an illness or to remove someone's suffering. When you know someone who is very sick and you say, "I will pray for you," that is intervention prayer. You might also pray for intervention to alleviate a situation of great devastation. In the first stage of prayer, you are not praying for intervention. You're just wishing.

First-stage prayer involves a very elementary way of thinking. With second-stage prayer there is a development of maturity, a greater depth, and a more constructed type of thought. This kind of prayer tends to take humanity and all of life into account more often. The difference between the first and second stages of prayer is like the mind of a seven-year-old versus the mind of a forty-five-year-old. In second-stage prayer, one can be heartful. One can feel very touched. But there is still a vast difference between second-stage prayer and the next stage of prayer: divine prayer.

In third-stage or divine prayer, one does not ask for anything. Divine prayer is difficult for most people to comprehend for this very reason: one is not wishing for anything. One is not wanting anything. With divine prayer, you are laying the predicament on the table in front of you with no wishes, desires, or wants. Once you start to ask for something in particular, you have distorted the view. Prayer is what goes out to ask for help because a predicament exists and that is it. There are no ulterior motives behind this kind of prayer. It takes an awful lot of work to be able to pray and not ask for anything. The mind not only has to be in an extremely unique time and space, but one also must have enough wisdom to be able to actually pray within the third stage.

"How can I not want a particular outcome?" people ask. This idea is practically incomprehensible to most human beings. Yet this is one of the main reasons that very few people know how to pray. This is also why so many prayers never get answered. Always keep in mind that even if what you prayed for does come about, it doesn't necessarily mean that your prayer was heard and answered. Maybe something happened that made it appear that your prayer was answered, or maybe the synchronicity was there so that a certain outcome was going to happen anyway. You don't know.

Divine prayer resides within the realm of understanding the paradoxes of life. Unfortunately, the minute we start school, we are taught to live on only one side of the fence. Either you stand here or you stand there. Either you think like this or you think like that. Either you're Muslim or you're Christian. This also makes it extremely difficult for most human beings to bring in third-stage prayer, because prayer takes both sides of the fence into account and encompasses the whole. Very few can understand this paradox, much less transcend it. This, in addition to the condition of not asking, is what creates the wall that makes divine prayer invisible to most. And that is why most of us relate to only the first and second stages of prayer.

The problem is that we are literally trained into thinking that we always have to ask. "Ask and you will receive." Grandmas teach it. Schools teach it. Even priests teach it. These are the only references we have in our educational system. As we know, when most of us come to the point of prayer, it's either, "Hey, save me from this illness that's consuming my body," or "Save me from this accident," or "Save me from losing my money," or "Save me from the torment of my mind." We even make deals with God. "If you save me, I promise to be good. I promise never to do that again. I won't ever ask for *anything* again." There are motives behind these prayers. And these motives actually seem to be quite justified. We know that a little positive thinking can help in these moments. It does make a difference. It is better to have positive thinking than negative thinking. But it has nothing to do with divine prayer whatsoever.

Here is an example of the differences between the various forms of prayer. First-stage prayer is: "I wish that my enemies would like me. I pray that they would understand me." Inappropriate first-stage prayer is: "I pray that my enemies will be killed and die off. I pray that those people who don't like me or agree with me will have lives that become hell for them."

Second-stage prayer is: "I pray that my enemies, in time, can understand where I am coming from. I pray that I develop more understanding and compassion for my enemies, and that my behavior becomes less offensive in their eyes. I pray for help to defuse this situation, to bring in more peace, to ease the suffering of it all."

Third-stage prayer is putting your enemies in front of you without judging them, and looking at the situation as clearly as possible. It is looking through their eyes to understand how they see you, and acknowledging that there is not much you can do about the discord that is taking place. Divine prayer knows that if this predicament exists for you at this point in time, it must also exist for many other human beings in this world — not just in the present but in the past — and that this predicament will, no doubt, continue to exist in our world. One who knows divine prayer says, "I hold in my hand that this predicament exists, and I pray because there are no easy answers."

One form of the first stage of prayer has been termed "group consciousness" or "collective consciousness." We all know that there's a collective consciousness of the United States, Japan, and Australia, as there is of all countries. How does this work? Whether we realize it or not, we all radiate our thoughts. For instance, we know that when one person has an idea, all of a sudden quite a few other people will come up with the same idea. This is one aspect of collective consciousness. To take this a step further, when there are enough people wishing for the same thing, it creates a movement within a particular nation or group of people, and their wishes and desires can sometimes start to manifest. America is the manifested prayer of the people of the past who wanted freedom from oppression, not just for themselves but for future generations. In fact, we are all a manifested prayer in the works, because of those in the past who prayed that the people of the future have better lives. Better laws. Peace. Enough food. More laughter and friendship. So a group consciousness can be strong enough to create dramatic changes in history. But that doesn't necessarily mean it involves the second or third stage of prayer.

First-stage prayer *can* translate into the second or even third stage of prayer, depending on the nature of the wishes. Most of first-stage prayer is for the self, but if it is selfless or contains something inherently good that serves humanity — and not just what is good for your genes, your DNA, or your race — then it can transform into the third stage of prayer. And that's when prayers are answered. This means that even if you don't ordinarily have the capacity to bring in the third stage of prayer, you could say that ignorantly you can find yourself in the realm of divine prayer. So, as you can see, it's not as though all prayers are fixed at a given stage. Prayer is multidimensional and fluid — there isn't a formula.

Let's take wishing as an example of first-stage prayer that can transform. One of the most precious rights human beings have in their lives is to wish. We are born with this right. Yet wishing has been left to the children. To wish has been misconstrued and misinterpreted so much that wishing somehow stops at the age of five or seven. This right has been taken away from the young ones far too early. And yet I tell you *never* to stop wishing. For certain wishes are, you could say, the breath that touches the lips of God so quickly and closely, especially if the wish comes from one's heart, and it has the elements to improve one's life, to change oneself inside, or even to touch someone.

If you see something better, for instance, you have a right to wish for that. Teach your eyes, your ears, and all your senses to learn to recognize grass that is greener, walls that have fresher paint, buildings that have more pride, rooms that are more welcoming, books that speak with more sanity and clarity. You have a right to wish for clearer eyes. A softer touch.

A word that emanates from the heart and not just the mind. An intent that runs as deep as the dinosaurs. And a sight that is not blinded by the sun and the blue ceiling of the day.

That's all I did. I saw what was a better country. A better way of thinking. A better way to walk, a better way to hear, a better way to write. And I waited for the right moment to come around—one of those unique, pristine moments when a falling star streaks across the sky. Such a moment may not come for three or four years due to the clouds or because one is a little too busy. Maybe one's head is too heavy to look up. But always have the wish ready to be made when that star appears or the moment is right.

So when the clouds disappear from the night sky, spend more time looking up, and make a wish as a child would wish. To send a sound beat of your own heart that eventually touches the heart of your Creator: what does it so easily is not pain. It's not suffering. It is but a wish from the heart—so innocent and quiet, yet conveyed with very few words. When a wish is ever so silent, no logic, no reason, no analysis can touch it or keep up with it. These silent wishes are the loudest of all. For a wish can draw out the magic of a falling star, or of a certain moment in time, if it is expressed with a very tender and soft word of a heart that runs deep. These are the wishes that are heard.

Beyond wishing prayer, the next stage of prayer—intervention prayer—may or may not be heard. It depends. Second-stage prayer is like an in-between level that gets a little closer to genuine prayer, because it doesn't just involve ordinary wishes, and there is more substance, sincerity, and reverence within it. Yet many think that's the ultimate kind of prayer. And it's not.

You can look at it this way. Third-stage prayer is nothing more than dialing the right phone number. With second-stage prayer, somehow you've dialed the right phone number, but it can be a bad line, depending on the circumstances. Even though intervention prayer comes more from the heart, and might have to do with a desire to ease suffering or bring in something of value for all living beings, the connection still may not be clear. First-stage prayer involving ordinary wishes that don't come from the heart, in most cases, doesn't even have access to the right phone number.

Typical first-stage prayer wants a lot of results. Immediate results. Yesterday results. Second-stage prayer also wants results, but it is more realistic in its expectations. Third-stage prayer doesn't expect results.

Divine prayer takes the past, the present, and the future equally into view. One doesn't expect that the prayer will be answered tomorrow or next week or next year. That's not the point. The point is that if a predicament exists today in this time, then it exists in all times.

Third-stage prayer realizes that it is not just me who is going through hard times. If this is happening to me, then it is happening to all of us to some degree. So it is important to acknowledge that there is a predicament taking place that is bigger than myself and my problems. Then prayer becomes strong.

Divine prayer releases one from any intervention or assistance for a given situation. Divine prayer is not just for one's immediate predicament; one prays for all times, with absolutely no expectations of any results, even within one's lifetime. One's prayers could actually affect someone ten thousand years in the future. You see, the person praying has enough faith that all existence matters. All time matters.

When someone is ill, you pray. But not to heal. How do you know what is behind the illness? When false pride is there, we think we have to go and heal everything. Divine prayer knows that if one person is ill and suffering, most likely many others are, too. So the one who is praying in the third stage prays for all. Although divine prayer acknowledges that unusual things can happen, it knows that an angel doesn't just come down and wash the earth with a bottle of bleach that kills all the bacteria and viruses.

Actually, no matter what stage you are praying in, it is wise never to expect results. Let's say you're a pioneer in America during the early 18th century, traveling across Oklahoma with your family in your covered wagon. All of a sudden, you see dozens of Indians coming to attack your wagon, so you start to pray like hell that somehow you and your family can make it through alive. No matter how hard you pray, you must keep in mind that the outcome doesn't necessarily depend solely on some form of intervention; it also depends on what you do and what the Indians do. Besides, the Indians could be praying for something else — for instance, that they destroy your covered wagon and that this is the last of the white people coming through their land! That's the trouble. Still, intervention can take place in the first and second stages of prayer. But most of it is so common that it takes a certain brightness within that prayer, as I explained in chapter 2.

Divine prayer doesn't mean you're not concerned with a situation of great suffering, it's just that you have a different understanding of reality. You don't have false hope. False faith. You're very sane and practical about time and space. A lot of bad things don't instantly go away just because you have the gift of third-stage prayer. They might, but one doesn't know. So divine prayer is asking for help because a predicament exists, but from a greater sense of reality and a greater perspective that is uncommon to the common mind.

Aarmon

Prayer is just not for our generation, prayer is for all the generations. Prayer is not just for one human being who is ill and suffering, but for all human beings who suffer.

One of the biggest lessons in my life came from my oldest son, Aarmon, who is now in his mid-twenties. Several years ago, a biological illness overtook him and began to affect his brain quite severely. Certain areas of his brain were not receiving adequate blood flow, and so they began to shut down. In effect, his world was getting smaller and smaller.

Before this happened, my son was just another typical young teenager who enjoyed his friends and his life. He was intelligent and sensitive. Now his mentality is that of a six-year-old. He essentially lost his life to whatever this disease is. Nobody really understands what happened. Not even the specialists have been able to pinpoint the problem.

To watch my firstborn son deteriorate before my eyes was not an easy thing. Aarmon realized that something was happening to him that he could not stop and that wasn't his choice at all. When he was about seventeen or eighteen, he would sit in his bedroom, holding his head in his hands and rocking quietly for hours. One could feel his mental pain and agony, as he tried to figure out what was wrong: "What's going on? What's going on? Something's wrong — what is it?"

One day Aarmon and I were talking about his illness, because he had asked me what was happening to him. I was trying to give him as much clarity as I could about his situation without holding anything back. At the time, we didn't even know if he was dying. But clearly, he was losing his world.

After a while, he looked up at me and said, "Dad, will I ever be able to love again?" He could feel the love of his youth disappearing, because his emotional and mental worlds were shrinking. Just a few years ago, he loved life just like any other young person. He loved to laugh and play games and get into trouble. He loved his friends and family. But now this love was leaving his personality, and more and more, it was becoming as though nobody was there. It was like he was going away.

"Will I ever be able to love again?" To hear that hurt my heart, almost more than I could bear. But I began to see that all over the world there are lots of young ones, not just my son, having problems. Prayer takes the wholeness of it all into view. From this perspective, my son was just another number among humanity. He was just another patient in a hospital. Just another name in a newspaper. Just another fact for medical science. That's all.

"I understand now," I remember thinking. "Prayer is not because it happens just to my son. Prayer is not just for those who are young and healthy. Prayer is realizing that one day we will find ourselves very old. We really will. Prayer is understanding that we live in a world where biology rules. Nature rules. Not us. We're not going to save the world, any more than we can save all the sick human beings. We can clean up our air and our water, but we're not saving the world. That's arrogance."

You see, those who can genuinely pray have an understanding of time, biology, the sciences, and the environment in which we live. They have an understanding, as much as possible at the present time, of the heavens, the stars, the planets, the moons, the galaxies, and all the worlds that the astronomers are bringing to us. They have an understanding of what it is to love, and what it is for the love to suddenly fly away, as though a gust of wind came and carried it far beyond one's reach. They have a good understanding of birth, and they have a very good understanding that we all must pass away.

What has created the vast illusion of seemingly never-ending life, good health, and success are the young ones who are healthy and don't get ill. The ones who are successful every day, who have enough to eat, who have enough money. And the ones who have gone on to reach their twenties, thirties, and forties. What is it to be successful? You can drive a car. People who know you come up and say "hello." You know where your wallet is. You can buy groceries. Your family is proud of you, and you can feel the sense of pride in yourself. You know where to put your left and right foot. You don't even have to think about it. When you go home, if you're lucky, you have a nice bed with clean sheets and the TV is still there to watch. Your hair is brushed nicely. And this has been going on for days and weeks and months and years. "Ah! I live in success. I bathe in it. It's ordinary. So what? I don't even think about it, I just do it. I mean, what's so wrong?"

The people who know prayer have a different understanding. They know what a short time we have to live. Yet how easily most of us hold onto the illusion of life that goes on without end, without problems.

But look how fast you have reached your age. Multiply that times two and you will find yourself reaching the next phase of your life even faster.

Those who understand prayer know that one day this generation will slip away, as have all the other generations. As we've dodged in and out of the shadows, somehow we have found ourselves alive in this generation. It's our turn now. But prayer is not just for our generation, prayer is for all the generations. Prayer is not just for one human being who is ill and suffering, but for all human beings who suffer. Does prayer just reside in the lineage of your own family? No. Does prayer have boundaries? No. For all people really do hurt. They do.

Lama Gheshala

This lama enlightens the mind by transmitting the light.

In the old days, it was well known that very few people had the gift of prayer. But when someone was blessed with the gift, it was clear. There was usually one person in the village, community, or tribe who had it. Everyone in the village would go to that person and ask, "Would you please pray for me, would you please pray for my family?" People had a better understanding of prayer back then. Prayer is a gift.

Lama Gheshala is a good friend of mine who has the gift. There is no doubt that this lama knows how to pray — quietly, naturally, kindly. He is known as a Geshe. In the Buddhist tradition there are different levels of lamas. It is very much like our academic system. You can get a college degree and just be a lama. If you want to get a Ph.D., you go back to the university for more schooling and then you become a Geshe, which is equivalent to a college professor. Lama Gheshala is like a professor in the school of Buddhism.

These Geshe lamas are extremely bright and intelligent. As the years go by, many of them become gentler, kinder, softer, and quieter. The young lamas tend to be very robust. They are the ones who go out into the world and do much of the work that people see.

Lama Gheshala doesn't like to teach. He just likes to do his prayers. Because of who he is, the lama has transcended the three stages of prayer so that all his prayers carry an inherent goodness for humanity. This man is at peace. He is a wonderful, simple, nurturing human being who is very kind and sincere. He also has a great deal of power. Yet only a few students study with him. That's what is so amazing. Lama Gheshala hardly says or does anything. He does not even perform all the traditional Buddhist rituals. He just "emanates."

Lama Gheshala lives in Monterey, California. A friend of mine, one of the lama's students who takes care of him, bought him a house in a neighborhood of the city that wasn't at all nice. The area was neglected and in shambles. When you looked around the streets, you could see that people had simply stopped caring. They didn't really care if their houses were falling apart or hadn't been painted within the last thirty years. They didn't mind if the neighborhood looked bad. They were just living. So this wonderful "professor" of lamas was living in a house that was as run down as all the other houses on the block. Inside his house it was quite nice, but the outside needed a lot of work.

I felt a little embarrassed about the situation, because this lama was so gentle and sweet. So I expressed my concern.

"Lama Gheshala, I'm sorry that your eyes have to see this." When one cares for someone, one naturally wants the best for that person. The lama just smiled and said, "No problem. You know, I'll just do my pujas and take care of it. Just wait and see. Don't worry." I realized that the lama didn't really care about his living situation. He was going to let it be. But once he noticed that *I* cared, he started to do something about it to ease my mind. He began to do his pujas, or ceremonial prayers, very quietly.

The lama was simply emanating. He was not condemning the neighborhood or the people. He didn't go around telling others,

"You have to paint your houses. You need to clean up your yards." He respected what is, understood the predicament, and just raised the consciousness. The lama knew that situations can change. So he opened up his heart and lightened up the darkness of the minds of those who lived in the neighborhood. The light gives people new ways to see. It gives them options. It makes them feel better about themselves. And when people feel better about themselves, they start to care more — not just for their own lives, but for their homes, their neighborhoods, and their communities.

You could say that Lama Gheshala let the sun come out. What is in the light that he was letting out? It is like the light of a movie. When you make a movie and show the film, what is in the light that's coming from the projector onto the screen? The director's intent. The lama's light was well designed for the neighborhood. Lama Gheshala's movie showed what happens when the whole neighborhood starts to care. The kids feel better about their surroundings. The adults feel better about their lives. After a while, people begin to come out of their houses and get to know their neighbors. So the people living in the lama's neighborhood received not just the light of the projector, but the light of the director. In essence, the light itself was the lama's prayer.

Before long, I noticed that the neighborhood started to change. People began to paint and fix up their homes. They started to clean up their yards and pick up the trash. They put up nice new fences. One house after another improved dramatically. After about six or eight months had passed, the lama had managed to get this entire block looking very nice.

"Lama, it is amazing what you did," I said.

"Yes, what a few prayers and ceremonies can do," he replied. This is how he is. The lama understood the nature of genuine prayer. But he took care of the situation because someone was concerned, not because he minded living in such a neighborhood. That is love.

* * *

One day Lama Gheshala called me on the phone and said, "Please, come over and help me clean up my yard." This lama is not in heaven. His feet are on the earth all the time. So I went over to the lama's house and, along with several other people, began to straighten up his backyard. We found piles of old junk that had been sitting around for forty or fifty years. Trash was everywhere. We set aside all the garbage to burn later in a bonfire.

I watched every move this lama made, and I saw him do something that was so touching. When one picks up a piece of wood that has been laying on the ground for a long time, one usually finds many insects living underneath it. Most people would just throw it on the fire. Well, the lama picked up the board and started chanting: "Auuuuuuuuu…," then laid it back down. I didn't say anything. He did that with every piece of wood. Then he told us that tomorrow we would burn the wood in the fire.

I returned the next day and watched the lama as he walked around and started picking up these boards that were scattered all over the ground. But there were no insects underneath.

"What did you do?" I asked.

"Oh," he said, "I told them that we were going to come the next day and burn these boards in the fire, and that they are going to have to leave." This lama enlightens the mind by transmitting the light. He has a constant relationship with his environment. To him, everything is a living force. And he respects this living force.

※ ※ ※

One day this wonderful lama developed an abscess on his foot, which eventually became infected. The infection kept growing and getting worse. Because he was a well-respected, highly educated lama, he naturally drew in a lot of other important lamas to come and do pujas for his infected foot. Some of the lamas were doctors of medicine in the

Buddhist tradition, so they brought their Tibetan medicine with them. They did puja after puja after puja. They threw divinations to find out what was wrong from the spirits. They even took the lama to a woman in the San Francisco Bay area who sucked blood from his wounds. So Lama Gheshala received very potent prayers, pujas, mantras, medicine, and tiny pills, which I call "bullets," that are filled with special herbs and blessings. He really received the royal treatment.

Yet the infection continued to worsen until it began to eat up his foot. The other lamas kept pouring on the pujas, but nothing seemed to work and the pain was getting worse. So the lamas pumped out more pujas and more mantras and gave Lama Gheshala more Tibetan medicine. Everybody was watching this poor man grow worse and worse. By now the lama was truly suffering because the infection was affecting his nerves, which was quite painful. This went on for weeks.

The wife of one of the main students was watching all of this happen. She was a bookkeeper who did not do any Buddhist practices whatsoever. This woman was very straight, down to earth, and wonderful to talk with. Finally, she said, "No more! That's it! Stop this and take him to the doctor!" So his students finally took Lama Gheshala to the hospital.

"You know," said the doctor who examined him, "this man is dying of blood poisoning. Gangrene has set in. One more day and he would have died." The doctor even had to operate to save his life. It was that bad. The lama suffered terribly and went through a lot of pain. He almost lost his leg. The doctors took off one toe. Now when Lama Gheshala gets sick, he says, "No, no, no pujas! Take me to doctor. Take me to doctor."

The next month I went to see Lama Gheshala and I asked him to show me his foot. Being so good-natured, he was laughing at his predicament. He said, "Emahó, I really learned something." He learned to recognize which medicine is *appropriate*. To be appropriate is not an easy task. We become mesmerized by legends, dreams, fantasies, and false hopes. We need to put ourselves in our feet and to develop good judgment about which medicine is appropriate for the given situation — the medicine of prayers or the medicine of physicians.

Be careful with blind faith. There is a common sense of both worlds. They each have their good points. The pujas and prayers are wonderful if you understand them and keep them in their proper place. But if your dreams are beyond what is common sense, you will get lost.

You have to be cautious when you're ill. You cannot just go to the far left. You have to understand how far homeopathic medicine can go. How far can the divine touch go? How far can prayer go? And when is the time to take hard-core Western medicine? Naturally, it can be confusing when deciding which medicine to take because we have a powerful mind that can create placebo effects. Yet stability is essential. It is important to be in our feet, to be right in our toes, to keep our eyes open, and to have healthy doubt.

We must develop the discretion to understand the nature of blessings and to what extent they can help. This discretion is very important to have. The Buddhists call it the "wisdom of discretion." Well put. When we don't possess the wisdom of discretion, we are, in essence, ignorant about what is taking place inside the body.

I get so many questions from people about various physical ailments, and the problem is that many of them simply need to go see a physician: "You're sick. Go see a doctor." On the other hand, many of us do easily fall victim to psychosomatic illnesses. People can experience sicknesses associated with emotional turmoil or a spiritual process as it is cleaning up what is inside. These latent illnesses can arise and leave very quickly. They often feel quite real but are actually of the mind. Interestingly, when you are experiencing the mind-based illnesses, you feel sick yet look fine, but when you are truly ill, you feel sick and look sick. I am not saying not to treat any form of illness. I am saying that each of us has to develop discretion about when it is appropriate to go see a doctor.

I recently spoke with a woman who is studying Western medicine, but her heart is with another medicine from the East because she feels it's better.

But it is not better, it's just different. Western medicine is very good medicine and it's improving all the time. No doubt, the medicine of the Chinese, the Tibetans, and the Africans all have their wonderful aspects and can also be very good. North American Indians have excellent medicine, too. They all have their benefits. But we must understand that there are certain boundaries to each type of medicine and become very sane about this. When is each medicine appropriate? And when is prayer appropriate? Just because prayer can be beneficial doesn't mean that you don't also need to see a doctor.

The Dalai Lama, for instance, is the most sane person I have ever seen. His mind is extremely clear and he obviously has the wisdom of discretion. It is very evident that this man has transcended his mind. But he understands what it means to be trapped within one's culture and tradition — it's a predicament.

One who understands the nature of prayer knows that we have to use our intelligence as much as possible to deal with the bacteria and viruses and other elements of nature that can harm us. We have to figure out which water is safe to drink and which water is not safe. That's what our intelligence is for. If we drink bad water, we're going to get sick. And then we pray because we drank the bad water and we're sick? There's a price to pay for our decisions, our actions, and our ignorance. So we need to use our education, common sense, and discretion to make sure we don't drink the bad water. We will get into trouble if we do. It's a matter of simple intelligence. That's not up to God. That's up to us.

Understanding Effective Prayer

Sincere prayer takes place when your heart is present. It isn't just putting out words.

There are very few human beings who genuinely know how to pray. You either have to be naturally wired for it, or something must take place in your life that creates the wiring for prayer to take place. It could be happiness, sadness, a tragedy, or a wonderful day that opens the door to prayer. Otherwise, you're just talking to a wall. You're just going through the motions. And that's what happens with most people. The paradox is that prayer is in everyone's heart, but that doesn't mean one can always pray. The right circumstances have to arise to activate it.

Would you like to know a trick of the trade understood by those who know how to pray? It is not a complex thing. It's very simple. Whenever you find that your heart has been touched, just speak to life. Remember that you live in a glass house and your thoughts do not only reside inside your head. Life hears you. When you speak to life through your heart, that in itself becomes the prayer. And when you are not in your heart, do not attempt to pray. Don't waste your breath, for this is the time to prepare. Constantly get ready so that when your heart is open, which doesn't happen too often in this world, you can speak with greater depth and sincerity. The signal goes out further. The medicine is stronger. And when your heart closes, begin to prepare again for the next time. Continue to speak to life, if you wish. Talk to yourself. Connect inside. But know that this is not the moment for genuine prayer to show its face.

The ones who know how to pray know that prayer is also observing what the situation is while feeling the goodness of life. It is knowing that the goodness has to be there someplace, around the bend or past the shadows: "I see that things can be better, yet I cannot see how this will come about. So I pray because of what I have seen. I pray because I know there is more." Prayer is offering the faith that medicine can be created to come down and do what needs to be done to provide help, but from a greater perspective. It is creating the communication link with life, looking at what the reality is without judging it, and knowing that situations can change. Something out of the ordinary can happen.

One who understands prayer says, "I know my limits and my strengths. I know what I can and cannot do. I don't have the control wheel or buttons to push to change things. Who is in charge of life? Me? No. There is something much bigger than just me." It is the mere humbleness itself that is the prayer. "I don't know. I didn't put the sun up into the sky. I don't know. I didn't build this earth. I don't know. I don't make the future. I didn't take care of the past." You could say that true prayer goes where the mind cannot see and cannot follow.

What makes prayer strong is being honest with the circumstances, understanding your predicament, and realizing that there isn't much, if anything, you can do about it. All you can do is ask for help. Let's say that I am stranded out in the desert and I need help. I want to understand the reality of my situation without denying the seriousness of it. There's no water. I may die. It doesn't look good. "I want to understand" becomes the prayer. It starts manufacturing medicine to help. My job is to hold the honesty of my predicament and then start walking as I have been walking. But remember that it can take time. Sometimes solutions appear very quickly and sometimes they come about more slowly. Have patience. Don't lose faith. Faith and hope are the sons and daughters of prayer.

If you feel you do not know how to pray, pretend that you're a baby and you don't know how to tell your parents what is wrong or how to ask them for help. So you do what you can to communicate with the adults by means of your feelings and gestures, and the parents understand because your intent is there. It is the same with prayer, with speaking to life. Life will get the message.

Here is an example of how true prayer is activated. Imagine that before you is a big glass dome, and inside it is your child. There is no food for your child. You cannot hear your child. The child can't see you but you can see your child, for it is like you are looking through a one-way mirror. You can observe what your child is going through, but you cannot give anything to your child or offer any help.

That will start to open your heart very quickly. Prayers will begin to come through immediately because you see that an actual predicament is occurring and there is nothing you can do about it. In time, you may find that ways and means are offered so that the glass barrier between you and your child starts to soften. Tools are supplied. Education, wisdom, and insights are provided. Your instincts are enhanced. You could say that simply acknowledging that you cannot do anything about the situation starts to turn the predicament into medicine. That is what real medicine is.

How effective is prayer? It depends not only on the stage of prayer, but also on who is doing the praying and how naturally connected that particular person is. How developed is one's spirit? Is there innocence involved? What are the circumstances surrounding the prayer? You cannot look at prayer from a linear perspective, for the paradox is so intertwined with it that prayer can transcend all these elements, depending on the situation.

In most cases, I don't want people praying for me, not only because I don't know what they're praying for, but also because I want only the prayers of people who are sane and healthy in their mind and heart. The effectiveness of prayer depends, you could say, on the consciousness of the person praying. The more consciousness a person carries, the stronger the prayer. Yet a person might have a lack of consciousness and great innocence. When there is great innocence with an intent, prayer is strong because it's clean: there are no ulterior motives behind it. When there is motive behind it, prayer usually goes nowhere. It is just empty words that dissolve into the air.

Motives that one could call "clean" are very different from those that most adults have. They're not even quite motives any more. These motives are more natural, something like when an innocent child goes to touch you. Is there a motive? No. The child just wants to touch. You can see and feel that it is clean. But when somebody doesn't have a clean motive and that person is reaching out to touch you, it's obvious and it hurts. Clean motives are with us all the time, but we need to pay attention to see them.

When you have consciousness and you also have the innocence of life in which the innocence has become wisdom, then the prayer has matured and provides a different function. It affects life very differently because now there is wisdom backing up the prayer and not just innocence.

When someone comes to you and you happen to have this innocence, you can make things happen for that person. You are able to serve as a catalyst for the prayers of others. You don't know how it works, but all you do is close your eyes, hear what somebody is asking for, and it just seems to happen. All children have this innocence. It is quite natural. How easy it was to be kind when we were young, without a motive behind it.

When a child prays, the signals can travel so very far, so easily. But when many adults pray, their prayers don't go too far. Who taught the children the principles of prayer? No one. It's just that there are no motives behind their prayers — just innocence. No disappointment, hurt, or hatred — just innocence. No obstructions, no filters over their eyes — just innocence.

But as we get older, we start to lose our innocence and become angry, frustrated, bitter, and mistrustful of life. We leave the beauty of prayer behind. By the time we're in our thirties or forties and we try to formulate what prayer is, it will seem like something that is very far off, something quite removed from our lives. This is when people begin to feel *alone*, because they don't have this sense of prayer.

But when you have innocence and a sense of true, devotional prayer — you're not alone. A presence is there. You're not just speaking to the air. You're not just speaking to the walls. You're not just speaking to yourself. You know there is something out there in existence that is far more than most humans can perceive. Some people manage to hold on to the innocence, and then they become a channel for prayer itself. They might be seventy or eighty years old, yet they still understand prayer and the innocence it requires. These human beings are not alone, because they understand.

Prayer is almost a manipulation of light. It is a play of light, so to speak, but with light that is *alive*. It is care and living light. Prayer provides a little more inspiration to keep us going for another day. Prayer is a way of helping to remove obstacles that would have completely devastated someone for years to come. Prayer, you could say, is love, so that people don't have to go through their "karma" or experience suffering, because it's not always necessary. Yet sometimes suffering is the best thing that can happen. Prayer is an understanding that oversees the difference.

Sincere prayer takes place when your heart is present. It isn't just putting out words. It is gathering. Contemplating. Letting the situation touch your heart. It is coming to terms with the predicament with as much honesty as possible, and realizing that it's really no one's fault — that's just the way it is. Put it on the altar. You could say that you are offering up the predicament so that this in itself becomes the prayer, then giving the prayer time to work. But it needs honesty. When there is no honesty, prayer is useless, nothing but wind blowing. It is just that most of us haven't been taught how to pray. We may have been taught how to memorize a prayer, or how to kneel down and hold our hands in a certain way. But are we really praying? People turn prayer into practice, but life is not practicing.

If you're not sincere, but you're praying anyway, there's nothing going out. It's like people who are being nice because they want to get something. Those who have the wisdom can see it. They can see when people are faking so they can get what they want. That's the glass house. Nothing is hidden. So if you're just putting out garbage, who will respond to that? Will that touch anyone out there?

Very seldom in anyone's life does the opportunity arise for genuine, devotional prayer when the door to the heart is open and you are connected. When this happens, your prayer is free of ulterior motives, desperation, fear, greed, or want. You are not trying to shape the outcome of the prayer. You are not trying to manipulate it in any way whatsoever.

It is something like parents who hope that their child has a good life, although they don't know what the child's future will hold. It's a natural wish that most parents have: that their children are happy and do well in life. But at the same time the parents acknowledge that life can be difficult, and that they do not know which direction would be best for their child's life to take. This is prayer without asking for a specific outcome, without getting one's sticky fingers in the way.

I really cannot speak for you when it comes to prayer. But from my own account, I have found that I cannot pray all the time. I always find myself speaking to life, but that is not the same as sincere, devotional prayer. It's like somebody saying, "I want you to smile." If I don't feel like it, my smile isn't genuine. When I smile, I smile. But if I can't, I can't.

There are very few times that I pray in any given year, but when that door opens up, I pray with everything I have. When it's not open, I do not pray. I don't even attempt to. Why pray? It is just spinning words for my pride. At times many of us have felt that door open to some degree. Once again, this is when it comes down to honesty: is the door open or not?

When it comes to divine prayer, it takes a unique time and space for it to come in. When it happens, you feel an atmosphere of not just reverence but an actual holiness around you. In this state, there is *no doubt* that the door has opened up to divine prayer. And that is why prayer is so effective when you are in this state. When you are in the environment of divine prayer, you pray only for what is appropriate. You cannot really go wrong.

Think of it this way. We know that there are those people who compose or sing one extraordinarily beautiful song and that is it. They can't produce any more. Others can create two or three such songs, then all of a sudden the magic seems to go away. And that is also the case with prayer. It's rare to be in sync with it, when everything works. It is like receiving a heartfelt kiss, or making love when it is beautiful the whole time, or having a good day when everything is perfect. These things don't happen all the time.

When the door to pray does open so that you find yourself in a particular space where the energy is extremely strong and real, if your intent is genuinely from your heart and you ask something of life, what you ask will come eventually. Just give it time. Life has all the time in the world. Let's say you come down from that space the next day and you aren't feeling good about yourself. Now you want to change what you have just prayed for. No matter what you do, you cannot change it — unless you reach that same point or higher. If you can bring in a greater reality with even more heart, then you can change the prayer. The energy has to be of equal or greater value.

That is why, once you understand this, you will find yourself not praying for anything but goodness. You will pray that the goodness of life reveals itself to you, and that you become that goodness. You will pray to wake up. To be more present. To keep your heart open. To help when you can and to know when you cannot. To understand the nature of the mind, the human being, the planet we are living on. You will pray that every cell becomes good.

So do not pray if you are not in your heart. That is not real prayer. In the last thirty or forty years, how many times have you found yourself in that space where prayer was genuine and the connection to life was real? It is *very rare*. The trick is recognizing that the door is open and taking advantage of it. Always be on guard. Prepare, work, and get ready for the day when that door cracks open. I've seen these doors open up for people who just let the opportunity pass them by. When this phenomenon is taking place, they're too shocked to do anything about it. Then the sky closes up and ordinary life sets in. They missed it. Remember that like a good life, a good day, a good moment, a good situation — so does the opportunity for prayer arise. So be a good girl scout. Be a good boy scout. When that door opens, take advantage of it. And don't forget that when you truly speak from your bones, your voice is as loud and travels as far as the voice of any angel, any teacher, or any god.

SPEAK TO LIFE

Talk to life.
Speak to life.
You may not see anything but a tree and a sky.
You may not see anything but a sun.
If you do not see anything, have faith.
Whoever put your heart in your chest,
have faith and speak to that.

We all have to walk away from each other.
But life never walks away from us.
Never.
You can call me by phone
and I may answer or I may not.
But when you call life from your heart,
life always hears.
You can come to me
and I may be too busy
to hear what you have to say,
but when you speak to life from your heart,
life is never too busy to hear you.

Once you start to talk to life,
you don't need to be an American Indian,
you don't need to be a Catholic or a Jew,
you don't need to be a Buddhist or an Atheist.
You do not need a book.
You do not need a formula.
You do not need a special word or a mantra.
You don't even need to say or know one prayer.
You have it.

For the real communication
is as you would speak to a good friend.
Just speak to yourself inside
and learn to connect with life.
Very quietly.
Very softly.
Because life is very, very personal.

THE WINDS OF YOUR HEART

CHAPTER 4

THE LIVING SACRAMENTS

Once you can transfer the essence of the sacraments from the church to yourself, you have understood the goodness of religion.

In this world, there are living sacraments that exist not only in various churches, but also in nature, in our cities, in our communities, and in our homes. When the sacrament is real, there is actually a beautiful, benevolent spirit within it that is very much alive. Not all churches have sacraments that are embodied with spirit, but when there is a living presence within the church, it has an effect on us. It's like being radiated by plutonium, but the effect is beneficial.

If you simply hold this understanding, you will be able to go into any church or temple — whether it is Protestant, Catholic, Buddhist, or of another faith — and receive from the sacraments in a way that is extremely personal. Despite how harmful the church may have been in the past or how you feel about its religious practices, remember this. When you find the sacraments that are actually alive, get the heart of them. Receive what they have to offer, for this is what will help you. Once you can transfer the essence of the sacraments from the church to yourself, you have understood the goodness of religion.

All religions have their own sacraments, but with different names, different labels, and different stories behind them. Catholics have their holy Eucharist. Christians and Hindus have their religious icons — sacred images of various saints or teachings of the church. Buddhists have their thangkas — paintings illustrating Buddhist deities and teachings that are traditionally created by monks. Occasionally you will see a thangka that radiates an aliveness because it is instilled with spirit, either by the person who created it or by the one who received the thangka and looks after it.

A long time ago, the esoterics, the mystics, the people who spent a lot of time looking up at the stars, began to realize that they could actually draw spirit into a piece of paper, a cloth, or a stone — using a stick, a pencil, a brush, or a chisel. This can happen in one of two ways. When someone is creating an icon or thangka with reverence and prayer, the artist becomes like a conduit for spirit to come through and become embedded in the piece of cloth. Then there are those human beings, whether or not they are artists, who have the capacity to draw in a benevolent spirit simply because they are hard-wired to do so.

Several years ago, a good friend of mine came across a very large thangka of a green Tara, a female deity or Boddhisattva in the Buddhist tradition. A couple of days before he found the thangka, this man had been attending one of my workshops in Paris. After the workshop ended, he was resting in bed at his hotel, when all of a sudden something caught his eye and he turned to see a phenomenon of living light and objects in the air. Somehow, he knew that the light was alive. My friend was stunned by this because he had never witnessed a living light before. After a few minutes it stopped, and he found himself wondering, "Am I going crazy? I must be seeing things."

The next day this man was back home in Switzerland, when he felt a strong compulsion to get up early that morning and go into town. That was unusual. After so much traveling, he was usually so tired that he stayed in bed for a few days. When my friend got to town, without hesitating he headed straight to the store where the thangka was displayed and said, "That's it. I'll take it." This beautiful thangka had been for sale for quite some time, yet no one had bought it. But now this man had the eyes to see the thangka for what it was.

When I teach in Switzerland, I stay in this friend's home, so I got a chance to see this particular thangka soon after he bought it. What I saw was surprising: a living benevolent spirit was present in the cloth. I wondered how long it was going to remain in the thangka, because a spirit can leave from a piece of cloth, a rock, or whatever object it inhabits. But after some time had passed, I realized that it was here to stay. It had a home.

There are good reasons why we walk into a particular house, why we were born to a certain mother and father, why we find good water to drink. It is the same when a living sacrament exists in your village, in your town, or in your home — there are good reasons. My friend's thangka, like all living sacraments, is really something to share. And because my workshop was held just blocks from his house, all of the workshop participants were able to visit his home and witness what it was like to be in the presence of a living sacrament.

Someone asked me if spirits like those that live in the sacraments are sometimes drawn to help a human being personally. It depends. You can draw in a particular kind of spirit for your plan, your design, your destiny. As we all have our expertise with certain subjects, so do the various spirits. But they do not necessarily carry the quality of benevolence. If the spirit is benevolent, it will draw in and affect many people. If not, it will affect only you. It's designed just for you. And these benevolent spirits are not here just for humans. Animals can be affected as well.

How does a living benevolent spirit stay in an object or a piece of cloth? Let me put it this way. When you look down and see the tiny ants, spiders, and bugs, can they comprehend you? Can they understand your mind? No, although once in a great while one can. Besides, they're extremely busy within their own worlds. That is like the vast difference in the scale of evolution between most human beings and a living benevolent being, which exists in a different time and space where we are nothing but the dream. They're in the greater reality, we're not. We're the ones who are dreaming. That's the difference. And that's how a benevolent spirit can live in a cloth. From the spirit's point of view, it's not just a cloth. It's not just a piece of stone or metal that exists only in our world. It's also of another time and space.

In the living sacraments one can see what I call the "Buddha line"—a well-defined line of any form that has such great intent and understanding that it becomes an icon in a spiritual sense, whether or not it was created with a religious purpose in mind. It almost takes on a life within itself. Michelangelo, for instance, was a great artist who knew how to draw the Buddha line. One can just see the life in his work. Some architects know how to do it. So do a few movie directors, whose movies reflect the line. But when certain people who have been touched by spirit or who have understood the essence of religion create a Buddha line, they instill it with the nature of spirit. Spirit is *in* the lines, it's *in* the paper, although it also exists in another dimension.

You can see the Buddha line in some churches. Throughout history people have built extremely elaborate churches and temples. In ancient times the temple was revered and honored. These old temples were quite extraordinary. Their beauty and architectural style were designed not only for appearance but for a living purpose. The style of the walls, the floors, the windows—all of these details were there for a reason, not just to create a building that simply stood there looking beautiful.

Today we don't have this kind of thinking. Most of us do not have any references for building something with a living purpose. But the people of the past understood what the temple meant and how to use it. They knew that a temple or a church can become alive. Now it is mainly the architects who are constructing the churches, and the whole system of how to build them has changed. In the past, churches were built with a knowingness of the sacraments that were going to be living within them. The creation of a church wasn't just left up to the architects and builders. The feelings, thoughts, and intent of the mystics, lamas, and priests who understood the purpose of the temple were designed into the church. Modern architects and builders follow the directions of those with the vision as well as they can, but there's still something missing. In the past, there wasn't such a separation between the builder and the intent of those who truly understood what the temple was for. Today there is a much bigger gap.

Our Inner Temple

The real intent behind a church is to give us an external temple that is a reflection of our temple inside.

The purpose behind the living churches and temples, among other things, is to help people understand their own inner temple. The external temples provide us with a focal point that exists in the same physical dimension in which we live, and this is what helps us to connect with our own temple inside. When someone receives the Eucharist or a piece of bread or anything that is embodied with living spirit, this is the bridge that bypasses the "selfish genes" that tend to control us and make us think of nothing but survival. This is what gives us hope that we are more than our reactions, more than our hunger, more than our desperation. "Somehow I can now remember what I had forgotten because I've been too busy going to work, taking care of my family, paying the bills, finding food to eat."

The beauty of life is that all beings have a temple inside. You can think of your inner temple as having somewhat the structure of a physical temple, but it's made of Uncaused Light. Each temple is unique unto itself. It's like a home. But it's *your* home. Your temple is the totality of all that you are. It is constantly being constructed within your own thoughts. The walls are you. The floor is you. Everything within it is you. And your inner temple changes as you change. As the spirit changes, the walls change. The ceiling changes. One's temple is really quite simple. Yet no matter how simple it is, the temple is beautiful because it's living light. Your temple is as divine as that of any god. It's as beautiful and wonderful and quiet.

You as the spirit live within this temple. Nothing else exists in the temple but you. It is the same for all sentient creatures. A physician can cut into your body with a scalpel. A mother, a father, a friend, or a foe can get inside you energetically. Someone can feel empathy for your pain or joy. Yet no one but you can enter your temple. There isn't one being —

not even a god—who can walk into your temple. It's *yours*. And within your temple, you are in communion with the Creator.

The dream of it all, the reflection of it all, is what takes place within the spirit that always resides within the temple. Even if you are alive in the physical, and even if your spirit is drawn into your skin and you awaken, it still lives within the temple. What all of us are naturally trying to do is to find our temple. That's the journey. And when you do find your temple, you will understand the nature of real peace.

When the external temple becomes a reflection of our own temple inside, the true function of the church has been realized. It is really a matter of feeling and sensing that there is another way to live. There is another way to be. If we can establish and hold contact with our inner temple, we'll see this. And when we touch our temple inside, this also helps to awaken the spirit and draw it closer to our skin.

That, in essence, becomes the quest. That becomes what one could call "the process." That becomes the path. Somehow when we receive a taste of our inner temple, it makes us feel whole. It gives us back ourselves. It reminds us that there is a reason for life. There is great purpose for life. And we find that mercy and forgiveness seem to become much easier to understand and to act on.

The Eucharist

When the Eucharist is living you could say that the whole building becomes alive.

In Catholic and Christian churches throughout this world there are various Eucharists. On rare occasions, a beautiful benevolent spirit exists within a Eucharist. Catholics believe that the Eucharist represents the embodiment of Christ. Yes, there is such a phenomenon as a living body of Christ, a living body of Buddha, or a living body of any religion. This living body is present and it's real within certain sacraments. But does this mean that the actual spirit of Jesus lives in a Eucharist? No, not necessarily. The benevolent spirits residing within the sacraments have been around for billions of years according to linear time—long before Jesus even existed. But most religions love to claim: mine. We decide what lives in the sacraments to feel as though we are in control. We'd better be in control, especially if we're putting money into it. We love to control time and space. And yet there's no control, as we think. If you could see spirit, you would see that there is no difference in the spirit of the various religions of the world.

The benevolent spirits are not Catholic. They're not Muslim. They're not Jewish. They're not Indian. Most won't even know who Jesus is. Jesus who? One could say that the beings that inhabit the sacraments are not typical. They're highly evolved. Very bright. They carry the qualities of benevolence. Beauty. Love. Kindness. Light. They support, help, guide. They're father-like. Mother-like. And they're *extremely* full of the fire of presence.

When you enter a church you will generally find the Eucharist within a golden container off to the side of the altar, usually to the right. During the mass, you'll see the priest open the container with a key and take out the chalice that holds the Eucharist. In the fire dance I do at my workshops, I've noticed something interesting. In relation to the altar I lay out in the center of the room, the benevolent spirits that come are always off to the right. One would think that they would be in front of the altar, but they're not. If you were to ask me why, I don't know.

Not all churches have a living Eucharist. Most are dead, in essence. They are just stone. But there are still many churches in which the Eucharist is alive. When the Eucharist is living you could say that the whole building becomes alive.

Finding a Living Sacrament to Sunbathe Under

Do you have to pray like hell to sunbathe?

Here is something you can do as a research project. Develop a schedule to visit the various temples and churches in your community. All you have to do is sit on the pew or kneel down. Let the silence take place and see what you can feel. Try to sense if there is a benevolence in the sacraments and find out for yourself if this particular temple is alive. What would that feel like? In the stillness you can sense a presence that speaks silently yet loudly, although it is not like sound. It has a depth. When the Eucharist or other sacraments are alive, people are naturally drawn to this church. However, just because you see many people in a church doesn't mean that it has a living Eucharist.

When you find a temple where the sacraments are alive, watch the people who go inside. Notice how they react and what they have received as they leave. Then go to the temples that are not alive and observe the people and what they do in these particular churches. It is similar to those times when you meet human beings whose eyes are as cold as ice, who have become hard in their mind. You could say that their temple is still there, but it's very far away. Then it is easy to for them to be harsh and cruel. But when you observe people who are warm and receiving, you can sense an emanation coming from their bodies that is reflected in their mind and speech. A living presence is there.

I have taken many people into these living temples and most cannot feel anything. To them, the church is just a building. Then there are those who can feel a presence that is alive. These people tend to have a greater sense of what consciousness is. You can see that they have done a lot of contemplation and they're very in touch with life.

So first you have to ask yourself, "What is my state of awareness? Do I sense things differently?" Each home is different. Each town is different. You must be able to sense the external environment and not just yourself and your own internal environment. And from where are you looking? Are you looking from your heart? From your mind? Are you looking from your desperation? Are you looking with eyes of infinity? Eyes of a soaring hawk from above? What is most important is to be sincere with whatever your state of awareness is and to come to terms with it. Find out where your blindness lies. Learn what you can and cannot see, what you can and cannot sense. It's not how much you see or how little you see, it's your honesty with it that matters.

When you do find a living Eucharist, keep your eyes open. You might think that you can feel more with your eyes closed, but you can actually sense and receive much more with your eyes open and relaxed. You can fantasize anything you want once you close your eyes and go into your own world. You can play head games inside your mind. So don't close your eyes. You're on planet earth. It's daytime and you're not sleeping. See what is there in front of you. Look with your peripheral vision, not with direct vision. Be natural. Be yourself. Don't let your body all of a sudden walk like a stick. Just relax. And sunbathe.

This is what helps us. When we sunbathe under a living sacrament, we receive a little boost. A better petrol that has more charges in it. A bit more clarity for our day. It soothes our headache, lightens up our load, eases our hurt and disappointment. It gives us fuel for our heart, our body, and our mind, so we can go and live the life we want. Isn't it nice to get sunbathed by a good friend? Don't you have your favorite movie star? Your favorite room? Your favorite dress? Your favorite sunset? Your favorite moments that you love to be radiated with?

We have all suntanned ourselves beneath the sun. How wonderful it feels to sunbathe, to be radiated by the sun's rays. Do you have to pray like hell to sunbathe? Do you have to suffer and crawl on your knees for days before you can get that nice, golden tan? Do you have to break off a few branches from a tree and whip yourself before you can receive the light of the sun? That's what we've been taught.

"I have too much joy. I'd better start to suffer a little bit. I'm feeling too good. Uh-oh. Something's wrong. You love me? Something's definitely wrong."

To find your peace, re-educate your thinking. Life does nothing but give and give and give. Does the air ask for anything in return? *Learn to sunbathe, without thinking that you need to suffer.* How much good karma do you need to sunbathe? It's that simple. But because of our past education, to receive from life seems very difficult, confusing, and mysterious.

Always remember that there is much more living amongst us than most of us can see or comprehend. But we can teach ourselves to perceive these living phenomena that exist on this planet. There aren't many. But make it your job to go out and find one. Once you've found a Eucharist in your community and acquired a sense of it, it becomes easier to recognize other living sacraments when you come across them, because the "wiring" within you has been reconstructed. Then you have something nothing can take away from you — not time, not even death.

When you find a Eucharist that is alive, remember not to equate it with the church. It really has nothing to do with religion or the church. It has to do with the person who blessed the sacraments and helped to connect the spirit with the Eucharist. Generally that is the priest, although it doesn't necessarily have to be a priest. It could have been a nun. Anybody in the vicinity who works closely with the Eucharist could have been the one who actually drew the spirit into the Eucharist.

So do not give up on the churches just because you may be put off by religion. Use these temples for the purpose with which they were built. You can find a living temple on a hill or along a spring. You can find it in a tree. You can find it in a child's bedroom. You can find it in a restaurant. You can find it in a bar. You can find it on the highways. You can even find it in your enemies. But to do this you must understand that there is a way to think that is different from how most of us have been taught. Out there in the world we need a wishing well, so to speak.

We need another kind of resource in our community where we can go to recuperate and replenish our heart. We need someplace to go that is well connected where we can get good food and good water. And that is what the living churches and sacraments are for.

The Eucharist and the Beads

I saw that great benevolence lives among us — it's just not apparent to most.

Many years ago, my girlfriend Nya (pronounced Nee-yah) and I drove to Big Sur to spend a few days at a monastery that is run by a branch of the Catholic Church. The monks and nuns there spend all of their time meditating, praying, and working on their various projects. They don't participate in the community in any way other than to provide accommodations for those on retreat.

At the monastery there are several rooms available for guests. Anyone can rent one of these rooms and remain for as long as he or she wishes. Guests give the monastery a donation they feel they can afford. Meals are provided, and the food is even passed through an opening in the doorway to each room, so guests don't have to see anyone for weeks or even months if they don't want to.

We decided to stay at the monastery for five days. The first night after arriving, Nya and I both made up our minds to attend the church services for the nuns and monks. After Mass, the monks invited everyone to participate in the ceremony of the Eucharist. We didn't really know what to expect but decided to go anyway. About thirty of the people who attended the Mass walked over to a big round room and sat down in a circle around an altar in the center of the room. Everyone was quiet and still. One monk went into a small room to the right, took the chalice with the Eucharist out of the special tabernacle where it was kept, and placed it on the altar in the center of the room. Then he stepped back and sat down with everyone else. No one said anything. My understanding of the Eucharist was that it was supposed to hold the body of Christ in a symbolic way. So I assumed that everyone sitting in the circle just prayed and meditated on the Eucharist.

My inner vision had started to open up at this time, so I decided to use it to examine the Eucharist. At the time I didn't have much faith that life was alive or that there was any reality to ceremonies like this. I was skeptical.

"Let's see if this Eucharist is real," I said to myself. "Let's see if anything comes out of it." Most of the people in the circle were sitting in deep contemplation with their heads bent down. You could see that they had been doing this for quite some time. After about fifteen minutes had passed, I was getting a little discouraged and bored. I didn't know much about meditating or praying. All of a sudden I saw something move above the Eucharist. What looked like blue smoke was rising out of it. But it wasn't smoke. Now I was getting interested!

The blue smoke rose into the air and made a sharp, 90-degree turn so that it was angled like the hands of a clock reading "9:30." It looked almost like a snake. I could tell that the smoke was alive. Somehow I knew that there was a "face" at the end of the blue smoke. It was not a face as humans would envision, but it was a face nonetheless. The line of blue smoke stretched out parallel to the ground, paused by a nun sitting in the circle, and began to "look" directly at her. I remembered noticing this nun at the mass, and I could see that if anyone here was a saint, she was. Here was someone who had the light. She wasn't a typical nun at all. The blue smoke looked at her for a long time and then quickly flowed back into the Eucharist.

"Whoa! No wonder everyone sticks around!" I thought. "They know that something comes out of the Eucharist and blesses them. Something is *alive* in there, giving out blessings." After it went back into the chalice, I thought to myself, "Well, that's the end of it." But then the blue smoke emerged very slowly once again. This time it bent at a sharp 90-degree angle and looked at the person next to the nun. After a minute the smoke moved on to someone else, watched them for a while, and then quickly descended back into the Eucharist. The smoke seemed to come out of the Eucharist slowly but return to it quite rapidly. The next time it emerged, the smoke stayed out for a long time. It started to slowly circle the room, scanning and looking at each person in turn, but it just paused in front of certain individuals. I could see that it was blessing only these people.

Because the smoke had started circling the room just to my right, I knew that it would take a long time to reach me. I was the third person toward the end of the line. During this time in my life, a great deal of movement and change had been taking place within my mind and heart, and many unusual things were happening to me. Still, I had a lot of doubts about myself.

"Okay," I said to spirit. "I want acknowledgement. If this process I'm going through is real, if it is so holy and good, I want the blue smoke to acknowledge me, because I know it's real. If that smoke acknowledges me, you've got me. You've won. I'm yours. I'll do anything you say. But if I don't get acknowledged, I'm going to quit the process of waking up."

As the smoke made its way toward me, I started sweating and feeling more nervous because I knew that the blue smoke could see who we were. By the way it moved and paused and watched certain people, it was obvious that it could see right through us. I started thinking about all the bad things I had done in my life. Now I almost wished I couldn't see what was going on.

"Oh my Lord," I thought. "It's going to see all the shadows I have inside, all the awful things I've done. What's it going to do when it looks at this garbage can?" By this time I was squirming with anxiety. In a way I wanted it to go right past me because I thought I was so inadequate. But deep down inside I also hoped that the smoke would stop and acknowledge and bless me, because then I would know that this process happening to me was real and it was good. So I was caught in a fix, hoping yet not hoping.

I tried to think of something to calm down my mind. "What was that chant? What was that prayer?" I began to recite "Hail Mary" and whatever prayers I could remember to give myself some white paint. I tried everything imaginable to whitewash myself—because it was coming. When the smoke had nearly reached me, I started to compose myself. I was trying to be cool. Yet my heart was pounding with anticipation because I felt that what it did would affect the rest of my life. This was it.

Slowly the smoke proceeded to pass me. It went by me! At first, I was disappointed as hell because it didn't recognize me. Then I began to feel relieved that the smoke hadn't looked to see how "bad" I thought I was.

"Oh boy, what am I going to do now?" I thought to myself. "See? This isn't real. All my visions and everything people told me about my spirit weren't true. I've just been fooling myself." All these thoughts raced through my head, as I relaxed and let go of my pose.

Suddenly, as the blue smoke hovered by the person next to me, it turned and came back to me. That was odd, because it had never returned to anyone else in the circle. It looked and looked at me for a long time. I could feel an intensity building up within it. Then the smoke started to come toward me so quickly that I didn't even have time to think. It went right for my heart. When the blue smoke went into my heart, it hit me like a two-ton truck. I felt like I was knocked out for a minute.

After the smoke hit me, a tremendous wind began to blow outside! It literally sounded like a hurricane. The other people in the circle began to get concerned, looking around and wondering what to do. In my inner vision, I saw a gigantic oak tree in front of the church, protecting it from the wind. I didn't remember seeing an oak tree there when we arrived at the church, but in my mind this vision was extremely clear. The tree was absolutely immense. Nya later told me that she also saw a big oak tree in her mind at this time.

The onset of the wind was so dramatic that I forgot about the Eucharist that had come into me. By this time, everyone was getting very scared. It seemed as though the wind would tear the church down. But I knew that the oak tree was protecting us. After about ten minutes, the wind finally died down. Years later I learned that, when spirit is manifesting, at times it can actually move the air to create a wind. It can even create a storm.

When the wind stopped, the monk who had brought the Eucharist into the room got up and picked up the chalice. Somehow he knew that the ceremony was over. "That's really something," I thought. "These monks know what's going on. They can obviously see this." I was impressed. I also felt better about myself. It was over, so we all got up and went back to our rooms.

* * *

The next morning Nya and I took a walk. It was so foggy that we couldn't see more than a few feet in front of us, but we found a trail and walked up into the hills. After hiking for quite some time, we climbed above the fog and came to a clearing on the hill. In the middle of the clearing we found the same oak tree we had seen in our minds the night before. It actually *was* that oak tree. This was the biggest tree I had ever seen. It was so big that the ends of its huge branches were touching the earth. We were amazed to find the same tree that we had seen in front of the church in our visions.

After we got back to the monastery, a nun approached us and said, "You two aren't supposed to walk up there. Didn't you see the signs?" She pointed out the signs indicating that the land behind the monastery was private property. We realized that the heavy fog had hidden the signs from our view so that we hadn't known we were trespassing.

"But it was so fogged in that we couldn't see anything," I said. "We just went for a walk."

"Well, that's true, it was foggy," she replied. "But nobody can walk back here. This whole area is off limits to everyone." So the dense fog not only made us miss the signs, but it also hid us so that no one but the nun had seen us walking on the land behind the church.

I spent most of that night restringing a necklace of wooden mala beads that had been given to me. These beads meant a lot to me. I didn't pray on them often, but somehow I had an affinity for them. Later that night I had a good idea. It was about midnight but I knew that the church was always open. Now that the beads were restrung, I wanted to have them blessed. So I walked into the church and went up to the Eucharist. I placed the beads on the tabernacle and knocked on the little metal door where the Eucharist was kept.

"Hello, I know you're in there," I said. "I saw you come out yesterday. Would you please come out again and bless these beads for me?" I knelt down by the tabernacle and waited. After a couple of minutes, I saw the blue smoke emerge. It didn't come out through the cracks in the door as it had the previous evening, but emerged right through the center. It hovered over the beads, and then descended very slowly and rested on them for two or three minutes. Then the smoke rose up quickly and went back inside the Eucharist. I went up to the tabernacle, knocked at the door once more, and whispered, "Thank you. Thank you very much for blessing my beads." Then I went back to my room.

The next day, much to my dismay, I found a mala bead I'd dropped on the floor. Because I had strung the beads in a specific order, I had to take off every single bead and restring them again so this one bead could go back in its place. It took me hours to restring the beads. Then I started wondering if I should ask the Eucharist to bless the mala beads again.

"Oh my god, what should I do? It was my fault I lost that bead. I can't go back and ask for the necklace to be 'reblessed.' The Eucharist is probably busy. But this unblessed bead might throw the whole thing out of whack." For hours I went back and forth in my mind, agonizing over what to do.

Finally, with great reluctance, I went back to the church around midnight, placed the beads before the Eucharist and knocked on the door again.

"Please, will you come out and bless these beads again?" I asked. "I know you blessed them last night, but I dropped a bead so I had to restring them all." After I knelt down, the blue smoke emerged again, but this time it came out much faster. Once more it descended onto the beads, but it rested on them for only about thirty seconds this time. Then it disappeared back into the Eucharist. I knocked on the door a second time and said, "Thank you! Thank you very much." I was happy. That's how I was in those days — almost like a child when it came to dealing with spirit.

* * *

On the last day of our stay at the monastery one of the nuns knocked on my door. It was the same nun that the spirit from the Eucharist had first looked at and blessed. I felt a presence within her that was very strong.

"Can I ask you a personal question?" she asked.

"Sure," I replied.

"I saw you wearing these beads around your neck. What are they? Where did you get them?" After I told her the story behind the beads, she asked, "May I hold them?"

"Of course," I said. So I took off the beads and gave them to her. She held the beads with great reverence and then asked, "May I put them on?" After placing the beads around her neck, she closed her eyes and went into a deep meditative state for about five minutes. When she was finished, she opened her eyes and said, "May I tell you something about these beads? What I feel from them?"

"Yes, please do."

"These beads have been prayed on with a particular intent for hundreds of years since they were first made. They now carry this intention. Whatever the intent was, it has been passed on from person to person through these beads, and they all prayed for this same intent to work. Everyone who has had these beads knew what the intent was, and now you have them. Now the intent is here to manifest." She didn't know what the intent was, but she could feel that there was great purpose within the beads. The reality behind the nun's words struck me, and her reading of the beads helped me to open up and trust life a little bit more.

What I was learning was that life is alive. A Eucharist can be alive in a way that I never could have imagined. I realized that the heart and goodness exist and they are very real. And I saw that great benevolence lives among us — it's just not apparent to most. There is far more to life than meets the eye.

The Mystic Church

Remember that it is not a church that will save you. There is nothing to save.

I was raised as a Catholic and spent a great deal of my early life going to church. In fact, I was an altar boy for a few years. But I had no real feeling for the church at that time. I attended Mass and became an altar boy because my parents wanted me to. A lot of the other young boys I knew were caught up in similar situations. They went to church because they had to.

Now nearly three decades later I found myself on retreat at the Catholic monastery in Big Sur — going to Mass and talking with the nuns and monks. Yet I still felt hurt and confused, like many others, when it came to religion and the church. So I decided to question the nun who was so interested in my beads about the Catholic and Christian churches. I knew I could trust her.

"What are you doing up way up here in this hermitage?" I asked. "What's your job? How are you involved? This doesn't seem like a typical Catholic church."

When the nun saw where I was coming from, she opened up her heart and immediately started to re-educate me about the essence of religion and what the real church was all about. She explained that there are actually two churches in the Christian and Catholic traditions. One is for the lay people who are too busy to immerse themselves completely in the study of religion or God. They're too involved with work and raising families. So they go to church on Sundays to get a little comfort for the rest of the week or to make amends. They just want a little religion.

And then there is the other church—the mystic church—which has been in existence for centuries. The nun explained that the monks and nuns who belong to this church don't follow the instructions of the lay church. They just pray and contemplate. Whether the sun or the moon is in the sky, they pray within the solitude of silence—without asking. They have their own independent community and their own traditions. These are the real mystics who carry on many of the old traditions. You could call them professionals—the ones who study and meditate and are more tuned into the truer nature of spirit. Many have a passion for it, actually. They can be found everywhere. But there aren't many relative to the number of priests and nuns in the lay church.

The monks and nuns of the mystic church don't teach people about God or spirit or the Bible. They don't give Masses for the public, although sometimes their services are open to those in the community. They went into the church for themselves, to communicate with life on a personal, one-to-one basis. The lay church thought it could save other people. But the nun said, "No, you can't save people. There isn't anything to save."

The monks and nuns have always been working with the spirit where there's no control. The lay church controls. It runs the big organizations throughout the Western world. But the mystics know that one doesn't control life. Their approach has nothing to do with gaining parishioners or power for their church. It's prayer. That's all it is.

As this beautiful nun re-educated me, she helped to ease my hurt and misunderstandings. There was a reason I came back around into what I was born into: to remove my ignorance. For me it was a liberation to be re-educated about religion. It was a tremendous relief to see that there really was a reason why so many women and men of the past had devoted themselves to walking through the deserts. Praying morning and noon and night. Helping people. Putting books together.

Most people hold their focus on the lay church. And their hurt continues, having no respect for time or for their lives. So make it your job to re-educate yourself about religion and find the goodness that lies within the church. To be a mystic — a modern, conventional, everyday mystic — you must update yourself.

And please realize that you can connect with the essence of the real church without becoming a monk or nun, or a member of any religion. There are many students of life who are not in religious orders and follow no particular spiritual traditions at all. The real church, you could say, is the earth. It's the water. The air. You do not have to know the words of any prayers in any books. You do not have to go on a spiritual path at all, for you have been ever since you were born. It is your own life experiences that are your best teacher.

Remember that it is not a church that will save you. There is nothing to save. You are a child of life. It is just a matter of having the passion to transcend the mind, to transcend the paradoxes of life, and seek what they call the spirit. It is learning to be honest with yourself. And it is simply realizing what it is to be alive as a human being. That in itself will become the medicine that makes the alchemy to create the change within you.

The Coffee Filters and Religion

It is not to take away your tradition. It is to become the tradition as it was originally meant instead of just understanding it conceptually.

Countless philosophies and religions have existed over the centuries. Many of these philosophies have caused a great deal of discord, harm, war, and confusion. We know that people will kill just because others do not believe as they do. Hundreds of thousands have been murdered throughout history in the name of some god. And this is still going on today. Besides this, when people have greed, it takes hold and uses religion for its own purpose. In fact, religion and politics essentially walk the same line — they're just on opposite poles.

Because of the way history has unfolded, a great many of us have been hurt by religion — whether we were hurt personally or we saw the hurt inflicted on others. For some of us, the infliction of the bruise is still occurring and the hurt continues to trouble us. As a result, many of us have rejected various religions and traditions. We've become suspicious of such organizations, and for good reasons. Some people have even become angry toward organized religion or God.

Yet what is at the root of these traditions? A good intent. It's just that the original intent of many traditional religions has become obscured or forgotten over time. That means it's up to us to unlock the hurt and re-educate ourselves about what religion actually means and what it was originally intended for. How can we uncover this good intent?

Let's take Christianity, which has brought something into this world that many other philosophies have never touched and cannot comprehend, and that is a hope and a faith that touches the human heart in a way that brings blood — living blood — into us. Living blood flows through our veins when we become cognizant not just of our own existence, but of something much greater than ourselves. Hope and faith are essential for us to have because of the conditions of the spirited human being living in nature. So Christianity has given us two amazing elements that are very human and of the heart.

Then what distorts the good intent behind established religions? It is what I call the predicament. You see, various traditions and religions exist that are quite wonderful, and there are people who become teachers, lamas, or priests in order to help bring out this good intent. The problem is what one could call the "coffee filters" — the filters and veils of our mind, our feelings, our ulterior motives, our hurt, our greed, and our desperation. When even one word is spoken that originally came from, you could say, the voice of spirit, by the time it has gone through the coffee filters, that word can be completely turned around and used for a person's motive. Many teachers then speak the words based on what they think they heard.

This is essentially how most traditions are corrupted. All we have to do is turn around and look behind us, and we will realize that there isn't too much sanity in our past history. We are the same blood and bones of this history. To come to terms with this and to uproot these distortions is not an easy task.

It is so difficult for any human being to be totally clear and to allow any amount of the spiritual force to come through without distorting it, because the predicament is so strong. Once you begin to have compassion for this predicament, you will see that a lot of people are essentially doing the best they can, whether or not their teachings are harmful, because this is all they see.

To truly hear the voice of spirit, one's coffee filters must be totally de-stained. Otherwise, the words and ideas of religion can become twisted. There also has to be a transcendence of one's mind. This is where it comes down to honesty and care. To transcend your mind you must genuinely care enough — more than your thoughts, more than your ideas, more than your concepts, more than your feelings, more than all your experiences.

Years ago, I began to get a sense of all the coffee filters I had developed due to my upbringing, my education, my experiences, and so forth. I had no idea how many filters I had or how thick they were. But I knew they existed. So when the spirit would come into me, I knew there was no way I could trust what I saw or heard. Even though the experience was beautiful, wonderful, and full of bright lights, I couldn't rely on my interpretation of it. I knew that first the experience would have to go through my filters, then I would perceive it, and finally I'd have my subjective and experiential understanding of it. So I realized that I was caught in a fix. Trapped in a predicament. If only I were two years old and had no coffee filters — then I wondered what I would see and hear when the spirit came in. But I was in my twenties, and soon I would be in my thirties, forties, and fifties.

I discovered, however, that my saving grace was honesty. When I developed enough honesty to recognize the existence of my filters, enough sincerity to ask for help, and enough courage to see what my predicament was — that became the ticket out of my predicament and the medicine to clean up and transcend my coffee filters, no matter how many layers there were.

What happens when enough honesty, effort, and sincerity emerge out from one's mind and heart? Look at it like this. Imagine that you're a boss and you see that a young woman working for your business is genuinely trying her best. This employee is very sincere, somewhat innocent, and has the skills to succeed, even though she may not know it. If you have a good heart, you will do all you can to help her. If you don't have a good heart and you're full of greed, you won't care. But if you do care, you will become a mentor. You know that this kind of care and dedication is rare, because most people don't really put in much effort. They just finish their work because they are going to get paid, doing the absolute minimum that they have to. And this is how many of us live out our lives.

But when someone goes beyond their means, help will come. This is true for all realms of life. No matter what predicament we are caught in, no matter what forces are against us—life sees. Don't forget that there is no hiding at all, for we live in glass houses. The "movie pictures" we project out from our minds and hearts are clear and bright, and when sincerity and honesty arise, as I've mentioned before, there are many benevolent beings and spirited friends who see this and will come to do what they can.

I could not have removed my coffee filters by myself. If it wasn't for the help I received I would not be able to see as I do. But my sincerity was there. What honesty I could draw up was there. So I waited, *hoping* that my filters would diminish. And they did.

In spite of the coffee filters that entrap most human beings, I still knew that a goodness had to be present in all religions, although not always easily perceived, despite what I had seen, what I had learned, and what I had been told. It had to be there. Even if some aspects of a particular religion are distorted or full of drama, it may also contain elements of great beauty. But it is up to us to determine that. It takes our discretion and intelligence to understand this. Don't leave it up to the priests. Of course, some religions and philosophies, like communism, have elements that are dangerous or cruel, and it would be best to change them to some degree. But remember that certain aspects of even these philosophies also have goodness in them as they were originally conceived and not as they have come to be interpreted.

You see, it is not to take away your tradition. It is to become the tradition as it was originally meant instead of just understanding it conceptually. You start to pump blood into it. You become more alive, more real, and more genuine with your religion. The price you will pay to do this is to change the conceptual world of what you think your religion is. Then you can go from conceptual mind to conceptual heart, but with living blood.

The point is not to let go of your religion, your culture, or your heritage. You can't, because it's too difficult to suddenly change skins. You can't change names the instant that you want to. It is a process. But once you understand, you become more than your name. You become more genuine. You become more real. I am not saying that you shouldn't explore other religions and integrate them into your life, if you wish. But you can use the tools of your lineage because that is in your foundation.

The Gift of the Holy Spirit

The universe is dark compared to the Holy Spirit, for its light is that immense. Yet the Holy Spirit is also like a down feather, very soft and tender.

When I was living in Santa Cruz in the early 1980s, I became good friends with two archbishops. One of them belonged to the Catholic Church of Antioch. There are actually three Catholic churches. Two I've already mentioned: the Roman Catholic Church — the lay church — and a separate branch of this church where the mystics are found. The third is the Catholic Church of Antioch, which is much older than the church of Rome and based in India, although there are branches throughout the world. Both of the churches are essentially the same when it comes to the Catholic teachings, prayers, and ceremonies. Yet the Church of Antioch is very small in comparison to the church of Rome. It's completely different in its approach and in its interactions with the community. I found it to be a very humble church. In the church of Antioch, the priests can marry and have children. They live with the community instead of trying to separate themselves or give the impression that they are higher than others. One of the archbishops I knew had a family and he was extremely reachable, which I thought was quite healthy.

These two archbishops used to come by to see me for counseling on a regular basis. As time passed, they opened up and we got to know one another very well. They were both good men, extremely sincere in their interactions with me.

After two or three months one of the archbishops approached me and said, "Emahó, we would like to give you a gift. My friend and I have decided that we would like to offer you the position of a Catholic bishop in the Church of Antioch because of your teachings and the work you are doing. We realize that your work goes beyond the boundaries of what a bishop does. But legally this is the most we can offer you."

Before I could respond the archbishop went on to say, "We know you're going to turn down this offer because of the way you are. You don't teach by means of traditional religions, but your way is very much in line with how we personally try to teach. We can see that you have the understanding and you walk with it. You have the spirit and that is really what it's all about. And we also know you won't go out and create a church of your own.

"So we have some good reasons why you should accept our offer. One is that it will give you legal protection. It will also give you credibility. You'll be officially recognized and licensed in the state of California, and no one can dispute your right to teach. Once you become a bishop, you'll always have that position for the rest of your life. But our main reason is this: we want you to have the gifts of the Church, the Holy Spirit, and the sacraments. We think it will help you to receive the sacraments. And this is why it would be good if you accepted our offer."

"We also want to let you know," he continued, "that to become a bishop in our church and in other churches takes a very long time. It took me twenty years to become a bishop. That's about the average length of time it takes to get to this level in the church. But we want to give it to you in one night, and we've figured out a way to do this so it's legitimate. We're going to start you off as a deacon, then as a priest, and so on, until you reach the level of bishop. You must be ordained in each of these positions in order for it to be legal." He told me that to do the entire ceremony would take a few hours. Twenty years would be condensed into an evening.

After the archbishop had proposed these ideas to me, I told him I would think about it, although I really wasn't interested at the time. Then one night it suddenly became clear to me that I should go through with the ordination. It made sense somehow. I called the archbishop and asked him to ordain me on the next full moon, which was only a couple of weeks away.

"Good," he said. "I'll get it ready. Bring your closest friends as witnesses."

One week later, my friends as well as the witnesses for the archbishops assembled in their chapel for the ceremony. I had spent days beforehand preparing with the archbishop, because I had to learn a lot about the Church of Antioch very quickly. The entire ceremony was quite elaborate and it must have lasted at least four or five hours. As I was being ordained, the archbishops placed different robes and headpieces on me for each initiation, and gave me various rings and scepters. I felt a little self-conscious wearing the bishop's traditional hat and robe while my friends were looking at me and trying not to laugh, because this huge hat was beginning to tip over, and they knew I never wore robes or religious clothing of any kind. But still, I felt very respectful of the sacramental clothing and objects.

The ordinations were as elaborate as they normally were, except that the archbishop recited the prayers extremely rapidly to shorten the ceremony. If you've ever heard Buddhist monks praying, you know how fast they chant their prayers. Well, this is what the archbishop did — in Latin. He would say each prayer as quickly as he could — so fast it was hardly audible — and then call out, "Next position!" Then he would go on to the next prayer until he finished. "Next one!" So I went through the entire process as quickly as possible.

At the end of the ceremony when it came time for the final sacrament of the bishop, I knelt down before the archbishop. I noticed that he wasn't speaking so fast anymore. All of a sudden, he changed. He became quiet and very present. Now the archbishop said the prayers slowly and with reverence, as he laid his hand on my head and called in the Holy Spirit. After a moment something remarkable happened:

the Holy Spirit came into me, filling me from above. That was the first time I had ever felt the Holy Spirit, although I had heard about it since I was a child. But when the Holy Spirit came into me, I knew that's what it was. There was no doubt. And it was very personal.

The Holy Spirit felt like a white-silver flame that kept burning and burning from within me. I felt like I was an oven. And this light, like the heat of the sun, was filling me everywhere. It flooded into me so strongly that I began to gasp for breath. The light was *so intense* that I almost passed out. But of course my pride wouldn't allow me to do that in front of the archbishop and all my friends! So I did everything I could to stay on my knees. Even after the experience was over, I was still filled with it.

Although I had been raised a Catholic, I had never seen anything in the church that had to do with the true essence of spirit. So I thought the Holy Spirit was only a title. To me, it was just a concept. But after the ordination I had no doubt that the Holy Spirit was in fact very real. I no longer had disrespect for any tradition or religion. My understanding changed. And I naturally began to respect the sacraments of the church even more.

To the Christians and Catholics, the Holy Spirit, also known as the Holy Ghost, is the mediator between God and humanity. Actually, in all religions, it's very much the same: an intermediary of some kind exists to help bridge the gap between the divine and humanity. Some people think of angels or archangels as messengers to God, but when it comes to a mediator like the Holy Spirit, you could say that the profile, the job description, is unique. Angels and divine beings can be mediators, too, but in a different sense. Even for them, to make actual contact with a human is extremely difficult — almost impossible — although they can still help in other ways. This is because humanity and these divine beings live in different dimensions, with different atmospheres, so to speak. And the frequency radiated by such beings can be too much for many human beings to handle. So sometimes even angels need mediators, too.

Here's an analogy. Let's say that there is a particular race of human beings who have adapted to marine life so well that they inhabit the bottom of the ocean. Living on an island are a specialized group of people who have learned to dive deeply to the bottom of the sea and communicate with this marine community on the ocean floor. For thousands of years they've been doing this. No one else has the lung power or the capacity. No submarines, deep-sea submersibles, or diving gear have been invented yet. As a result, when people want to communicate with the deep-sea humans, they have to go through these islanders who have the ability to contact them.

So it takes a special kind of "middle person" with the qualifications, the wiring, and the capacity to connect both worlds. It takes someone very close to a particular dimension in spirit or in the divine who can also communicate with human beings. It takes an "in-between" who can live in both atmospheres. And that is how you can think of the Holy Spirit.

How else can the Holy Spirit be described? It is a messenger. A highly concentrated angel. It is the dharma, the guru, the transmission of light. The Holy Spirit is like the space between the earth and the sun. It can connect this space, enliven it, juice it up. The universe is dark compared to the Holy Spirit, for its light is that immense. Yet the Holy Spirit is also like a down feather, very soft and tender.

The Holy Spirit bestows. It is the arrow that transports the light, the messages, the movement. When the arrow hits its mark, it releases the blessings and delivers whatever is in the intent of the bowmaker. The presence of the Holy Spirit is rare. Under certain circumstances it can reveal itself as one comes to a crossroad. Unlike the phenomenon of the benevolent spirits that can live in the sacraments indefinitely, the Holy Spirit hits the crossroad, comes in, and leaves. When the Holy Spirit came into me, it stayed for only a few minutes, yet the effect was profound.

For the archbishop to actually draw in the Holy Spirit as he ordained me was a unique event. Yet he was able to do so as a result of his genuineness, his heart, and his connections. He had a gift. But just because you become a priest doesn't mean you have earned the right to draw in the Holy Spirit. It is the same with a lama or anyone who has a position in a religious organization. Just because you wear a robe, possess various credentials, or have studied for thirty years doesn't mean that you have any capacity at all to draw in spirit. It doesn't even mean you are a good person. Not all priests and bishops are good. Not all lamas are good. Not all fathers and mothers are good. Not all brothers and sisters are good. Care enough to develop the eye and the discretion to see the difference. It isn't the robe. It isn't the organization or club to which you belong. It is your genuineness and your ability to connect with spirit. So whether it is a priest, a church, a sacrament, or anything in this world, always remember to look for the genuineness, the living essence within.

CHAPTER 5

THE PETROL STATION

The trick is to get the energy of the heart nourished within yourself so you can start to generate your own petrol.

When spirituality walks with us on a day-to-day basis, how should it be addressed? Throughout history it has been addressed as religion. It has been addressed as fasting. It has been addressed as putting on certain colors of clothing or reciting a particular mantra. But maybe the essence of spirituality can be summed up by means of something very simple and down to earth that we can all relate to: a petrol station. It's wonderful once you understand it.

Let's say that I build a petrol station. I paint it with bright colors and make a nice sign that says "open." Then I sit back and wait for my customers to come. All I am is a filling station attendant. That's it. And I have good premium petrol to sell. When you come in with your car and say, "Hey, Emahó, I want to get some petrol," how would you like it if I said, "Okay, I'm going to put forty liters in your car." You would say, "What? No, that's not right. *I'm* supposed to tell *you* how many gallons I would like. Give me *twenty* liters."

"Yes ma'am! Can I wash all your windows?"

"No, not today! Just wash the passenger side."

Now that you have petrol in your car, how would you feel if I were to tell you where to go? "You have to go this way, and then you turn right on Highway 66, and you turn left over there..." You wouldn't like that at all. No one would. Yet a lot of people like a teacher or guru to do just that. They want the teacher to tell them how much petrol to put in their car, and then they want the teacher to tell them exactly where to go.

"Where should I go? Please tell me."

But when you ask the petrol station attendant, "What's ahead?" I'll say, "Here are some maps."

"Oh, all right. Then what's over there?"

"Oh, let me tell you. It's a beautiful drive."

"What about over here?"

"Oh, you have to be a little careful over here. You had better get some water, just in case."

This is real spirituality. You see, my objective is to teach you what one could call "spiritual autonomy." Spiritual autonomy is very much like being a citizen instead of a slave of your country. You're not bound by a dictatorship or a monarchy. You have your independence. You can run your own business. You can do whatever you wish with your life.

That is the true nature of spirit. You see, breaking the spiritual code of life is an individual experience that cannot really be taught, for it can be understood only within your own framework, your own mentality, your own experiences. The job of any teacher is to show you this and to connect you with life. It is not the teacher's business what is in your heart and why you are here on this planet.

My main job is to be your springboard, to ricochet your dreams and wishes into a direction that reflects back to you. It's to help you get there, to where *you* want to be. It's not my job to tell you to go north or south or east or west. Nobody likes to be told what to do. To follow the adventure of a wish, of what you truly want inside, is wonderful. My aim is to help you radiate your heart out to life so that your intent, your wishes and hopes, can become a living reality.

As it is, spiritual autonomy means that I don't want my customers to come and stay at my filling station. That's called the ashram. Get your petrol and move on. I'm watching my soaps on TV! Once you get your petrol, what you do with it is up to you. Go wherever *you* want to go. It's your car. It's your life.

When I was a teenager I used to drive a motorcycle around town. To pay for petrol I had a newspaper route, but I still didn't always have enough cash. My father never gave us an allowance, so we always had to work for our money. Sometimes I could only get twenty-five cents or fifty cents worth of petrol. That still bought a lot of fuel back then. So I kept having to go back to the filling station quite often because of my predicament at the time.

The same is true of my petrol station. There are some customers who pull in and buy only a gallon of petrol at a time. They will come back quickly to refuel, and that's all right. Others can fill up on a lot of petrol and take off on their own for a long time — until they know how to produce their own petrol. One day they might even have their own filling station. In fact, some of you may be feeling more and more what it is to be a filling station attendant. So remember not to forget what a good attendant is and what your job is as a customer.

There is nothing wrong with asking for help from others. We know it is necessary at times, but ultimately you have to get back into your car and drive away. Once you drive off, I'm fine as the petrol station attendant. It is *you* who has to go out into the desert. This is a very personal process that only you can walk, as an individual.

Close your eyes and you will see what I mean. I cannot be you as you go away into your own world. When you lay down your beautiful, tired head on that nice, soft pillow, what happens? You go into your own dreams. As it is with passing away. No one can die for you but you. No one. No one can breathe for you. *You* have to do it. Who is going to think for you? This is our inherent independence. Life is showing us this all the time. Yet it's one of the most difficult realities to realize.

Some human beings do have a natural sense of this reality. A number of people have come up to me and remarked, "You know, Emahó, I've been looking for some sort of a path. But I'm feeling discouraged, because the organizations and religions I've looked into are so structured. And they have so many rules: don't do this, you have to do that." What about these people? Are they kept out of the gates of heaven because they can't tolerate so many rules and they value their independence?

Actually, a lot of people don't like this independence. Many people do need help, guidance, and instruction. They need formulas and that's all right. But again, let's consider the reality. Who was born for you? This is something that most people intellectually understand, but the trouble is that it's not realized. If you were to fully realize this simple, ordinary fact, it would change your life. It would have a tremendous impact on all your actions and thoughts throughout the day. It would start to penetrate every moment of your life. You would never forget it.

It takes a great deal of courage to come to this realization: it is my car, my life, my mind, my heart. How will you know that this realization is affecting you? You will begin to feel more and more alone. You'll feel that there is more and more distance between you and the rest of the world. This is what most people don't like, and I don't blame them. But although you are beginning to feel more alone, in reality, this is the ingredient for your strength. And actually, you are getting closer to people through your heart, not more distant.

The problem is that we're used to thinking as a group, as a society, as a couple or a family. So when people start to feel this separation and loneliness, they often look at it as: "There is something wrong with me" or "I'm not good" or "I'm not being friendly." No, it is just a symptom that you are beginning to realize this greater reality — the reality of what happens every time you close your eyes. It is your world. It is you who has to go to work. It is you who has to go into a store. It is you who has to deal with your situation. It's your car. How much strength do you have in your car? How much strength do you have in yourself, in what you know and how you walk through the world?

Here is another way to think about the petrol station. I know that there's always someone smarter than me. Someone with more wisdom.

Someone with a greater light. And that's good, because without those human beings who are able to show me a greater sophistication of movement, of thought, of being—how else can I learn? In my heart, I always ask: "If there is someone much more than me, come teach me—as I teach my sons, as my father has taught me." There are wonderful teachers out there in the world. It does help to go to various workshops. It's nice to hear someone speak. And personally, I'm thankful that I see the same faces come back over and over again.

But there is a predicament and that is time and space. Eventually my workshops will stop. And so will those given by other teachers. Then what are you going to do? Your teacher won't always be around. Even your mother can't always be with you. It's wonderful to have her at your side when you're young, but you still have to go out and play. When you get older, you have to go to work, visit friends, run errands, or turn over and go to sleep. This is true no matter who you are with, whether it is your wife, your husband, or your children. We always have to turn away from each other. And one day we will find ourselves leaving this world and heading into another time and place. This will happen to each of us, that's for sure.

This is a greater reality. Keep your mind and heart turned toward the greater realities of life as much as possible, even though they may seem harsh or uncomfortable to contemplate. Why? Because there are massive energies backing up these realities. And in time, these energies will start to back you up, too.

Look at the two doors: the entrance and exit to this world. Each and every one of us has our own two doors—the door that we came in through and the door that we will leave through. They don't belong to anybody else. No one has a key to your doors but you.

"Hey Betty, can you die for me, please? You know, I'd like to pass this one up."

"Hey Joe, can you be born for me this lifetime?" No. We know it doesn't work that way. The two greatest doors ever invented: they speak.

What do they say? It's transitory here. This doesn't last. All teachers, friends, wives, husbands—you can't hang onto anyone. When you find yourself walking alone, then what really matters? What are you left with?

The trick is to get the energy of the heart nourished within yourself so you can start to generate your own petrol. When your heart begins to radiate on its own, this is what creates the connection with life. And attracts your friends behind the two doors. Yet it takes a lot of effort to be independent with this. It is not easy, as many of us have discovered. But once you get radiated enough—by a teacher who is genuine, a living sacrament, or life itself—or you receive enough good petrol, by whatever means, something kicks in and you have your independence. Wisdom begins to filter in. It's a matter of drawing the force of your own spirit in, so that you become independently healthy.

We know it's good to be touched in our hearts. It rejuvenates us and gets us going again. The light is different. Things are clearer. All of a sudden, hope arises and we can see differently. We gain another perspective, and we start to feel alive again. When we haven't been touched for a long time, sometimes we develop a hardness on our faces and a distrust of other people. But suddenly a door can open up that softens the hard lines and gives us a new way to go about our lives.

To be touched in the heart is like receiving petrol—good fuel to keep us going just long enough until we are able to manufacture our own. Maps are needed, too, because of how we have been taught to function in this world with our two physical eyes. But once our inner eye opens and wisdom comes in, we see another map, and we walk through this world far differently than before.

A BLESSING

My wish is to give you a blessing,
a blessing in a different way.
A blessing of a person who was fortunate enough
to be born in the Western world.
A blessing that will help to touch your heart.
A blessing that will help to open up your mind.
And it's not as I think.
But a blessing to bless you as you think.

Healthy Discretion

There is a price to pay for independence of body, mind, and spirit, and that is to wake up and see what else is going on in the world and how it's affecting all of us.

Years ago, a healer from Australia came to visit me in Santa Cruz, California, and we soon became good friends. Australians are very kind and wonderful people, and this man was easy to be with. I could see that he wanted something from me, but he didn't quite know what it was that he wanted.

My friend used to be an advertising executive in a big firm. After an accident in which he almost died, he became a healer. He grew his beard and hair, and decided to change his life. This man really had something in his hands. Everywhere he went, he would put people on a table and do healings. You could see that he really loved his work.

After a few months, he went to Europe and Russia and continued to do his healings. One day he called me from Russia.

"Emahó," he said, "you've got to come to Russia. The way you teach, you could end up with tens of thousands of people coming to see you."

"Oh really?" I said.

"Yeah, man, they're just so hungry here. I've got thousands of people already coming to listen to me about my healing work, and I'm doing all these teachings. Come on over. I'll set you up, and hey, you'll be a big star."

After I heard this, I knew where *not* to go. I didn't want to teach where people had too much desperation, naiveté, or fear. I didn't want to attract people who would believe in anything, who were easy to "catch."

When you take away healthy discretion and substitute it with desperation — you're in trouble. It's the blind leading the blind. In any society, it's easy to be ignorant. No matter where you live, it's easy to be blinded by your flag, your country, your hurt, your wants — too easy.

But I discovered that Westerners as a whole have good, healthy doubt. They don't believe just anything. They think about it. Listen. Question. And that is what creates good character inside.

When I go out and do my work, what I'm doing is hunting. Any intelligent teacher goes out and hunts. Some teachers hunt for the naive. Some teachers hunt for the ignorant. I hunt for the stubborn. Why?

These people are not going to sell out. They're not going to listen to everything that comes along, no matter what predicament they may be in. They're going to doubt what they hear and whittle it down carefully to make sure it is good. You can trust these people. They've been stubborn like this for a long time. They tend to be very quiet and individualistic people.

Please don't believe in anything I say without thinking it through first. Don't be foolish. In all aspects of our lives, we have to learn to dissect, take apart, investigate. We need to have good, healthy criticism and doubt to the point where we can say, "Okay, now this I know. And this I don't know." That's the most important thing.

One thing that blinds people so easily are robes. When people see someone in a robe of any kind, they immediately go into a mode of submission. Human beings are practically conditioned to do this by belief structures and imprints that have been built in for tens of thousands of years. It's well designed. But one doesn't judge a book by its cover. It is no different with what people wear. Just because someone puts on a robe or has credentials plastered all over the wall, does it mean that the person is holy? Does it mean that the person is kind? Or even sane? It takes time and effort to take apart our mind, to take apart our philosophy, to take apart what comes in through our eyes and senses, so that we have enough discernment and discretion to stand on our own.

Don't we teach our children how to live in society so they will do well when they are adults? We know it's important. It's a matter of education. It takes a lot of training and understanding to have the wisdom of discretion, and it has to take place within us. Healthy criticism we'd better have — until the naiveté has subsided and enough wisdom is there so that we don't need criticism any more.

Several years ago, I remember speaking with a young lady who was extremely confused. She was only in her thirties and she had cancer. Both of her breasts had already been removed and she was going through chemotherapy. Her doctor had told her that the cancer would most likely invade her brain and the rest of her body within two years.

During this time, the young lady was working with a lama who had a large following of students. She had never done any spiritual practices until becoming involved with this one. After this young woman became ill, she didn't feel like doing her spiritual practices anymore. But she was told by the lama that if she quit, the demons would come and get her, and she would never be able to be part of the dharma for the rest of this lifetime or any other lifetime. She would be lost forever.

When one is truly vulnerable and naive, like this young lady who had just lost both breasts and would soon lose her life, and an ignorant spiritual teacher who is dressed in robes feeds her a story like this, what will it do to her life? What will it do to her mind? After I assured this young woman that the lama's ideas were ridiculous and had no basis whatsoever in reality, it eased her fears, and she stopped her spiritual practices shortly afterward.

This is why it's important to stand on our own two feet, and to educate our mind so that we become very skeptical in a healthy way. If we can develop healthy doubt and good self-esteem, then no matter who is talking to us or what book we are reading, we will have the discretion to know the difference between what is good and what is not so good, what is dishonest and what is sincere, what has substance and what does not.

It is not just a matter of eliminating our ignorance, naiveté, and self-doubt. It's much more than that, because we can be highly intelligent and yet still have no heart. Then what good is life? We can become very wealthy and yet lose our soul. We can become very poor and yet lose our sight. There are so many different ways to be in this world; it's up to us to find out how we wish to live out our lives. It really has nothing to do with a choice of religion. It has nothing to do with our neighbors, our teachers, our parents. It has nothing to do with our children or our grandparents. It essentially has to do with just you, the individual. It is just between you and life itself.

There is a price to pay for independence of body, mind, and spirit, and that is to wake up and see what else is going on in the world and how it's affecting all of us. It is not easy to see the tricks of this world, because that means we're going to have to develop a responsibility for ourselves. That means we'll have to change how we are — how we've been the last ten minutes, the last hour, the last day.

I remember hearing a story about a famous purse snatcher who used to stand outside of shopping malls and study all the female shoppers. Somehow he always knew which women to steal from, and which women *not* to steal from. This thief was so successful that he made a very good living just stealing purses. Finally, he got caught. Most purse snatchers get caught within a few months. But this man lasted ten years. He was that good. And I recall that it was by some fluke or just bad luck that he got caught. Normally, he wouldn't have.

A team of psychologists on the police force wanted to find out why this man was so good at his profession, so they spent some time questioning him.

"How can you always tell which women to take the purses from?" they asked.

"Easy," he said. "Come on, I'll show you." So they all headed out to a shopping mall.

"See this woman? Piece of cake. That one, she'll put up a little fight. This woman, easy. But now that one, boy, don't get within ten feet of her."

"But how on earth how do you see this?"

"Isn't it obvious? Look. On a scale of one to ten, the women between five and ten are a lot more aware. They're going to fight for their purses. If I'm a little bit desperate, I might go for a five. But if I'm patient, I'll go for the woman who's between one and three."

So the psychologists talked to these woman and asked them if they would volunteer to participate in a study to determine why some were so vulnerable while others would fight for their purses. After numerous sophisticated tests, the psychologists still couldn't figure it out. The purse snatcher's natural discretion put a big dent into the philosophy of these people who were trying to understand the human mind. And yet, to the purse snatcher, it was something so simple and obvious.

What I'm trying to say is that sometimes life is not all that perplexing. Don't make it more complex than it is. So many things are as obvious as how much water we should drink. But when we try to explain something by putting mysticism, great reasons, and wonderful stories into it, we've lost. The veils descend over our eyes.

The psychologists kept going back to the purse snatcher, trying to understand how he could see what they couldn't see. But all he could say was, "Well, it's obvious. Look! Can't you see it?" This man was very honest with himself. That's it.

And this is what *we* have to do with ourselves, as we clean up our naiveness inside. In other words, we must develop honesty. Otherwise, we can get into trouble. Other people can take advantage of us, and then all of a sudden we become victims.

I have two sons, and I do not talk to them about my teachings at all. I teach them from a father's point of view as well as I can. When my sons were younger, I encouraged them to find their own answers, but if they got stuck I provided as much help as I could. I knew how important it was for them to learn to stand on their own and think for themselves. I taught them to doubt me. "Don't trust me, watch out for my tricks." Now when I am honest and sincere, they know it. When I am playing games, they know it. My sons have become comfortable with this, so they know when other people play games and when they are sincere.

Like most parents, my wish for my sons is that they grow up to be independent and not have the wool pulled over their eyes, so that whether it is a governor, a priest, a guru, or their best friend who is standing in front of them, they have the discretion to say, "No, I can see your games," or "Yes, I can see that it's good," because they've learned to trust themselves inside.

Standing on Our Own

This work is about being alive in one's heart. Not enlightened—alive. Living through one's heart.

I remember when my sons were babies. Like all babies, their mother and I fed them until they caught on and could do it for themselves. After a while, we could almost hear them thinking, "Something isn't right here. There's something very wrong." Finally, after a few months they figured it out: "I've got it! Let me feed myself. Give me the spoon. Let me do it. Let *me* do it!"

A society gets sick when the people in that society say, "You feed me. You tell me what to do. You tell me what to think. You do it." That's when we get into trouble. *You* do it.

Remember when we were young? The adventure was to learn that word, to learn that experience, to learn what a particular expression meant. "I want to feel what that is. Let me do it, let me do it. Let me drink for myself. Let me hold my fork. Let me walk on my own. Let me put on my clothes. Let me drive the car. Let me think for myself." It was such a natural desire when we were children. Yet as we got absorbed into the adult world, although we tried to retain our feelings of independence, over time most of us learned to develop self-doubt, to stop believing in ourselves, and to lose contact with whoever and whatever gave us life.

You see, my intent is not to teach anyone how to be spiritual, for I do not advocate that whatsoever. My intent is to encourage all children to stand on their own so that when they grow up, they will have a better sense of their world, their neighborhood, and themselves. My purpose is to teach one how to wake up as a human being, to become a better human being. When it really comes down to it, this work is about being alive in one's heart. Not enlightened — alive. Living through one's heart.

These particular teachings are also geared to strengthen our ego, not to destroy it. Because of the teachings that have come in from the East, so many people are trying to kill their ego. But that's a big mistake. A great misunderstanding. It's a terrible thing to do to people, especially to kids, and it just induces more fear and ignorance. The one thing we do not want to do is attack, kill, annihilate our personality. It frightens us to death inside. Kill myself? How many years have I invested in myself, in learning to get along in this world, going to the store, and answering the phone? My personality brought me to this point in time. And now I say, "Hey, thanks a lot, but adiós. See you later!" With this attitude, we're going to have a big fight on our hands.

Instead of cutting our head off, it's to educate ourselves and to strengthen our personality. It is healthy to have a strong, colorful personality. We need this in society. We don't have to obliterate it to connect with life, to wake up, or to achieve what they call enlightenment. Actually, it's just the opposite. It is far better to walk with our personality: "Let's wake up together." I've found that it is essential to have a well-developed, healthy ego and personality to seek the spirit, to look for something more in life, just as it's important to get back the natural sense of independence we had when we were young.

It takes a lot of time to learn how to stand on one's own. It's not a simple process, but something that is usually a lifetime endeavor. So it's important to head toward independence while at the same time having the humility and sincerity to speak to life and ask for assistance: a paradox. Do not ever be too self-sufficient to ask for help from life, for even if your teacher walks away, and even if all the petrol station attendants disappear, life itself is always there for you.

Our Foundation

I don't want to start another club. There are already too many.
I trust your life as it is—your direction, your likes, your wants.

Like the petrol station, these teachings have been designed as much as possible so that they do not turn into a spiritual organization, a club, or a particular philosophy. My purpose is not to take you out of your philosophy. It is not to encourage you to abandon your religion, your path, your business, or your family. My emphasis is for you to continue doing what you have been doing. If you have a personal practice, if you are Christian or Buddhist, continue your practice.

What these teachings will do is provide a foundation for you—not to become someone else or belong to something else, but to continue to do what *you* like to do. What feels good to you. These teachings, like life, are very, very personal. They have nothing to do with your neighbor, your mother, your father, your son, your daughter, your grandpa, or your grandma. They have to do with you personally. It is no one else's business what you do with your life. You can be a good teacher, a good manager, a good employee, a good cook, a good salesperson, a good computer wizard. You can be a person who answers the phone well, a good taxicab driver, a mother, a father, a citizen. No matter what you do, these teachings are designed to connect you with what has given you life.

So many clubs exist on this earth—clubs that meet every week, every month, every year. There are wonderful clubs out there that help people. But they won't last. They will only continue on until the times change. Clubs may endure for many hundreds of years, but they will always change in time. Many will disappear. We have seen that. Look at history. What club, tradition, or philosophy has lasted without changing or fading away? So what does that say? We stand alone, basically. And in that aloneness, it always comes back to our own self: what is real inside that we can take with us forever?

I don't want to start another club. There are already too many. I trust your life as it is—your direction, your likes, your wants. *That* I trust. For many people, it is easier to be identified with a group or a club. How lonely it can feel not to be a member and to stand on your own. But to find what we are all inherently searching for, no word, no label, no thought can touch it or even come close. When you see that the sky, the earth, and the air that you breath is alive, what can a club do with that? Can a club connect you with what has given you life?

Who is the person in your shoes, walking into that club? How solid is your foundation? That's what matters in the long run. Wouldn't it be nice if you could travel to India and not be confused about what you see and feel? What is Life? What is God? What is society? Millions of people hold different beliefs, whether they are from Russia, Iran, China, Africa, or America. What should you trust?

The hardest part in any process or any endeavor is the beginning. It can be a very confusing phase. The most important part of any business, family, tradition, culture, or society is the *foundation*. When your foundation is weak, there isn't much reality backing you up. Then when something suddenly comes along and starts to pull the carpet from beneath your feet, you'll know why: your foundation wasn't solid in the first place.

When the foundation is real, when the foundation has a tremendous amount of honesty built into it, you can bring any guest into your home and not be disturbed. You can bring any philosophy into your mind, and not get confused. When a human being's foundation is solid, the heart is open. A common sense is present. No philosophy can bend you. No religion can confuse you. You can go anywhere in this world and be very comfortable, without wondering what to do or how to think, without asking "why?" For it's simply that you're at ease with your mind and your heart.

Who is Right?

To realize the person in your own shoes, to realize the gift of self — you could say this is the secret of life.

Why else should we develop a strong foundation? Here is another way to look at it, from a greater perspective. The following is just a hypothetical example to make a point, so please don't take this literally. Let's say that you're in spirit. Next to you is your guardian angel and you're both hovering over earth. You ask, "Is it time for me to go down?" And your guardian angel says, "Sure. Where do you want to go?"

"Right over there." All right. Boom.

So now you are born in a Roman Catholic culture. You are born and die and reborn and die and reborn and die until you become a very good Roman Catholic to the point that now you're either a nun or a priest. Then you find yourself in spirit once again and all of a sudden your guardian angel says, "You know, I think it's time for you to be a shaman."

"A what? What's that?" Boom. Now you're an American Indian. You're going to be a little confused for a few lifetimes until you adapt. After you get used to that, you're back up in spirit and the guardian angel says, "You know, let's do Buddhism this time."

"What's that?" At first, you are confused about this, too, but in time you adapt. So you continue to be reborn as a Buddhist for a while. Eventually, you will understand the problem: we can see only through the eyes of our particular culture or religion. We are bound by history. We're almost enchained by customs. "This is the way we do it, this is the way we are." What are the Germans like? What are the French like? Very different from each other. The Americans, the Italians, the Russians — what are they like? Very different.

"Well then, who's right? Tell me. Who is really right in this world?" Whether you are born in Italy, France, Russia, Malaysia, or China, for the most part, you are stuck with how the people of your culture think, how they look, how they eat, and how they feel.

It is a predicament. Wherever you are born, you have to wake up from that predicament. Take my heritage, for instance. I had to transcend being an American Indian. Whatever your culture's customs are, you have to wake up from those customs and transcend them. If you do not transcend your customs, if you do not transcend your heritage, you are stuck. You are blinded by it. I'm not saying that a strong heritage is bad at all. There is goodness in all cultures, but when you are entrapped by your culture and you take it too seriously, you will fight for it. You will go to war for it. And we have, haven't we? Every country has. "Hey, if you don't believe like I believe, you're in trouble." Don't we kill for a word?

You see, it basically takes an astronaut's point of view to transcend your heritage, your upbringing, your perspective of life. It takes a great stretching of your mind. It takes becoming a good anthropologist. It takes an understanding of history. It takes a good telescope to see what is really out there. It takes coming to terms with the fact that this generation will go and another generation will take its place, as our generation has taken the place of the last.

To widen and stretch your perspective is not easy, I know. It's not all that comfortable. But you see, it's your future. Your future really does matter. The next day really does matter. The next five years are really going to matter to you. But it is far easier to stay as is than it is to change. We know that. It is much easier to hold on to our hurt and disappointment, to *our* thinking about how this world is, than it is to completely restructure ourselves inside.

Always remember the bottom line: when you pass away, your grandma doesn't follow you. Your mother doesn't follow you. You can't take your flag with you. You can't even take your passport. Now what are you going to do? Now what's your philosophy? Now what are your ideas? Now what is your sense of reality? Can you take it?

Many people grab any philosophy and pull it into their lives because their foundation is not solid. Most of us easily accept anything that is written in a book. If it is in print, it's the *word*. It has to be true. Most of you have probably heard about the *Tibetan Book of the Dead*. This book has brought a lot of confusion into the West because the Westerners who have read it believe that this is exactly what happens for everyone after death. According to the Tibetan Buddhists, one encounters various transitional stages, known as bardo states, after passing away. In a sense, these states do exist, but not as the Tibetan Buddhists describe them — *unless* you happen to be a Tibetan.

If the North American Indians were to write a book about what it is like after one dies, you would see that it would be totally unlike the one written by the Tibetans. It would be much more personal, with a lot more feeling. If you were to travel to Africa, Siberia, or Mongolia and read their book of the dead, each book would be completely different. You could go to all the various shamans throughout the world, and each would write a book that is very unique when it comes to what takes place after death. If you were to talk to the Christians, their book would also be totally different. "The Christianity Book of the Dead." "The African Book of the Dead." "The Shamanic Book of the Dead."

So who is right? Which book is correct? We all live in our own world and see from our own perspective. Only if you are Tibetan do you experience the bardo states as they are portrayed in the *Tibetan Book of the Dead*. If you are African, what takes place after death will happen exactly as an African would perceive it. And the same is true of the American Indians. What do you want? What do you expect to see?

After you pass away, you don't suddenly meet the Tibetan Buddhist deities and gods. You will meet death as an American Indian. Or you will meet it as a Westerner. You'll meet it as a German, a French, or as a Swiss. What is in your mind is due to who you are, not because a Tibetan is living on the other side of the world, and not because an African, an American Indian, or a Hindu is living in their culture. That isn't life. Life is you as you are — the person in your shoes. Even your dreams are your dreams. If you are a Westerner, your dreams aren't American Indian. They aren't Tibetan. They aren't African. They are your dreams, your hopes and wishes, your feelings and thoughts. They aren't Hindu. They're yours. A Western world. Western thought. Western upbringing. This is your gift.

You know, spirituality can be so corrupt. There's so much drama. The only proof you need that you are spiritual? Look down at your feet. You have your feet. That's your license. You have your hands. That's your proof. Your evidence? Simply the mere existence of your life. It is your destiny that I trust the most. For I know that life itself is your best teacher.

The best chance you have is you, all that you are, simply because life has given you your life. This is very clear. So keep walking in your own shoes, continue whatever practices you have been doing, but with a trust in your own life. To realize the person in your own shoes, to realize the gift of self — you could say this is the secret of life.

WHO WALKS?

What do we live for?
A retirement?
A gold watch?
What do we strive for?
Success is important.
It's good and healthy
to be successful as a human being.
But what is the purpose of life?
Will your boss walk you into your dreams?
Will your employees walk you into your afterlife?
Who walks?
You and no one else.

CHAPTER 6

FIND SOMETHING TO LOVE

Find something that you love and hold it in your heart, because when you go on your detours, that love can bring you back easily and quickly.

When it comes to connecting with life, it's difficult to do it with the mind, but through the heart it's a different matter. It is the same with any process of waking up: the easiest way is through your heart. Well then, what can help to activate your heart? Here's a secret: find something that you love—something you can contemplate and feel and hold in your heart as much as possible. It could be your child. It could be your husband or your wife. It could be a little bird that comes to the front of your yard. A puppy. A flower in your garden. A movie. A piece of music. Or even an act of kindness. Let that be your ticket to help you connect with life. Let that be the key that unlocks the wisdom living deep within your bones. Although it is important to acknowledge your frailties, don't be overly concerned about your disabilities or weaknesses. Instead, get the love. Find it and nourish it and keep it alive.

If there is nothing that you are in love with in this world, if no one has come into your life who has brought that feeling of being loved—time to do some work. If you don't have anything to love, go look for something—*anything*—that attracts you, that gives you a feeling of passion, whether it's a book, a home, a sunset, or a sprinkling rain. Whatever it is, study it. Build it up. If you don't get to touch it, then just see it. Water it. Protect it like you protect your children, like your father and mother protected you. Nourish it like a little campfire, and do not let that fire go out. In time, you can find yourself with another campfire. Another campfire. A little candle. And pretty soon, you have a whole bag of things that you love.

Naturally, there's a difference between loving a human being and loving a rosebush. The impact on your life is going to be different. It's just that when you are actually loving another person, the effects are dramatically obvious, in comparison to loving a fish, a flower, a rock, or a hobby.

When we are in love with someone, what does it do to our lives? We automatically brush our teeth better. We're more conscious of our cleanliness and our appearance. We clean up our house. We're more aware of what we say and what we do. We're more courteous to other people, because of our happiness inside. Our lives take on less effort. Somehow what was difficult and heavy all of a sudden has a lighter tone to it, and it becomes easier to walk through our day.

So be a good gardener. Nourish your love and your passion. It's quick and easy access to your heart. It keeps you there. You know, it's so easy to get sidetracked in life. But when you go on your detours, the love can bring you back easily and quickly. It's a wonderful tool. And here is something else: every time you find something that you genuinely love, it can affect the "compasses" of that hologram, that tiny spirit deep inside you, as the Uncaused Light of spirit, radiating in all directions at once, begins to point in the direction of that love. This in turn helps to draw the spirit inside closer and closer to your skin.

The love you have for your loved ones, the love you have for something in this life, use it as a telephone to life, just as you can use the predicament as a telephone. Use what is already easy for you. Because love is the direct route. Otherwise you have to go through the mind. And do you know how long it takes to go through the mind? A very, very long time.

Once you find that love, put your faith in it. Even if you see ninety-nine percent shadows in this life, and even if ninety-nine percent of the day is very constricted and hard on you, just take that one percent of whatever or whoever you love and keep heading toward it. Let it help you. Don't give up. And if you do give up, get back up.

As your love starts to grow, it's like a light that keeps getting stronger. It's like a new road out in the country that you start to travel down every week. At first it's hard to find your way, but in time it gets easier. More familiar. Do you know what love is? It is creativity. Love does not want at all. It's not even in the books of wanting. It just is. But as you allow, its creativity starts to come through. More tools appear to help you. Doors open up. New opportunities arise.

Look what happened in the past when certain human beings had a love and passion for electricity or machinery. They gave us the light bulb. They gave us the washing machine. Although our washers and dryers have given us far more free time, do we care who invented them? Do we realize that we would be spending four or five hours at the river every day, beating our clothes on rocks to clean them? Look what that one good act did for humanity. As it is for our spectacles, our glasses: someone who cared made it possible for us to see the world so much more clearly. The passion. The love. The science. The effort. *Thank you.* In essence, 99.999 percent of all humanity rides on the coattails of only a few individuals. One act of kindness transmutes tons and tons of inappropriate acts. One act of passion deactivates immense amounts of complacency.

After you have found something to love, you can ask yourself the question: "Now that I love this person or this thing *so much*, where is this love coming from?" Is it coming from something external? Is it coming from the stars? Is it coming from the sun? Was it always in the air? Is it coming from the object of your love? No, it is coming from within your own heart. Who is issuing the love? You are. You're the one who is literally manufacturing this love. The feelings of your love are just reflecting back to you, like you are looking into a mirror. But most people think the love they feel is coming externally from the one they love. They reverse it: "Not me. It's coming from you."

Once you become conscious of the fact that it is *you* who is actually issuing this love, what are the implications? That forces your mind to consider this: "My god, if I'm the one who's been issuing and nourishing the love all this time, I *am* this love. I *am* this kindness. I *am* this goodness." This changes the entire picture about the nature of relationships. If you are the issuer of this love, what does that say about you? Remember this when you aren't feeling good about yourself.

Shutting Down the Love

When you do fall in love, use it wisely, for that is the easiest and fastest way to tap into wisdom.

The only thing that I've ever known that truly is alive, that really does matter, is love. Any organism can work. Any organism can be sophisticated. Any organism can be clever. But very few organisms can truly love. Like music, love is rare to find in the universe. There are insects that do produce music. Without crickets, I wonder what the night would be like. But we all know what a beautiful piece of music can do, when it is created by a human being from the heart. It can tap our heads. It can tap our hearts. It can make us cry and laugh. It can make us dance.

It is the same when we fall in love. When this happens, it's as though the sky has opened up. The earth has opened up. The electrical field of every cell in our body becomes intense, and we can even feel the love vibrating inside. Most of us have felt what a love like this does to us. We know how wonderful it is. But for so many, to be in love has become extremely dangerous, for it has turned into hurt and disappointment. Soon bitterness takes its place. In time, one resorts to being alone, and the world doesn't look so bright anymore.

When something activates this love in your heart, you have the ability to shut it down. You can totally close down this manufacturing plant within yourself or you can leave it on: it's your choice. But it's much harder to keep it on than it is to turn it off.

Find Something to Love

I know it's not easy to go through all the early stages of what love can do. The neuroses, the desperation, all the confusion. The rules of society. The doubts. But try to have the courage to withstand all of it.

Whether the person loves you back or not is not the point. The point is that you finally have the love inside, vibrating you like a bell, like a drum. A love that is constantly drumming and sending out that vibration. And when that drum beats loud enough and long enough, something above will hear. It will finally reach a certain point, a certain destination, and the reflection will come back. It's just that most people do not allow the drum to beat for long enough or with enough intensity. They get disturbed by too much disappointment and confusion. They are not prepared, like good boy scouts or good girl scouts, to hold onto this love, to nourish and protect it to the point that the vibration will never leave them.

If you feel that the drumbeat is vibrating to a certain person — good. And if that person does not want you, it's all right. Don't let the drumming stop. For you see, real love means that you genuinely care that the ones you love are happy and doing what *they* want to do. You support them, even if you're not getting what you want. Love is not to possess.

Reflect back on your past and remember all those times when you let the drumbeat stop. It was *you* who stopped it. No one else. It wasn't the one who disappointed you. It wasn't the one who turned away from you. It was you. The love was coming from your own heart. But we always seem to point the finger at someone else. So go back and make peace. Pull out these thorns.

That doesn't mean that love will ever come knocking on your door again. For one never knows. But once you've been radiated, it's forever. It's just that the drumbeat is not as loud.

If you have this kind of love vibrating in you, protect it like you're pregnant, like you're caring for a baby in your womb. Nourish it until it is mature and can never go away. And those human beings you know are in love, whether they are men or women, protect them too. Why? Because this kind of love is so rare. Whether the love is in a seven-year-old or a ninety-two-year-old, respect it.

Society teaches people to keep love only a short time, to play with it like tennis, to treat it like a game. Practically all of us have been scarred on so many levels by those we have loved. And then the scars become our guides of how to conduct ourselves with the next person that we meet. Instead of love, it's a negotiation. This becomes the intelligent thing to do to supplement what it is to be in love. Do not negotiate. Negotiation is only for business. Leave it in business.

Fall in love and be in love as much as you can. When you do fall in love, use it wisely, for that is the easiest and fastest way to tap into wisdom. And be realistic with it. Don't have expectations. Have as much tolerance and patience as possible. Just know that sometimes things work out and sometimes they don't. It's all right.

We need the love and passion that the young ones bring to us — the ones who haven't been hurt and disappointed yet — because this love is really the life force that constantly brings new blood into the adult world, into the adult mind. Without the young people, we would sink fast.

That is the beauty of innocence. Many adults who understand this protect the innocent as much as possible, to keep love running through society. For real love, as I understand love, is the glue of life that holds everything together — all the atoms, all the molecules. It holds together the people, the trees, the heavens, the stars, the winds, the clouds, the frogs. It doesn't want. It doesn't expect. Life's love is the farmer: what do you want? I give you the free will. I give you your life. What do you want? It's up to you. You want to dream? No problem. Dream of what? No problem, just give me time. That's how much life loves us.

Find it somewhere in your heart to care more than your pain, more than your disappointment, and understand what is behind love. Then you can have the forgiveness of a nation, of a human being, of an act, even of yourself. You can see the love behind war, behind chaos, behind illness. You will never lose faith or hope, because you know this love is there. As long as another person is happy, as long as one person is in love in this world, there is nothing but hope.

The Roses

Go back and unearth the love of all those people you threw away.
If you loved them once, the love you had in your heart is still there.

When someone you love has left you, or you have left someone you once loved, even though the reality is that you are not together anymore, the important thing is never to stop loving that person. Never stop loving anyone you have loved in the past.

I know that love can die down. I understand that relationships can get difficult. And all of a sudden you find a new love. Well, what about the old love? Is it gone?

Think of your past loves as beautiful roses. Like all flowers, they are designed to be cared for and nourished. Do not throw away beauty. I wonder why so many people, so easily without even thinking, throw away so many beautiful flowers. Yet this is what we do with relationships: "Oh, I love you. I'll always be in love with you. And I know you love me for who I am." As time goes by, suddenly there's a difference of opinion. Now it's one big fight. After a while: "I don't love you any more. Next!"

"Now, I love *you*. You are the one and only for the rest of my life. I love you very, very much. You know me so well — so well that you have caught me in all my games. And I don't like that. Next!"

"Oh, now I have found my true love. I really love you. Oh, yes, forever and ever. Yes, you're just so wonderful, you have truly touched my heart. What? How can you say that? I don't love you anymore because you've hurt me too much. Next!"

My point is that this is what we do with our roses. We throw people away, just like that. Each love was a rose. Just because certain people have make you angry, or just because they have made your life harsh — never stop loving them. You may not find agreement with your minds. You may not be able to live with each other. That's understandable. But never stop loving them. Because they're roses. And because of what it does to the mind: "So this is what you do with love."

In whatever way your past loves crossed your life, they helped you. How many years does it take to finish high school? How many years does it take to really get to know someone? How many years did you devote to helping the one you love? For how many years did you receive that person's help? And then you just want to throw it away?

We all need a lot of help along the way. It takes a lot of very good roses, if they cross our path, to help us. It takes so many beautiful roses to develop a genuine love inside, to get your heart to truly open up. Hurt is hurt. Disappointment is disappointment. Agreement or disagreement, that's all it is. But people are roses. Don't throw them away.

In essence, that is our altar: the relationships we have had along the way. Sometimes we did not treat our loved ones too well, whether they were girlfriends, boyfriends, wives, husbands, friends, sons, daughters, grandmas, or grandpas. But we always have another day to rearrange our lives, to look at our altar differently.

So go back and unearth the love of all those people you threw away. If you loved them once, the love you had in your heart is still there. In your mind, you threw it away. But if it was genuine love, it's still in your bones. Bring back that love and nourish it. And when you are truly nourishing it, out of the blue you can get a phone call or receive a letter from your old love. You can run across that person in the streets.

Just because other people will throw you away so quickly, don't you do it too. Just remember to let people be. People cannot help but do what they do. Give people time to change. Give people plenty of time to understand. And if they never understand, it's all right. But *you* learn to understand as fast as possible.

Be wise with your life. Do not expect anybody to be kind to you. But you learn to be as kind as possible to others. Do not expect anybody to listen to you. But you learn to listen to others. Do not expect anybody to respect you. But you learn to respect others. Do not expect anybody to be courteous to you. But you learn to be courteous to others. And in time you will begin to be a witness of this world, as you keep your mind quieter and just watch.

Do not forget about the roses. To keep the love you once had alive in your heart is one of the most important things that you can do for yourself. You will see the quality of your life get much better. You will even see the quality of your mind change. It is better to die with a dozen roses in your heart, of all the loves and friends that you've had, than to let them go, no matter how angry they made you or what they have done to you. Do not throw away your own heart.

Finding Somebody

What is it that you like? Reflect this back upon yourself, without thinking of someone else. And in time, someone who has the same likes as you do will see your light.

A lot of people approach me with the question: "I'm looking for someone to have a relationship with but I can't find anybody. What should I do?" Well, today everyone knows that you can go on the Internet and pick out exactly the kind of partner you want: size, color, hair, weight, and so forth. Naturally, you hope that the description matches the person when you go meet them. Usually it doesn't, from what I hear. You can also search through hundreds of newspaper ads to see which words capture your heart and mind. Personally, to choose like that would not be easy for me.

To put yourself on a particular road during the day to meet someone is an extremely difficult thing to do, period. No matter where you live, no matter what your profession is, no matter how poor or how wealthy you are, it's not easy to find someone you can truly love.

After most people reach the age of twenty-five or thirty, they have been hurt *so much* by relationships. They've been lied to, stepped on, and accumulated enough pain and disappointment that finding something genuine in a relationship is very difficult. Now we don't want to go for walks alone. Or we want somebody to help us do the dishes. Or we want someone by our side just so we can say we have a relationship.

If you find yourself feeling a little desperation when it comes to finding a relationship, you are in trouble. You are attracting the wolves. The sharks. If you want somebody, do not be hungry. The only time to be hungry is before you eat. So take care of the hunger and desperation ahead of time, before you go looking for a relationship. I often tell people: please don't seek spirit out of desperation or ulterior motives. This is really no different.

I know that those little, innocent hungers are hard to stop. There's nothing wrong with having these kinds of desires. But it's important to acknowledge them and bring them out. Don't swallow that hunger. Keep it on the fireplace mantle, on the dresser. If you deny the hunger or try to hide it, that is when you'll run into problems. Simply be honest with it. If you have a sincere desire to find a relationship that is of the heart, just make sure that is leading your motivation to find somebody.

You can also do this: wrap up these little hungers up in nice box with a pretty ribbon. And after you meet your true love, you can say, "Oh, I've got a surprise for you." Most likely she'll love it. Then she'll say, "Oh, guess what? I have a few of those boxes too. Here's yours!"

If I see that people have a lot of ulterior motives or they're just playing around, I tell them to look on the Internet or in the newspaper. They aren't serious. These people aren't looking for a relationship that has any real depth, they're going for something more superficial. Maybe their motivation is purely sexual. Or perhaps it's loneliness, or a desire for security.

But if I see that someone is looking for something that is genuine and of the heart, I recommend something very different. One could say it involves a process that is internal, not external. If the ulterior motives and desires have died down, and you don't have all the hurts and disappointments bothering you, I will offer the following advice.

First, give yourself plenty of time — months or years — to find someone. You must allow the space and time for something to connect, with no provisions, no directions, and no control measures. Stop searching.

Then simply go inside and feel yourself. Go into your feelings and your heart, and feel what it is that *you* like, what it is that *you* want. How do you like to be touched? On your shoulders? Do you like your feet rubbed? Do you like your back scratched? What kind of lotion to you prefer to use? How do you like to brush your hair? How do you like others to communicate with you? What kind of music do you enjoy?

You have to reflect this back upon yourself, without thinking of someone else. It's like becoming a friend to yourself. A boyfriend to yourself. Or a girlfriend to yourself. Continue to ask: "What is it that *I* like to do? What kind of movies do I like to see? What kind of books do I like to read? What kind of places do I like to visit?" Nourish and rejuvenate this part of you inside. Think about it. Support it. Become very good at it. Watch the children, for they naturally nurture what they like and reflect it back onto themselves.

After a while, what happens? This kind of reflection creates an aura about you, a light that gets brighter as you keep building it up. You become like a lighthouse, a beacon of light that keeps growing and expanding. And in time, someone who has the same likes as you do will see your light.

You see, everyone has certain unique and beautiful qualities that they have mastered, although most people hide them and look at them as nothing special. Once you can recognize these qualities, these particular lights in others, you will find yourself asking, "Why do I like that person? It is because I saw something in that man or woman that *I* like. And I would like a small bit of that."

This is what naturally opens up communications and relationships: interest in another person. Even if it is just one molecule of something genuine you have in common, someone can easily be attracted to you. And you to them. With care and sincerity, you can start to pick up a lot of qualities from so many people.

What I'm saying is that there are a wealth of potential friends and lovers out there for everybody. Just understand that all people have their own unique qualities. Don't just say, "Oh, that's just a person. Oh, I don't like that." *Every person counts.*

Even though there are many human beings we can connect with, the numbers are still relatively few compared to the population of all the world. We are all so different. Is a shark going to love a bear? No. Is a fox going to love a mouse? No. Yet, believe me, no matter how we are or who we are, there are still quite a few people in the world who can connect with us from head to toe. There really are. But they can be almost impossible to find. Why? Because we haven't nourished our light inside. And because we control ourselves all the time, which can throw us out of synchronicity. That means we could miss someone by a century. Or by one minute.

When we really begin to connect with our hearts, synchronicity naturally starts to take place. Synchronicity is something that can happen more than once every few years. It can happen all the time. We can get to the point where we actually walk with synchronicity so that it touches our lives far more often.

Find Something to Love

One of my earlier teachers was an American Indian woman named Roberta. She was a wonderful teacher. Before Roberta and I met, she traveled to a retreat for Sikhs in the Southwest. She had just begun practicing the Sikh religion. About 1,500 people were attending this retreat. When Roberta arrived, she parked her car and got out to talk to someone. Suddenly her car went rolling down a hill and slammed right into another car, which happened to belong to the guru. It didn't take long before Roberta and the guru fell in love. This lady had synchronicity that was unbelievable. She always seemed to be in the right place at the right time. But there was a predicament: she was a student and he was the teacher. So it took an impact to bring them together and help them get past the usual stages and protocols of life.

When synchronicity doesn't seem to be present in our lives, or when we resist and hold back, we'll find ourselves staying home when we should be down at the grocery store so we can have an accident with someone we need to meet. So get out there and let the synchronicity take you places. Relax and allow life to happen, even if it means you might get bumped here and there. And continue to nourish the light within yourself.

Do not give up on love. Find something that touches your heart. And keep it touched as much as you can. Remember that you don't have to find a romantic love to open up your heart. It can be anything at all that touches you personally, for do not forget that life is, after all, very, very personal.

*Though I have all faith
so that I could remove mountains,
and have not love, I am nothing.*

*And though I bestow
all my goods to feed the poor,
and though I give my body to be burned,
and have not love, it profiteth me nothing.*

*Love suffers long and is kind.
Love envieth not.
Love wanteth not itself.
It is not puffed up.*

*When I was a child,
I spake as a child,
I understood as a child,
I thought as a child.*

*But when I became a man,
I put away childish things.
But now abideth
faith, hope, love — these three.
But the greatest of these is love."*

— 1 Corinthians 13:2

CHAPTER 7

HURT AND DISAPPOINTMENT

Do not let hurt and disappointment be your compass or your god.

Some of you may have heard the story about the young teenager, Bethany Hamilton, who lost her arm while surfing. She was only thirteen years old at the time. This young lady loved to surf. She was so good at it that she had already won a number of surfing contests, and her dream was to pursue a successful career as a professional surfer. One morning Bethany was out surfing with her friends and family near her home in Hawaii. All of a sudden, she was attacked by a very large shark that bit off her entire arm, along with a big chunk of her surfboard.

The other surfers managed to get Bethany safely back to shore, and she made it to the hospital where the doctors were able to save her life. Within a month of the shark attack, Bethany was back on her surfboard riding waves. Two months later she returned to competitive surfing, where she placed fifth in a surf meet. The loss of her arm is *not* going to stop her. Now, at fifteen years of age, she's one of the most sought-after and admired surfers in the world, because of how she managed her hurt and disappointment—the two biggest obstacles in most people's way.

Although this young girl showed an unusual amount of determination, strength, and faith, I think that an older person probably would not have handled this setback nearly so well. The young ones usually cope far better when it comes to real hurt and disappointment.

What does it take for us to get back on our boards and surf the waves of hurt and disappointment, the dangers that lurk out there? Not many people will even get on a board and ride the waves of life, of everyday existence. So many fall down too quickly, too many times, and simply don't get back up. Others become bitter, because they've experienced too much pain and hardship in this world.

Do not let hurt and disappointment be your compass or your god. Don't let a shark, a business person, a politician, or a government stop you from getting back on your board. Do not allow another human being — not even a neighbor, a husband, a brother, or a sister — to keep you off your surfboard, just because they may have cheated you or taken a big bite out of you — out of your pride, out of your arrogance, or out of your ignorance.

As long as we are human beings, the waves of hurt and disappointment will come into our lives. Life is not fair. It is not designed to be fair. But that's really not the point. The point is how we manage the hurt and disappointment, and how we look at it along the way. This is what makes a difference in our lives and helps us to become better human beings.

Closing the Heart

A matured heart will always get hurt, for hurt is one of the most wonderful indicators that we are alive and not a cold piece of stone walking around this earth.

When someone has hurt us a great deal, the doors to our heart can close down very quickly and remain closed for decades. What a strange mechanism. We can lock the doors and seal up the windows like a punishment. How easily we can say, "There's no way I'm going to forgive you. And I can hold these doors shut for twenty, thirty, forty years. Just watch me." And it's understandable. I don't blame anyone for doing this. For it takes a tremendous amount of courage to forgive — to open up the curtains, unlock the doors, and let people into our lives. It is our decision to let people in — in to be a friend, a lover, a counselor, a helper. It is our life. Our choice.

Hurt and Disappointment

A matured heart will always get hurt, for hurt is one of the most wonderful indicators that we are alive and not a cold piece of stone walking around this earth. We know we are not dreaming. And whatever scars we have, they have made us more than we were. So let yourself fall down into the mud or run into a wall. Let the adventure take place. When something goes wrong in your life, you never know what is behind it. What a lot of people consider to be misfortune, bad tidings, or bad luck is not necessarily bad at all. Maybe it is your gold, your saving grace. Maybe it's a blessing. And maybe not. You don't know. Time will tell. Either way, it's how you stand back up after being knocked down that matters, and that can create a most wonderful medicine just for you.

Although hurt is not a comfortable feeling, do not be afraid of getting hurt or disappointed by another person. If you do not understand the heart, and you put up walls or run away when the hurt has been, let's say, too deep and too painful, what happens? You also run away from life. You create a separation between yourself and other people, between yourself and life. And this keeps opportunities from coming toward you. It keeps people away from you.

Throughout life we all get hurt and disappointed, but it isn't really because of people. It is because we are spirited human beings, just another species, living in nature. If we cannot understand this predicament, we're going to hang on to the hurt and disappointment. It will make sense to hang on to it, for it's got us by its logic. But we have to be more clever than logic. And we have to have more heart than logic. Otherwise, we're bound by our mind, by the sense of logic itself.

When human beings, like any species, are disappointed and hurt too much, there's an alteration of direction. Now we want to hit back. Punch back. Get back at the source of the hurt. We become critical and sad. In time, so many of us lose the joy and beauty we once had in our faces, because we've lost faith in humanity.

But there is something that can bring back this beauty, and that is to open up our heart — and not just at Christmas or when someone close to us dies. I've noticed that the women and men who have opened their hearts begin to look younger. I have seen it wipe away the lines of age and worry in their faces, because it brings back a very innocent joy with wisdom behind it. It restores their sense of self.

Hurt and disappointment are probably the most invisible yet potent elements that cover and hold and keep people from moving and growing. One intense, deep-diving piece of hurt can keep us locked up for the rest of our lives, even if we've read all the books and all the magazines, trying to find a way to work it out. Even if it is hurt of oneself, it's still hurt. It's a very delicate thing, this hurt and disappointment. Yet despite the fact that we all get hurt and disappointed, it is a gift to be a human being, no matter where we are born. It is the most precious gift of all. Remember this.

The Biofeedback Patient

Sin is not the problem. That's a false front. The real problem that blinds humanity, that really holds us down is hurt and disappointment.

In the past, the concept of sin was brought in to help the ignorant, to keep people heading in a good direction. But sin is not the problem. That's a false front. The real problem that blinds humanity, that really holds us down, is hurt and disappointment.

Basically, all human beings are intelligent enough to understand the mysteries of life. But first we have to get past the drama of hurt and disappointment, which is not well understood by society. What society understands is sin. Society understands the implications of doing bad things to other people, stealing, and cheating. Society understands what it means to lose a business, a child, a friend, or a parent.

But hurt and disappointment have somehow become woven into complacency. Human beings eat hurt and disappointment and don't think much of it. It's kind of like it goes with the cornflakes. Getting hurt and disappointed is just something that happens in life, along with everything else we have to deal with: going to work, making phone calls, meeting deadlines, putting petrol in the car. Yet it's so important to understand what hurt and disappointment can do to our lives.

Here is a story about what hurt can do to us, if we let it. Many years ago, I was a biofeedback therapist. In my practice, I used various medical instruments and electrodes to monitor brain waves, skin temperature, blood flow, muscle tension, and sweat gland activity. When people are hooked up to biofeedback instruments, it's like they are taking a very sophisticated lie detector test. They cannot lie. And they can use the feedback signals from the body to relax their muscles, cope with pain, lower blood pressure, and improve their health in other ways, as they learn to make adjustments internally.

One of my patients was a woman who came to my office for migraine headaches that had troubled her for most of her life. She was a wonderful lady, a fast learner who had a quick mind.

Migraine headaches are the most difficult, next to cluster headaches, for a person to manage. When people get migraines, the blood has been shunted away from the extremities, the feet and hands, and into the central core of the body as well as the head, which then has to accommodate all this extra blood. The blood vessels in the head begin to expand and expand until they're pressing on nerves in the brain, and that's what causes the migraine and the pain.

Biofeedback teaches patients to get the blood out of the brain and back into the feet and hands, which eases the pressure of the blood vessels in the head and relieves the pain. But it's not all that easy to do when people have been "training" themselves for years to hold the blood up in the head. Today there are medications that open up the capillaries in the hands and feet and increase blood flow. But they don't always work, because the conditioning is so strong to shift the flow of the blood elsewhere. It's a difficult habit to break. So biofeedback teaches people how to communicate with their hands and feet and get them warm again by bringing the blood back to these areas. It's actually a matter of learning to use one's conscious will — not one's free will, but the will of the body and personality.

In this particular case, I was able to teach the woman with migraines how to get the blood back into her hands. But we just couldn't get it back into her legs and feet. No matter what I did, even after working with her thirty hours a week for three months, she had a big block. I even tried electroacupuncture. Nothing was working.

So I gave up. I put down the biofeedback equipment, stopped all the treatments, and started to talk with this lady: "Tell me about your life. What are you feeling? How was it when you were young?" After two sessions it finally came out that she hated her legs and feet because they had always been somewhat big. And I could see it was true — her legs and feet were a little large compared to the rest of her body.

To make matters worse, when this lady was a little girl, the other children made fun of the way she looked. You know how kids are — they can be very cruel. As a child, she was so hurt by their ridicule that she disassociated herself from her legs and feet. She wanted nothing to do with them. So she shut down the communication and completely blocked off any feelings to this area. As a result, she started to get migraine headaches. And her feet became cold all the time.

"They've always been ice-cold," she said. "You know, I've tried niacin. I've tried all the B vitamins. I've tried exercising. Nothing has ever worked."

After we talked for a while, this woman began to realize that she had literally shut down the fuel to her legs because of the hate that developed after she had been so hurt. It's like the brain was telling the blood, "Hey, don't go down there. It's no good. Trust me. Not nice. Stay up here." The brain was telling the feet: "I don't like you. I'm going to pull away. You're not going to get my blood, feet. Look what you have done." So, punish. Or withdraw. It's a very complex relationship.

So I had to bring her awareness back to her feet. In this case, the biofeedback instruments turned out to be useless. It took a lot of work to get this woman to accept her feet and re-establish a relationship with them. She began rubbing her feet, thinking about her feet. It was difficult, but she did it. And sure enough, it started to open up the doors for the blood to flow right in.

"That's really something," she said. "Do you mean that we really have the say-so?" Yes, we do. Blood, in. Blood, out. It's a very interesting phenomenon. We have the power to cut off the circulation to our fingers, our feet, our toes. I've seen this happen over and over again. We can increase the blood in our brain and give ourselves tremendous pain if we want. What hurt can do. And what our will can do. What do you want in life? Be *very* careful with your feelings and attitudes.

There is a simplicity in how the brain speaks to the body. The body says, "Yes, master." Yet who is really the master? It's not the brain. The brain simply gets the messages. It's not even the chemicals and hormones pumping through our bodies. Who is ultimately the master of what manufactures the chemicals that tell the brain whether or not to send blood down to the bottoms of the feet? *You are.* You're the boss. Yet how easily people give up.

Here is something else to think about. There is a link between your emotions and water. The body is made up of about sixty percent water, on average. If you were to take a drop of water out of the body and look at its molecular structure, you would see that water basically has the appearance of crystals.

When water is pure, it looks like snowflakes with intricate and beautiful designs. But once the water becomes flat and polluted, the crystals become deformed or dissolve. The water is dead, so to speak.

The water in your body also changes its crystalline form according to your feelings, your thoughts, and your state of mind. When you feel good about yourself, or when you are touched in your heart, it alters the make-up of the water and blood within your body. You become like one big crystal, so to speak, with a unique and beautiful design. When you feel depressed, the water looks quite different.

That's why the appearance of your face can change so much, depending on how you feel—whether you are frustrated and angry, sad or happy. It's profound. Yet what is actually happening is that you change inside first as the crystalline structure of the water changes, and eventually the change shows up on your skin. Imagine what hating your feet for twenty years can do to the very nature of the water within you.

So it's important to relax with your life, with yourself, even with your hurt and disappointment. This means accepting yourself as you are, feeling more comfortable with your dark sides and light sides and heaven sides and blue sides and yellow sides. It means being kinder to yourself, more forgiving of yourself. And it means understanding what hurt and disappointment can do: it can embed itself into your very cells and stay there for years, stealing your precious days away from you. It can overshadow your life for decades. Don't let that happen.

The Homeless Man in Santa Cruz

We're all bag people. We carry the weight of our hurt, our pain, our neuroses. And we endure it.

When I was in my thirties, I lived in Santa Cruz, California. The residents of Santa Cruz have learned to be as tolerant as possible to anyone who comes to their community. As a result, there are a lot of unique people who live in the streets of Santa Cruz. Some are called "bag people," because, being homeless, they keep all their possessions in bags that they carry with them.

For about two years, I remember watching one particular man who was always carrying at least three or four big plastic bags. I spotted him all over town, walking down the streets with his bags. Every day he wore a brown winter coat, with two or three other shirts on underneath, and heavy shoes—even in the summertime.

I always found myself wondering, "What on earth is in those bags?" They were obviously very heavy. After observing this man for a while, I could that see there was really nothing in his bags that most people would consider to be of value. But to him, they were valuable.

One summer day it was very hot outside. I was watching the bag man as he struggled under his load. He was really sweating. After walking about ten feet, he would put down his bags, rest a few minutes, get ready, then pick up his bags again and walk a few more paces. He didn't even take off his coat.

After following him in the car for some time, I finally decided to approach him. "Go help the man," my mind said. "Be a good person and give him a hand." By now, he was walking along a side street, which was good because I didn't want anybody to see me. So I got out of my car, walked across the street, and said, "Can help you? Let me carry your bags, at least for a block or two."

"No!" he said. "Get away! Get away! They're mine!" Ah. I got it. We're all bag people. We carry the weight of our hurt, our pain, our neuroses. And we endure it.

Then we have the pride to say, "You're not going to help me. It's *my* weight." This man was one of my best teachers. He just tore right into my brain, right in to my conditioning. A breakthrough. He showed me what my predicament was, what we all do to ourselves.

I began to remember all those times when people saw that *I* was hurting. In my face, in my expression, they could see all the weight I was carrying. When they tried to help, I rejected it. "No, I'm fine. I'm fine. No, it's okay." Nothing but my pride—my stupid pride—was in the way. "No, don't help me. I'm fine." Is this the message I was also sending out to life?

So I began to look for the bags that I'd been carrying inside my head and my heart. How long have I been holding onto them? This was my investment. How many years have I invested in my protection? I go to sleep with it. I have dinner with it. I take it to the movies. I might even catch cold if I let it go. And when I add a little more weight to my bags, guess what goes with it? An ounce of pride. A little more weight? Another ounce of pride.

This is what takes place within all of us. It's not easy to turn our eyes inward to see this. But our own predicament is as extreme as that of the bag man in Santa Cruz. We just don't realize it. And then we wonder why we have problems.

Do you know what is painful? When we let go of our bags. Because we are so used to carrying around the weight of our bags, what will we go through when we put them down? A separation. Feeling a loss. Feeling inadequate. Feeling naked. "It hurts. There's too much light. Something's wrong. I don't feel normal. I can't stand right. I feel too vulnerable. Give me back my life." This is what suffering is. It's not easy to wake up or to open the heart.

How many years did it take for our bags, our shields of protection to become a part of our lives? Did it just happen? All of a sudden, did somebody say, "Hey, here you go! Here's a good shield for you. What about this bag?" No. They developed over time. Do you know how much time we spend in complete devotion to getting all this weight on our shoulders? Many hours. Many, many moons. Many years.

And then we say we want to take it off, just like that? Nope. We're not going to let it go that easily. It's going to be a fight. This is where we need to have compassion for our personality.

Watch the children. They run around. They go into other people's yards, climb trees, drink and eat whatever they want. They don't worry about putting on a coat. It's the adults who say, "Come on, put on a coat, sweetie." Yet the kids are warm, playing outside in the snow. They're spontaneous with life.

But as adults we have surrounded ourselves in shields and walls because we've been hurt and disappointed too much. We've lost trust in our own feet, lost faith in life. And we have become comfortably numb. We've stopped taking chances, because we might get hurt. We might get disappointed. Imagine walking around with a heavy coat of armor protecting us. Yet this is what a lot of us do all the time. "Please protect me. Please protect me." And it works, to some degree. But we are spiritually, religiously, and ignorantly walking ourselves into four walls, as we build up these barriers around our mind and heart.

To awaken the mind and heart is to get the blood to feel nothing there, no more shields. Just openness. Yet we are *so* protective — especially in front — how much are we going to let in?

When you understand how conditioning works, our habit of protecting ourselves makes sense. Human beings walk forward. As a result, we run into people. We get hurt as we go through various experiences. We learn to be on guard. Whenever we open our eyes and look forward, we are on the defensive. We already have our shields up. We're automatically deciphering what we see and hear, deciding which words to bring into our mind and which words to keep out.

How long does it take before we really open up our arms to a friend, whether it's minutes, hours, days, or even years? Even though we try to absorb new ideas and bring new people into our lives, as adults most of us find it very difficult. There seems to be a force that constantly holds our arms up in front of us, that shuts down our ears so we don't really hear what's being said. As a result, we develop distance from others. We become isolated within ourselves. It is like we're standing alone inside a castle surrounded by stone walls. And it becomes extremely difficult to create a change in our lives.

Although the mind has the space in front of us completely within its grasp, it doesn't guard us from behind or to the sides. We don't have the conditioning to protect our backs. If this is the case, what if we were to approach ourselves from a different direction? From behind. As we start to sense ourselves from behind, we're activating completely different parts of the brain that we don't normally use. We begin to perceive and feel ourselves differently. We feel our vulnerableness. Our shyness. And this helps us to open up and receive, despite our shields. Using peripheral vision, not pinpoint focus vision, can also help us to relax our guard and receive more from the sides where we aren't as protected.

You could say that much of what you are reading in this book comes from this direction, for it is the basis of these teachings. They basically leave the front as is, acknowledging what is before us: our conditioning, our mistrust, our doubt. And it has to be this way. This is a part of growing up. It's healthy to have doubt. It is healthy to wait and see. These teachings do not fight with society, they walk with society. They support our traditions instead of taking them away.

It is the same with our shields. You don't have to rip off all your shields or throw away your bags, especially if you're not ready. Some of them may even be good for you, although it's important to work on the ones that are harmful, that keep people away, that prevent opportunities from coming your way. Years ago, I used to take all this weight off of people. But many of them almost went insane. They couldn't handle it. So I don't do that anymore. I say, "You've got a nice shield. Very pretty. Boy, you really have a nice bag."

It takes an awful lot of courage to put down our shields and let go of our bags. And so many of us don't have enough courage. I didn't either. But in between my shields, I also knew there had to be a goodness in life. And this is what I held on to: "Just because I have many bags, just because I've been hurt, does that mean the world is no good? No. Have faith in life. The goodness is there. That light is there. Believe me, whoever put this heart in me is there." This is how I spoke to myself. And I continued to walk, asking for the courage to open up a little bit more. To have a little more understanding. A little more hope. And I didn't give up.

It doesn't matter if you have ten bags or one bag. What matters is that you started the faith, you started the courage, you started the hope.

Hurt and Disappointment

What matters is that you're being honest with your predicament. This is what makes the medicine to lighten your load, soften your shields, and penetrate the walls around you to let life in.

TAKE AWAY THE UMBRELLA

When the sun goes down,
infinity shows its face.
No more ceiling.
You get to see the stars.

You take away the umbrella,
and you get to feel the rain.
You take away your shoes,
you get to feel the earth and the mud.
You relax your mind and thoughts,
you get to hear your own heartbeat.
You take away the protection,
and you get to feel your heart.

You look far enough,
you get to see what you have not touched.
And no matter what face stands in front of you,
you see tens of thousands of years of humanity.
Timelessness in front of you.

Opening the Four Doors

Here is a simple visualization that may help some of you. Close your eyes. In your mind's eye visualize yourself in a room, sitting in a chair. As you contemplate your past, think about the things that you have or do not have: a friendship, a child, a business, a job, and so forth. Contemplate your own life.

While you are sitting in this chair, look at your hands. Feel your hands and rub them together. Now visualize something that you want, whether it is a relationship, a new job, a new understanding, or whatever it is that would be good for you. In your mind's eye, see a door before you. At first you will see only one door. Now also look to your right, to your left, and behind you, and you will see a door in all four directions.

Get up and open up all four doors. Now your job is simply to live your life in your room. You've opened up the doors. You've had the wish. Now just relax and go about your day. Even though you may want something, don't put it on the other side of the doors. Just open up the doors in the four directions — north, south, east and west — and leave them open.

What did you just do? You not only provided room for more spaciousness to come into your mind, but you also simply allowed, which creates opportunities. Most of us are dealing with a desire to have a relationship, not to have a relationship, a lack of self-esteem, or something of this nature. There are all kinds of wonderful therapies we can do to help us achieve what we want in life. But if you do this simple visualization, what is the effect?

Think of it this way. When you leave the door to your house open, what happens? All sorts of strange and interesting things can find their way inside. Unusual opportunities drift in. Certain people walk through. Your perception and feelings become somewhat altered. What are doors for? They don't just have meaning and purpose in the external world.

Inside their minds and hearts, people close the doors to opportunities all the time. When I look into people's minds, I usually see nothing but doors closed, windows shut, and curtains drawn. Sometimes they are open. But typically almost everything is closed off.

When you close a lot of doors inside — do you know what happens externally on your face? It's closed too. When you see people who are open, they are easy to approach. But if the doors inside are closed, it broadcasts the message: "I'm closed. Stay away. Keep out."

What do you think spontaneity is? What do you think creativity is? Open doors. Why are some people bored with themselves? No one comes in through their doors. Why? Their doors are closed. No creativity can come in. No spontaneity can come in. Closed. "I've done it, seen it, read it all. There's nothing else to do, see, think, or say. Hmmm. Why am I so unhappy?"

To open the doors is like opening up your eyes. To open the doors is to search and to seek, to let life be spontaneous with you. It is to bring into your life new blood, new people, new sights and sounds, new events, new things that you haven't seen, heard, or thought about before.

Although this is a visualization, you're still standing up inside, breathing in a "spaciousness." A different kind of spaciousness exists internally than externally. In the internal world there is also an atmosphere. You could call it a "dream" atmosphere. When you go inside this space in your mind and then you come back out, you will feel as though your mind has slowed down, like you've just awakened from a good sleep. You may also sense more spaciousness inside.

If you want to do this visualization symbolically, that is fine. But it's important to get to the point where you personally open your doors inside. And it is really none of your business what comes in. What matters is that you have put the wish out. But still, buyer beware. In other words, be careful what you wish for.

Diving into the Heart

Take advantage of the situations when you find yourself in a moment that is rare for any human being — in the depths of your heart.

It's easy to be a human being who is asleep, walking. But it takes a great deal of work and tremendous courage to live in your heart, because it hurts. The more you feel, the greater the sensitivity in your heart. Sometimes your heart can even ache physically. When this happens, we're often told, "Don't feel so much. Don't be so emotional. Stay out of it. Get into your mind. And you won't hurt." And that's true.

To open up the door to your heart is not easy. It's like those times when an arm has fallen asleep, and you don't want to let the blood back in because it's too painful. You don't even want to move your arm, because the pins-and-needles sensation is going to get worse. It hurts. That is what it's like when you're trapped in your mind. You're asleep. "Don't move it." When you start to open up the door to your heart, it's going to hurt like hell, because you're comfortable being asleep. It's painful to wake up.

But to awaken this heart of yours, you have to feel all the hurt and disappointment that you experienced growing up, as you've walked out your life. No one escapes it. It's not to get rid of all your memories. You want all your memories, don't you? Don't pretend something didn't happen or hide it underneath the covers. Remember every little detail, if possible — even the hurt and disappointment. It's painful to look at, isn't it? But that's what you want to do. And when you do look at it, hope that you have the good graces to forgive all those times you've been hurt and disappointed, so you can finally put down your weapons.

An open heart does not necessarily bring only joy and happiness as a lot of people expect. It's a painful process, because you start to feel your body and the world around you. But guess who will be home if you do? *You* will be home. And guess who will notice this? Children will notice this. They can tell the difference. Animals can tell the difference. And there are many adults who can also tell the difference.

To touch the spirit, to activate the heart, to connect with life, you cannot just skim the surface of your mind and your experiences of the day. You have to dive down deep. What takes you down very deep and fast into your heart? Hurt. That, or very good love. What else takes you down? Sometimes a good scene in a movie will do it. Can work do it? Driving a car? It's rare, but it happens. But how often during your seven-day week does it happen? Not often — not often enough.

Do you know what most people do when hurt takes them down into their heart? They miss the opportunity. Now that they've plunged into the depths of their heart, this is the time to plug into life. Yet they usually jump right back out because they don't want to feel the hurt. Human beings have developed a conditioning to walk away from hurt. Most people think that the minute you feel pain, you're going the wrong way. Go the other way. But that is what you *don't* want to do. As soon as you feel pain — look, walk, run in that direction. If you find yourself getting angry, that means you've run the other way. You've gotten angry because you can't deal with the hurt and disappointment.

Your job is to *stay down*. And don't point the finger. Do not blame anyone else: "*You* made me feel like this. *You* did this. *You* caused this." That's not the point. The point is that you are down. You have dived deep. The mind wants to point the finger so it can stay out instead of going in and taking advantage of this extremely rare opportunity. You are deep in your heart, and that's why you hurt.

Hurt will take you down so quickly it will make you cry because it feels so bad. "Oh my god, that hurts. I wish it could have been love, instead of this damn hurt. That would have been great. My bad luck. What did I do to deserve this?" But if it happens to be hurt or disappointment that has taken you down, use it.

If you don't feel the hurt, where are you? In your mind. If you don't feel the love or something else that touches your heart, you are also in your mind. The mind is necessary to get along in this world. But a student of life who truly understands the Eastern scriptures, who grasps what Jesus or Buddha were trying to say, knows this well: take advantage of the situations when you find yourself in a moment that is rare for any human being—in the depths of your heart.

So be aware, be attentive, and when you're down, take hold of the opportunity and feel that hurt. Just realize that in the beginning, when you're starting to look at the hurt inside, it's going to get much worse for a while. Why? Because you're looking at it instead of running away. That tells you that you're doing it correctly. In time the hurt will settle down. Then you can begin to look at the situation differently. When you begin to look into that space inside your inner heart, in time, your life will start to change.

THE PHENOMENON OF SELF

I have to take responsibility to realize
there are other people living in the world,
not just me.
And the whole world is not just my view.
In turning my eyes to this larger perspective,
to the Mother and Father of life
that have given me life,
the problems of myself,
of my mind and my heart,
get smaller and smaller,
and life becomes more important
than just me.

Life Is More Than Just Me

Why not plug into a telephone network that is connected to the whole world?

When I was practicing biofeedback many years ago, my intention wasn't to be a therapist. I just thought of myself as a technician who taught people how to relax and manage their pain. But after my clients relaxed for a certain amount of time, they began to talk, and before long, they started telling me their stories.

After listening to everyone's stories for about a year, I realized something: almost everybody who came to see me thought they had the worst pain of all. Nobody else could have a pain greater than their pain. Nobody could have had a life worse than their life. No hardship could be more difficult than theirs. This was especially surprising to me, because at the time I thought that certain aspects of *my* life, especially my childhood, were worse than anybody else's.

This is what I call "the phenomenon of the self," and it goes something like this: because I have been living inside my body and mind since I was born, I can only perceive, think, feel, eat, and live through my own body and mind — not through yours. So, in essence, I am a world unto myself. When I feel pain, to me it is the greatest pain in the world. When I find clarity, it is the greatest clarity, the most wonderful idea in the world. If I feel dumb, I feel like I'm the dumbest person in the world. But if you were to go out and conduct a survey, you would find that most other people are also claiming that they have the worst headache, the worst husband, the most difficult child, and on and on.

You see, there is something that matters much more in this world than your pain. There is something that has much more value than your emotional satisfaction. And that is to bring in an astronaut's perspective of life that takes all of humanity — past, present, and future — into account.

It is only you who can decide the priorities of life. What really matters? Be extremely careful what you emphasize, and look to see if there's an element of selfishness in wherever your emphasis comes from. Your hurt. Your drama. Your pain. Your stories. See if it matches the astronaut's point of view.

Simply understanding the phenomenon of self will lead you out of your hurt and disappointment. When your knees grow weak with fear or pain, this understanding will help to lift you up. And when your eyes burn with confusion and distress, it will dry your tears.

Our best medicine is using our intellect, reason, and common sense to see that there is a predicament in life and we are all in this together. All human beings are in the same boat. In realizing this, we make a quantum jump. Now we are connected to an international telephone system instead of a telephone system that's confined to only one country. Why not plug into a telephone network that is connected to the whole world? This is what gives us a strong foundation inside. It makes our prayers strong. It engages the winds of our heart, and helps to make those winds stronger. And it teaches us to see from a greater perspective — from life's eyes, you could say, and not just our eyes. Remember what happened when the astronauts first went up into orbit and brought back the pictures of our planet? Our world changed.

Every time we take our situation — our personal problems, our misunderstandings, our goodness — and we hook it up to the much larger network encompassing everyone else, it immediately draws in a much stronger reality to help us. It's not just *my* problem. This is what we *all* have been going through. This is what Grandma went through, but I didn't know it. This is what all the generations went through. What about our collective courage and our common struggle to live with more peace and understanding? What about the good life constantly coming into this world, whether it's an invention, a child, or anything to help the common cause of humanity? We have seen it happen time and time again. If I just think of "me, myself and I," what happens to everybody else? But if the whole community pulls together, what is the result?

When we just pay attention to our *own* hurt and disappointment, our macrocosm starts to transform itself from a telescope into a microscope. We reduce the capacity of our brain. We reduce our vision into a microcosm world. But when we begin to bring in a greater reality that encompasses everyone's pain, like smoke rising out of a microscope, whose power begins to increase more and more, in time there's a transition. Our lives begin to make more sense. And a different light reveals its face. Now we have the vision of a telescope. We see farther than before. More clearly. Yet we can still feel our own hurt.

Every wish, every prayer of all human beings who have lived and hoped for more goodness, more education, a better life for their children and for their country is always very much alive on this planet. Always. What is important is to connect with these living prayers and hopes and to realize that we are not alone.

Know that when you feel your hurt and pain, it's all right. There's nothing wrong. You know you're still alive. But every now and then, turn your eyes toward the sky and look up. And speak to yourself. Speak to whatever might be listening, as you radiate out your feelings inside. If you don't receive any feedback — no thunder, no car honking, no human's voice, no bird chirping, no wind through trees — just continue speaking to your own heart.

And remember that all people get hurt. All people get disappointed. All people get scared, too. Everyone basically wants the same things in life. A friend. Someone to touch. Someone to love. To grasp what sunrises really mean. And when we look up at the night sky filled with stars, everyone knows there is something more out there, that we really aren't alone after all. Everyone knows it.

The Tears of Humanity

We are the walking past, embedded in the present.

Did you know that most of what makes up your emotions, your feelings, and your thoughts is not yours? It is humanity's. You are *of* humanity. As one person, you're like one cell of humanity.

You inherit humanity's guilt, selfishness, goodness, beauty, joy, happiness, clarity, stupidity, hells, and heavens. All of it. There is nothing new. All any process of waking up does is to reveal what is, what has always been there. As you start to become more conscious, you'll see this. So be wise with your life. Be careful what you claim. A good ninety-five percent of it is not yours, but what has been filtered down through the generations. And that, you could say, is essentially what really makes a person whole.

In realizing this, you'll change the way you think about your pain, your disappointment, and your guilt. It's arrogant to think that it all belongs to you, for hurt and disappointment literally reside in the field of memories of all human beings. Don't be arrogant. You didn't invent it. Arrogance says, "Hey, this is my finger. This is my hand. This is my head, my face, my cheeks, my brain." No, it's actually humanity's brain. You are just using it.

Do you realize how many fathers have lost their wives, due to disease or war? Or how many women have lost their husbands? Have you thought about how many mothers have lost their children? *Millions.* And all this we inherit. This is what gives us our feelings and our passion. It gives us a good foundation to stand on, so we can, in essence, know what our ancestors felt, what they saw, what they dreamt. We're dreaming their dreams. We're feeling their feelings. We're going through their losses, too. We are the walking past, embedded in the present. And one day, our children's children are going to be dreaming our dreams and going through our wants, our struggles, with one difference — they will be smarter than we are.

When a human being understands that the feelings, the pictures, and the thoughts inside one's head are not just "mine" but humanity's, then maturity starts to emerge. The mind begins to expand. Consciousness starts to show its face. And one's tears no longer belong to just "me, myself and I"—they belong to humanity.

You see, the chemical make-up of each tear is the result of the feelings, thoughts, stories, and pictures that go into creating that tear. It takes a tremendous amount of beauty to produce one tear. When you shed a tear for yourself, you can literally change the chemical composition of that tear so that you are actually crying humanity's tears—not only yours but also those of everyone who has lived before you. This is how your tears, like your hurt and disappointment, can transform.

MORE TO LIFE

*To see from the eyes of life,
it took a realization
that there is more to life than just me.*

*We all have to get through the day.
We all have to get up in the morning.*

*It is not just me, it is us.
Things don't just happen to me,
things happen to us.*

*It is not only I who hurts,
it is all of us who hurt.
It is not only I who hungers,
it is all of us who hunger.
It is not only I who is confused,
it is all of us who are confused.*

*We are all in one big boat
traveling through space,
learning to live on this earth,
while our hearts beat
to give us another day, another sunrise,
to help us understand ourselves and life.
All of us.*

CHAPTER 8

FORGIVENESS

When you forgive you are more than nature, more than your hurt, and more than time. But remember that you simply have to care enough.

There is a medicine that we all have inside. It's a most wonderful and beautiful alchemy that our bones can emit. What activates the creation of this medicine? Forgiveness. It is *direct*. It can touch one's heart like few other elements can.

About fifteen years ago, I was teaching a five-day workshop in Shinoa, a small town in northern California. I'd been looking forward to some sun, but it was dark and cloudy outside, and the forecast was for rain all week. The first day of the workshop, something unusual took place as I began to speak. My eyes closed and I went into my heart in a way that didn't happen often. In this particular space I found myself in, there was a tremendous amount of depth. And the depth carried a feeling of great reverence.

After a few moments, I began to pray out loud. It was one of those rare moments when I was able to go into genuine divine prayer. And my prayer had to do with forgiveness. I asked forgiveness of all those who had ever crossed my path—in the past, in dream states, in other lives. Somehow my vision encompassed so much that I could see the predicament of everyone I had ever met and how it intersected with my own predicament, my ignorance, and my hurt.

Suddenly, in the middle of my prayer, sunlight began to stream in through a window and make its way toward me. Within a few moments, I was completely enveloped in sunbeams. I could feel the warmth of the light shining onto my head from behind. After I finished my prayer of forgiveness, the light receded. This was the only time the sun came out during the entire time I was in Shinoa. What I remember so well was that, while the light was shining down during the prayer, it seemed like the most important part of the whole workshop.

As it is, a most significant moment in your own life can also take place when you are forgiven or you truly forgive someone. Real forgiveness is a most touching means of activating your heart. It can even set a new course for your life. And once you have done one act of genuine forgiveness, it becomes much easier to forgive again in the future.

When you lay down your head on your pillow tonight, please try to go back over all those times when someone hurt or disappointed you. And somewhere in your heart, if not in that moment, then sometime in the future, try to forgive that person. If you have to devote months or years to working on that one act forgiveness, it's worth it.

Most of the time, you can't just say, "I forgive you." It's not that easy. Like a good oil rig, looking for oil deep within the earth, you have to dig down deep into your mind, so the forgiveness reaches those deposits of hurt. If the hurt took place a year ago, it's buried pretty deeply, covered up by many layers of time and experiences. If it happened ten years ago, you have some serious digging to do.

So spend some time in your quiet moments uprooting all these hurts and disappointments. Soon you will begin to feel much lighter, much freer with yourself. You'll notice that you have far more energy. But remember that there is a price to pay to put lightness into your mind, into your life, and into your heart. What is that price? Forgiveness.

***

Why is it so difficult to forgive? It has a great deal to do with nature itself, for nature remembers. Nature remembers its enemies well. It has to. The violence of nature is extremely strong, and it has no mercy on the innocent, the young, or the old. At a very early age, the young of any species have already inherited so much information about what to beware of, what to stay away from. Evolution and natural selection have programmed humans, like all species, to remember everything that is painful in order to stay alive.

When we get hurt, what is it that is being hurt? Our feelings, yes. But what is behind our feelings? Our instincts. We haven't completely shed the animal that lives inside of us. We are still caught in survival, just in a different way. Only five hundred years ago, many European nations were at war. Violence was widespread. Instinct was strong. The struggle to survive has been going on for thousands and thousands of years. There's no devil. It is simply nature, the instinct to survive, and our ignorance of how strong the animal still is within human beings.

Naturally we are not the same animal that roamed the earth tens of thousands of years ago. We're more evolved, at least in some respects. If we live in the Western world, we now have to deal with the economy, taxes, money, and work. We have moved out of survival to a great degree, but not completely. Instinct can still control our behavior and we won't even know it. Once we identify with this instinct, we're lost. As human beings, we must understand this.

When we are hungry, our behavior can change drastically. Some of us will become very desperate. All the goodness that was inside can be completely wiped away. All the moral values, all those wonderful qualities that reside in the minds and hearts of human beings can disappear, simply because our stomach has been empty for a little too long. Desperation and survival now run the show. And instinct has got us by our tails again.

What is the history of the ground we are standing on? Don't forget that the earth was flat not too many centuries ago. The last witch was burned alive just over one hundred years ago in Switzerland. I know a Swiss man who lives in the valley where this took place. He told me there are people living there today who still believe that this witch was evil and deserved to be burned. The earth, believe me, is still flat. Neuroses, hurt, disappointment, ignorance, hatred — they have no respect for our lives or for time.

Instinct does not forget. It had better not forget. And this is what holds back forgiveness. One generation after another, whether you are a fish, a bird, an insect, or an antelope roaming the grasslands — you do not forget. You learn very quickly to survive.

Today human beings have evolved into a more sophisticated species, with four brains, you could say, instead of only one, so it becomes much more complicated when hurt comes into the picture. Now it is more than just instinct. Now we have a choice. We have a higher intellect to make a choice — a better choice — about what to do with this hurt that is so instinctive that it wants to live forever. A hurt that doesn't respect time or our lives. A hurt that is designed not to forget.

But do you care *enough* to make that better choice, to transcend the forces of evolution, the animal inside? Most people do not care enough. It is too much work, too much effort. Actually, it can feel good not to forgive. This is another reason people don't do it. Holding on to their hurt gives them fuel. It gives them energy. It gives them a cause, a reason to live another day for revenge, a justification to hold back their love and affection. Refusing to forgive is a kind of food, just like anger or hatred. That's why people like to hold on to grudges. It makes them feel bigger and stronger. In a sense, they are. But it doesn't last. And it's very destructive. Yet because they receive a boost from it, many people think it's right not to forgive.

Remember what it felt like when someone hurt you? First it brought you down. Then after a while, you stood back up with this strength, this animal inside, this cause. When this happens, ask yourself, "Am I conscious enough to go against nature, or am I just reactive?" A dog can be very reactive, yet a dog can have consciousness, too. But some animals don't have much of a brain and they are almost totally instinctive. They see food and immediately take off to devour it. Is this what I am? Instinctive? Put a red flag in front of me and I will charge it? Put a plate of food nearby and I will attack it?

Again, do you really care enough to transcend the bonds of nature? That is the question. For humanity really does not live through bread alone. There is such a thing is as a spirit of life, a fuel that bread cannot give you, that an apple cannot give you, that a whole field of wheat cannot give you, that an ocean of pure water cannot give you.

Do I really care enough not to let my instincts run my life? Because one day I will not have my stomach anymore. I will not hunger for food anymore. One day I will not have my physical eyes to see anymore. One day I will have to leave my body behind. And then what will my cause be? What will I fight for then? What food will I reach for then? Who will be around to forgive or not to forgive?

One act of forgiveness is a most blessed event. You have to care more than the hunger of your stomach. You have to care more than the pain that someone has caused you. You have to care more than your sweet revenge. You have to care more than the scars on your body, the scars in your mind and heart. For anger does not care. Hatred does not care. Hurt definitely does not care. *You* have to care. You have to rise above it, and this is the hard part.

The act of forgiveness is no thunderstorm and no lightening bolt. It is no great cry out. The act of forgiveness is as soft as a feather. It is as quiet as a breeze. The act of forgiveness is more alive than the life that any planet can ever offer you. It is worth more than ten thousand or a hundred thousand lifetimes. When you forgive you are more than nature, more than your hurt, and more than time. But remember that you simply have to care enough.

Bending One's Pride

The act of kneeling touches the essence of forgiveness in a way that sitting cannot, whether it is forgiveness of oneself or of others.

What is forgiveness? Forgiveness is bending. When you ask a person for forgiveness, in essence, you are bending your will, bending your pride. One of the hardest substances residing within a human being is pride, whether it is appropriate or inappropriate pride. It can stand against any storm. It can withstand time. Pride has no boundaries. It is very much like cement. So when a person forgives, or asks to be forgiven, it is actually bending this cement.

In the movie *Braveheart*, there is a scene in which William Wallace is burying his beloved wife. Afterward, he falls to this knees and asks for forgiveness from his wife's father, because Wallace feels responsible for her death. You'll see that even in his anguish, the father finds the courage to forgive. Find the movie if you can and watch this scene from your heart. It is so touching, and it will help you to understand the beauty of forgiveness.

Here is another suggestion to help you feel the forgiveness that lies in your bones. When you are alone in your room, a church, or any other quiet place, and you are in a certain space in your mind and heart, kneel down. You can even play some music that touches you and helps to bring you into a more contemplative state. It is not just to sit, but to have the humility to bend down and kneel. The act of kneeling touches the essence of forgiveness in a way that sitting cannot, whether it is forgiveness of oneself or of others. Prayers are important, but when people are hungry, food is more wonderful. An act is what matters.

Kneeling isn't a natural posture for human beings. People stand up, sit, or lie down. They don't usually bend. So when you kneel down, there's a mystical quality to it, because it's so out of ordinary to bend the body in this way. You are also removing about half a meter of your stature — cutting down your mentality, your vision, your point of view.

You're humbling yourself, in essence. And you are bringing your heart closer to the earth.

When you are kneeling, it starts to activate the mechanics that allow forgiveness to take place. It's like flicking a switch that unlocks the internal ear and eye so you can perceive differently. It opens up the hearing, the sight, and the senses to look at life very differently. On the other hand, when you stand up, pride automatically sits in place and starts to put filters on your hearing and your seeing. When you kneel down, it's not so. But most people will not kneel because it's too humbling. Meditation also does not bend one's pride, because sitting is natural to do, even if you are sitting cross-legged. Everyone sits. So you can still hold your pride because you're sitting down.

Even bowing your head can place your body in a stance that helps to put you in a genuine forgiveness state. If you're talking to somebody, asking for forgiveness, and you tilt your head up with a little bit of arrogance, it's hard to be sincere, isn't it? The head naturally drops down in a certain gesture of humility when you sincerely ask for forgiveness from your heart. So remember to bend. It makes all the difference in the world when it comes to forgiveness.

Forgiveness and Time
To forgive, there is no negotiation.

Adults can find it extremely difficult to forgive. For children, it's much easier. Most of the time, they forgive unconditionally. When children get hurt, they're really hurt. But in the next moment, it's gone. They can let it go and forgive quite easily.

Adults say, "Well, let me see here, you didn't forgive me for this and this and that. Why should I forgive you for this and this and that? Now, if I forgive you, I need this and I want that, and then *maybe* I will forgive you."

I have occasionally come across adults who've forgiven, with no motives or bargaining, but most of the time when an adult says, "I forgive you," there are stipulations. I find that the grandmas and grandpas are the ones who tend to forgive most easily. They don't have anything to prove. They don't have to get your love. They've done it, seen it, heard it. They are able to make everything okay. You see, to forgive, there is no negotiation.

As we grow older, a conditioning develops that is like a rubber band. When we're young and open and receptive, the rubber band stretches way out and comes back very quickly. "Oh, that's okay," children say. "It's over. Now let's go out and play." But as we get hurt over and over again, we start to build up walls. We become defensive and angry. The rubber band stretches and stretches, but we don't bounce back the way we used to. Now, we don't let go. We hang onto the tension. The pain. The disappointment.

Every time we get hurt and disappointed, a feather goes over here. When a child gets a little hurt, here comes another little feather. "Well, it's no big deal. I mean, we all get hurt. I'll give you a few more feathers. You're not going to notice anything, little child."

But pretty soon, these feathers keep mounting and mounting. The balance scale keeps tipping and tipping. The hurt doesn't go away as fast. After a while, there's no such thing as fast. The hurt goes into the next category of *slow*. Very slow. In time, we start to exist in this state of slow, which gives us lots of hours, months, and even years to figure out ways to backstab the ones who hurt us. How can we wring their necks? Let's poison them very slowly. Revenge. Once it gets into the slow stage, we have time to think about all the details, and the ways and means of revenge can become quite ingenious. This is another reason it's so difficult to forgive. The memory is still there, living in the state of *slow*. "I still remember what you did. I still remember what you said."

Nobody forgets being hurt, no matter how much the one who caused the hurt loves us after that. Despite the dozens of roses, the new car, and all the best love this person gives us, we're not going to forget.

Life is so delicate. When we're hurt, we have a scar for the rest of our lives. It's not to pretend the hurt didn't exist. It's not to say, "It's over." It's never over. The mind knows that. It's how we deal with the hurt and disappointment that matters. How are we going to handle that memory, that situation, that experience? The hardest thing for all human beings to do is to be able to stand on hurt and disappointment to the point where they've come to terms with it and no longer let it affect their lives.

The conditioning, the remembering, the holding onto hurt happens on a larger scale, too, in a very quiet, deadly war that takes place within human beings in any society — a war that affects humanity from generation to generation. When a group of people get together with their concerns, gripes, and stories, these issues start to grow and grow. Then they're passed on from one generation to the next. A grudge can be perpetuated for *hundreds* of years.

When we are fed these stories as young children, what other references do we have? There's no other recourse, no other way to think. We want to be like Mom and Dad. We want to have a cause, too. Our friends think this way. We hear about it all day. It's constantly reinforced. The weight builds up. And we adapt to this weight. We buy the conditioning, the stories — hook, line, and sinker. It's not easy to stand on one's own.

Look at Europe. The various European countries are still caught in the trauma of what happened in the past, hundreds of years ago. Many Europeans continue to hold onto World War II, which ended over sixty years ago. England still thinks it is fighting Germany. France, Scotland, Ireland — they all hold onto their grudges. The same is true for many North American Indians. Most of my people hate Americans. They can't forgive the white people for overrunning their nation. They simply cannot let it go. The war of 1812 is still occurring. "What you did to great-great-great-grandpa" is still taking place in the blood. It's shocking to see this. Every human being who holds a grudge, who looks down on another nationality, who will not forgive another country and refuses to see its goodness, keeps this hatred and violence alive. As it is within our own mind and body.

You know, it is so difficult to change yourself. But to make that process easier, find something external that is gross, that really sticks out, and study it. Look at the actions of entire nations: do they take revenge, let their resentments simmer, or forgive? Because what happens out here in the macrocosm, in the external world, is a reflection of what is taking place inside you. That's one reason movies are so wonderful. What you see externally on the screen, you can transfer inside and create a change within.

Some people think they are their hurt, and they will follow their hurt. Some people think they are their hatred, and they will follow their hatred. And some people will follow their joy, healthiness, and goodness, which will give them the time and space to understand that there really is something more to life than what they know or have been taught.

It's not to forget the past, but to understand what the investments of the past can do. They can work for you or against you. Remember that hatred, hurt, and neuroses have a propensity to hang on to the past. Your job is to understand, as you walk into your future, what is good for you and what is not good for you. You don't live in the past anymore. Understand the present. Work with the present. And the results will come.

Forgiving Oneself

As a parent, when one of my children makes a mistake, do I condemn that child to hell?

Everyone, including myself, has done something wrong, probably many times. Many of us are very hard on ourselves for our past actions. If we continue to be so unforgiving of ourselves, it has implications for the mind and heart, which can even manifest, to some degree, inside the body. I remember coming home one day when my youngest son was about five years old. He ran up to me, very excited, and said, "Daddy, Daddy, come see what I can do! Mommy showed me how to use her computer." I watched while my son began to punch various keys, and all of a sudden something happened. He knew it and I knew it. "Uh-oh," he said. "I erased something." I didn't know exactly what it was that he erased, but he clearly knew.

My son felt so bad that he lowered his head onto his arms and said, "I do not like myself. I do not like myself at all." I could see that he meant it from his heart. Even though it was a mistake, how quickly this little five-year-old could close his mind, shut down his heart, and feel guilt and remorse.

As fast as possible I tried desperately to bring my son out of it. "Everything is all right," I said. "The program can be reinstalled. Your mother has backed up her data. It can be corrected. Please don't worry about it." This made him feel better but I could see that he still hurt inside.

How many times have we done this to ourselves? No matter what age we are, whether we get hurt due to our own actions or someone else's, we can invest so much time and energy into disliking ourselves and finding all sorts of ways to develop a separation between ourselves and life. Although children forgive others easily, they usually have a hard time forgiving themselves, like the rest of us.

As a parent, when one of my children makes a mistake, do I condemn that child to hell? Is my child destined to have a bad life forever for doing something wrong or getting a little rough with his brother? No. It's just a child having a child's mind, learning to get along in life. When you were five years old, did that make you lesser than your mother or father? Of course not. You were just not as mature. It takes time to grow up. You could say that life looks upon us in the same way, and would not condemn us or deny us forgiveness for the mistakes we have made along the way. Remember this when you're not feeling good about yourself.

Honesty and Forgiveness

The only time we can forgive is when the heart is fully open. We cannot do it with our mind, for the mind has no access to forgiveness.

Forgiveness is always appropriate. Yet sometimes there are certain people we simply will not forgive. Everybody else, yes, but not them. As it is with ourselves. We will not forgive ourselves for certain acts we have committed. We know that. So we're caught in a predicament.

This is where honesty comes in. Even though we are not going to forgive, we're being honest with it. That is what creates the alchemy to make the medicine to help us. If we have enough honesty, we'll realize that we're going to have a hard time forgiving everybody, just like that. We cannot always forgive someone who has hurt us just because we want to do it.

Forgiveness comes only at a certain time when a crossroad presents itself. The conditions have to be right. The heart has to be open. The willingness has to be there. All the magic has to be present for real forgiveness to take place — whether it is forgiveness of oneself or of others. It's kind of like heaven opening up its gates in the course of ordinary life. About the only time forgiveness can take place is during these moments.

Then what can we do? We have to be patient. And let life open up the doors for us. Instead of directing the forgiveness, we must wait for the right situation to occur when we have found the willingness and the courage to forgive someone who has hurt us. It will happen. In time, forgiveness will show its face and all we have to do is be there when that moment comes.

In the meantime, we can create a pact with ourselves, an intent for the forgiveness to take place sometime in the future. We must hold the understanding that we cannot just suddenly crack open our hearts. The only time we can forgive is when the heart is fully open. We cannot do it with our mind, for the mind has no access to forgiveness.

It is the same with prayer. As I've already mentioned, I can sincerely pray only under the right circumstances, even if someone asks me to pray. If it's not there, it's not there. I come to terms with the fact that I cannot do anything about it and just continue to live my life.

So take all the times you did something wrong or you were hurt by someone, put them in a little box somewhere in your mind or heart, and ask that the situation arise for forgiveness to take place. Ask that you have the good will and the good graces to open up that box at the right time and forgive.

If you are sincere enough, the opportunity will be created for that to happen. But until that time comes, put aside your guilt and don't be too hard on yourself. Just go live your life, for there's nothing you can do until life itself creates the scenario for forgiveness to take place. This in itself will begin to ease the burden of all that weight you have been carrying around.

※ ※ ※

This leads to something else that will help to ease your mind and heart. You do not have to love everybody. Please *don't* love everybody. It's not healthy. You don't even have to like everybody. Why? Because you can't. We are all such different creatures: bears living with rabbits, foxes living with squirrels, sharks living with seals. This earth is one big sandbox, and we are like little children playing in this sandbox, bumping into each other, throwing sand. All sorts of different species are thrown together on this earth, trying to get along.

You see, living with the heart, you don't have to like all people. There are many people I do not like, but I understand them. I can understand their ignorance and why they are the way they are. It is only when there is a transcendence of the mind and you see from your heart that you can understand people. You are able to love that part in their heart that is human, even though you do not like their behavior, their mentality, or the act itself. There is something in most people that you can always find to like or love if you are able to penetrate the barriers of hurt, pain, and prejudice. Like all human beings, you have a free will to decide whether to lift up a gun and fire it at someone you do not like. But if you have a big enough heart, you can see what brought a person to those circumstances, and you will not hate but understand. And if you are not yet at that point, simply know what you know, know what you don't know, and have the hope that someday you will understand.

Something else to remember is this: no matter what you do or say, some people will always hate you. Some people will always dislike you. Some will always be confused by you. Some people will always like you. And some will always love you. That is the way people are.

So make it all right if people don't like you. Once you understand this, you can say, "You don't like me? It's all right. I don't blame you. Life!" And walk on. You will find this taking loads and loads off your shoulders, as you begin to relax with yourself and stop taking everything so personally. It becomes easier to walk the earth, and to live in the sandbox.

You never know who you are talking to on the streets. You never know who is sitting next to you. Do you know what has been going on in that person's life? No. You never know who is in the car in front of you, the one you're honking at impatiently. Maybe the person behind the wheel is driving too slowly or he's not paying attention to the stoplight. But maybe he's also a father whose son has just died, and he's not feeling too good at the moment. You don't know. If you could go into another person's world, just for one day, you would never hate another human being ever again. If you could see the predicament and the complexities of this life, and realize how desperation and greed control people, you would not condemn or judge. You would forgive and understand.

FORGIVENESS

*When I take a look at my past actions
that I do not feel good about,
I'm very ashamed.
Do I wish life to forgive me?*

*As I would want life to forgive me,
then surely I would want life to forgive anyone.
As I would want life to forgive my child,
surely I would want life to forgive
every mother's and father's child.*

THE WINDS OF YOUR HEART

CHAPTER 9

WHAT LASTS FOREVER?

Head toward the elements that last — that are true any time, any place, anywhere, under any condition.

As the years go by, some of us find that our lives aren't working out, or that our days seem empty and monotonous. Why? Because there is very *little* reality within ourselves and our lives that is sustaining. We need to ask ourselves, "What kind of realities have I learned? How much goodness do they carry? How many realities have I brought into my life that are healthy and have good common sense? How many are stable enough to last longer than a few weeks, months, or years?"

We find that we can temporarily make ourselves happy — until the party is over, until our car breaks down, or until our relationship ends. The happiness never seems to last too long. So we keep going out, seeking, looking for something else to keep us busy or happy. And this does help. It keeps us going. But still, there's something missing.

What is real? What will sustain us from the time we are born until we take our last breath, and even long after our last breath, into the next life? What lasts from one century to the next and what is temporary? Remember that buildings come and go. Money comes and goes. Our stories and legends come and go. Our wars come and go. Our holidays come and go. We come and go.

If you want something solid, go for what is eternal. Don't go for what is temporary. Cars are temporary. Land and titles are temporary. Computer screens are temporary. Thoughts are temporary. Fantasies are temporary. Hurt is temporary. Revenge is temporary. Having a family is temporary. Most of that is so wonderful — just understand its nature.

But what can you do with love and courage? What can you do with kindness and forgiveness? What can you do with the wisdom of all the ages? All these are timeless. They are the same today as they were in the year 1593, and as they will be in the year 2593. These are the important elements to look for and to bring into your life, for they break the barriers of time and space.

These elements are real. *They're alive.* They are gifts of life that give us a unique medicine. But most of us do not pay attention to these gifts that feed and sustain us. We haven't been taught to look at these realities, to nourish them, or to understand why they are so important. And we have to nourish these realities within ourselves. No one else can do it for us. We can receive inspiration through someone else. We can get encouragement from someone else. But we cannot realize a permanent reality through someone else.

Let reality walk with you. Everything else is temporary — temporary realities sustained by temporary energies. Momentary satisfaction. But if you look for something that is permanent, something that will be as true the next century as it was ten centuries ago, your mind, deep down inside, knows the difference. It knows you have captured a permanent feeling, a permanent thought, a permanent reality. And this creates a transformation within you. You become more of the earth, more solid and grounded. You become more awake.

Hope, faith, and courage — just take these three. These three elements have woven every decade together, sewn with a needle and thread. They have kept entire nations going. So stitch with that needle — hope, faith, courage — and keep these moving through your life, even though the wind will go against you. That's the nature of life. These three elements can help keep you going during hard times. They can help you to understand the wind. They can create a change.

When we bring into our lives anything that has a genuine goodness behind it, we are tapping into an eternal energy. Behind this energy is a presence. And behind this presence is a reality. Behind these three elements of hope, faith, and courage there is something that binds all the centuries. It binds every person, every generation, and every family. Where there is something that is so binding, with such strong realities backing it up, you will find what one could call "primal energies," which have a presence behind them. And what is this presence? Who gave us our heart? Call it the Mother. Call it the Father.

Back in 1989, there was a very big earthquake in California. The epicenter was only ten miles from Santa Cruz, where I used to live. This earthquake was really something. The ground actually rose up in waves. It looked like everything above the ground — houses, cars, trees — was on a surfboard, riding these waves. Immediately you knew that the earth was not solid. This was so clear. Earth is liquid, period. Most of the residents of Santa Cruz felt this for the first time. As a result, a lot of people became anxious and uneasy for quite a while. It wasn't the shaking that was so disturbing, it was the realization that the earth is not solid.

What does this realization do to the very nature of the foundation inside our mind, to the structure behind every thought, to all our feelings and stories? It is nothing more than watching Grandma pass away. What can the mind do with that? The basis for all its foundations begin to crumble. You see, life is always telling us about the future. We don't live too long. Life here is temporary. *Everything* will be taken away.

Yet in essence, there is no death. The body dies, but we always live. The spirit lives forever. It is our spirit that has been traveling. It is our spirit that continues on after we pass away. And it is our spirit that will always carry with it whatever permanent realities we have realized.

The point is to understand the mind as well as the environment we are living in — a temporary environment with temporary teachings and temporary things to touch and see. We have a temporary body that needs to rest and that is lovely to live in. But give me something that is more than just temporary. Give me something that is always there, whether my eyes are closed, whether five centuries have passed, or whether I am sick, crying, or laughing. Give me the elements in my blood that are permanent, so that no matter what happens, there is a peace in my blood. No matter what takes place in my life, I know.

We all have a telescope and a microscope within our heart that can help us to perceive life differently. If we can find the courage to reach in and pull them out, we will see that no matter what human being we look at or what creature we observe, they, too, will pass in time. The smile and the friendship, the exchange of words and ideas will all eventually fade away, although the feeling of love for a friend can continue on. But what cannot be taken away is a knowingness and what is felt in one's heart.

Nature has a most wonderful way of changing things, making them disappear and go back to ashes so that we don't recognize them anymore. Learn to trust nature. You see, all our thoughts and feelings, everything about houses, tables, chairs, people, dresses, glasses, styles, and architecture all live within linear time. They can't exist for very long. But what about goodness? What about caring? What about a feeling for life? What lives forever? The heart.

Food For The Heart

We are all inherently searching for something that even the two doors of birth and death cannot touch or keep confined.

To understand what spirit is, like a person who understands archaeology, you must realize that your very short lifetime is but a moment in the entire history of the universe. A flash. Then you can ask yourself, "Do I have the courage to understand what takes place after this lifetime, or even to ask what happens? Or is it too frightening? Is it too big for me to comprehend? If I were to see what takes place afterward, would I change? Yes, I would change. Would my behavior change? Yes. Would my eyes see differently? Yes. My eyes would literally change."

Your eyes, your intent, your life would turn into an astronaut, because you will have realized the value of your life. This earth is speeding very quickly through space. It never stops. The land beneath your feet is constantly shifting and changing. One day the continent on which you live will be under the sea. Then where will you be?

When I leave this earth, what can I take with me? Can I take my wallet, my driver's license, or my books? I cannot even take these into my dreams at night. After I pass away, what is going to be of value to me then? These are good questions to ask ourselves. Constantly contemplating this will help us to transcend the smaller perspective. It will create enough weight to draw in the larger perspective of the astronaut.

Thinking about these questions gave me good reasons to change. It made sense to change my life into a direction that would be more healthy for me. So in planning out my future, like creating a life insurance policy, I began to work my day and my hour not just for this life, but for all my lives.

Try to pull out the elements that contain infinity, that no one can take away from you. We are all inherently searching for these elements, looking for something that even the two doors of birth and death cannot touch or keep confined. When we begin to understand the value and the quality of what is permanent and truly real, we'll notice it is something that a particular poem, phrase, or movie can evoke. We'll find it in someone's eyes or in a gesture that touches us. Then we can use our will to say, "I don't want to be touched only now and then. I want to be touched all the time."

In Milan, I visited a graveyard that was quite unique. It was practically a living graveyard. The people who contributed to this piece of land put beautiful works of art on top of the graves in the form of statues that said a lot about the lives of those who had passed away. You could see that some people experienced great pain and struggle as they lived out their lives. For them, life was too much. But others moved mountains, whether it was in relation to business, their families, or otherwise being extremely effective in their lives. A great deal of thought and money was put into these pieces of art to keep the memories alive for others to see. It was well done.

I saw this in New Delhi as well. Huge monuments with great beauty had been created in tribute those who had passed away. After visiting these cemeteries, I found myself asking, "What monument do I wish to leave for others to remember me by?" I wonder what will last longer: is it the touch of my hand or a kindness that I give to you? Is it a book or a candle? Or is it a large sum of money?

Once you understand what the journey of the heart is, you know what the real monuments are that we can leave. We have the mountains, but the mountains cannot last forever. We have rivers, but the rivers don't last too long. They are always moving and changing. Even the oceans don't stay as they are for all time, for they change, too. But with what can we refuel our heart? It must be something that will last longer than any mountain, something that will last beyond any experience, any contract, or any piece of stone. What lasts longer — a good friend or a stone monument to oneself? No matter how big a monument or how large a statue we make of ourselves, the wind and rain will eventually tear it down. But one thing that will always be true is friendship with oneself and others — *that* lasts forever. The warmth that I have seen in a loved one's eyes — that is something I can take with me, for my heart has been branded with that person's tenderness and kindness.

Traveling around India, Malaysia, and Italy, I saw how so many people wanted to hold on to eternity, building great monuments for their wives, their children, and themselves. But who cares about these monuments now? On the other hand, as I watched my grandmother pass her hope to me just before she died — a hope that was kept alive from one generation to the next — I realized that this is what is worth living for, this has substance, this is something that will last. It is simply a matter of putting things in the right perspective.

Jesus was so right when he said, "Give to Caesar what belongs to him. But everything that belongs to God must be given to God." And that is true — so very true. You can think of it like this. When you give your mind and body to your employer, it belongs to your employer, at least for the workday. He has hired your mind, body, and services for his gain or for the gain of the community. That belongs to his world. But your heart, your feelings, your beliefs belong to you. And that you give to the Creator. That belongs to the Creator.

Many years ago, one of the hardest things for me to learn was how to distinguish between what belongs to earth and what belongs to spirit. From what I have seen, understanding this difference is difficult for most human beings. As a result, a lot of people become confused. They think both belong together — but they don't. That doesn't mean that we should dislike our world or hold the attitude: "Material is not good. Spiritual is good." Just understand the difference.

Matter is born of the spirit. So one could say that the material world is actually part of the spiritual world. Yet the American dollar belongs to America, so to speak. The British pound belongs to Great Britain. What we can buy with a dollar or a pound, who made a particular product, and the exchange of business all belong here. The point is not to worship what belongs to earth, whether it is money, power, politics, or anything else that is made by humanity. It is to learn to live in the world, while turning our eyes upward. It is to take our minds above nature, above our biology, above what it means to live as social human beings, and to understand that we live simultaneously in two worlds. We are of the spirit. And we are within the body. But can you tell the difference?

To understand this difference takes a good deal of contemplation. Many human beings, for instance, believe that feeling good is something spiritual. But it's not. It's of the body. People think that just because they're happy or elated, it's a spiritual event. Yet what is making them feel happy are only "designer drugs" — the hormones and chemicals being manufactured within their bodies. The reason it feels spiritual is that they haven't felt these emotions for quite some time.

Many people also think that good fortune is a spiritual gift. Or they assume it means that whatever they're doing is right. But that isn't necessarily the case. It's just that a certain turn of events has crossed their path and things are working out a bit better. But it has nothing to do with the spirit.

The human body, we all know, needs good food. It helps. We know that good water makes a difference. We know that good laughter makes a wonderful difference. We know that a good sleep makes a big difference. We know that a good friend makes a beautiful difference. We know that to be fortunate makes a difference as well.

But all these "foods" are from where? These are all foods from this planet. They belong here. It's good to be well educated about these foods. But what is the food for you, the traveler who existed before you were conceived and will continue to exist after you leave? It is also important to educate yourself about this kind of food. You cannot find this food on top of a mountain. You cannot find it in the rivers. You cannot find it underneath the earth. You cannot find it in your home. Then where can you find this kind of food? My advice: look among the realities that last forever.

Polishing the Personality

Do you know how precious your life is, for you to spend your days working on polishing your personality?

Many of us try very hard to smooth out our personality. We spend a great deal of time, effort, and money attempting to eradicate our neuroses, soften our conditioning, and understand ourselves better. But haven't we found that we are still us? After all these years of working so hard at improving ourselves, don't we find that it's difficult to change very much? We're still stuck with ourselves. This is because we focus on the *personality*.

What Lasts Forever?

To completely change our personality is almost like trying to cut off our arm and replace it with a new arm. We're born with a unique personality, and after a particular age, it becomes essentially fixed.

Yet the personality is really not the issue. Naturally, it is a good idea to work out the neuroses that hurt people or otherwise cause problems for ourselves and others. But when people go into therapy, many of them work senselessly on the small neuroses that are essentially harmless, and if anything, add a little color and humor to their personality. Do you know how precious your life is, for you to spend your days working on polishing your personality?

When it comes to my own process, I only go after patterns that are obviously a hindrance to me. That's it. The rest I let go. Why waste my time? But it took me a long time to realize this. Years ago, I used to devote much of my life to understanding and living out what was inside my head — my pictures, my dreams, my conditioning — until I saw what the outcome was. My personality not only changed very little, but I realized that life was so much more than just my feelings and my viewpoint. Living as a cultural human being is a *very tiny percent* of what life actually is. Once you see this, using simple common sense, you will start to put all your time, effort, and investment where it should be — into those realities that will always be with you.

This physical world is just a momentary stop. Everything here lives in linear time. It doesn't last long. But don't we want something that lasts forever, something that we do not have to lose all the time? This takes us to the spirit of ourselves — the one who has seen much, done much, traveled much. Imagine the wisdom of our spirit versus the intelligence of the personality during each lifetime. How would the two compare? But what do we go by all the time? What do we hang on to all the time? Our personality. This is because of conditioning. Be this nationality. Be this "flag." Be this custom. This is the way we do it. Keep our parents happy. Keep our friends happy. Keep our neuroses happy. So instinctively we hang on. But there is an inherent wisdom in the traveler.

Here is a story that has to do with polishing the personality. In high school I had a friend, Robert, whose parents were from Germany. You could see that this young man was different. He was far more mature and much kinder than anybody else in the school. Robert seemed as if he were years ahead of us.

Right after high school, he started to put himself through therapy. I always admired this man because he seemed so progressive and far ahead of his time. He studied psychology in graduate school, and after receiving his Ph.D., he became a well-known therapist in Los Angeles. I didn't see him again until about twenty years after high school when we happened to meet each other at a convention hall. I could see that he was an extremely mature human being. I could also see that I wasn't very mature at that time. The contrast between us was obvious.

"You know something?" he said. "I'm going to tell you about my life. I don't know why, but I'd like share this with you. Immediately after high school, I went into all the best therapies I could find to clear up my mind. I worked so hard on myself."

"You know," he continued, "I have done everything imaginable. I had twenty years of therapy. I got the best help I could find to improve myself, my awareness, and my mind. And I really put my heart into it. I have put years and years and so much money into this. And you know what? I finally gave up. Because guess what I found? I am still me. Still me. Yes, I did get better. I'm 'polished.' And a lot of problems got worked out. But, you know, basically I am still me.

"When I realized that no matter how much I improved, I am still essentially who I am, I completely gave up. And now I'm just starting to live. I'm looking for something else other than just improving myself and 'polishing my personality,' because I still feel this emptiness inside. Something is missing, so I've been trying to fill myself up, and yet all I've done is polish myself up for everybody else, as well as myself. But how do I fill myself up inside? There's this void that is still there.

"If I could have done this process you're doing while I was involved in my psychology studies and therapies twenty years ago, I think I would be very different today. No doubt, if I hadn't done the therapy, I don't think I could have started to live. I mean, it was a tremendous stepping stone for me. I'm glad I did what I did, but that wasn't it. So I'm happy I stopped at an early age so I could finish my life and live, instead of living for my issues."

In essence, he put down his weapons. He willingly put down his shields when it finally made sense why to change his way of thinking. It was then that this beautiful, mature, and well-adjusted man started to have fun and enjoy himself, instead of just working on clearing up his issues with his parents or with society. He realized that you are who you are.

In my workshops, I often show a series of pictures of hot air balloons, which are surrounded by various objects and artifacts representing our inner mind and thoughts. The objects in these four illustrations diminish in size as the pictures progress, with one exception: a window outlined in black. The window always exists and essentially doesn't change its shape. Through the window the city of Budapest happens to be visible, so I call it the "Budapest window." The Budapest window signifies what one could call a neurosis. It represents something that is always with us that we cannot seem to get rid of. We've tried all kinds of therapies and nothing seems to work. It is like something we inherit from our parents. These Budapest windows are somewhat like our shadow. They seem to stick with us like glue wherever we go. This is what we are up against in transforming the personality.

The nature of mind makes us look out. We try to look in, but it's so difficult to find what is inside. And that's why it helps to understand these Budapest windows. Inside our mind there are so many neuroses hiding out, so much conflict and confusion taking place. It would help if we could simply be a little more compassionate with ourselves, give ourselves time, and allow the shadows and confusion to exist. Instead of fearing all this, what if we could just observe it? Walk with it. Let people make mistakes. And let yourself make mistakes, please. If you make the same mistake every day, wonderful, it's all right, just look at it as a Budapest window.

So you see, this young psychologist was way ahead of me. He saved me years and years of processing my imperfections, for he taught me about the Budapest windows, and helped me to realize that there really is something much more to life than diving into my personality. I knew there was no way I could eliminate my Budapest windows in the next thirty, forty, or even fifty years, for I was too neurotic and confused. It was impossible. So instead of spending my precious time just polishing my personality, I invested it more wisely.

When we turn our mind and intent in the direction of realities that have permanence, we naturally let the astronaut come in. We can all use our eyes to see as an astronaut. Every human being is well designed. Life is well designed. When we start to put a little more trust, faith, and hope into our own lives, in time a different perspective shows its face, and we realize, "My god, all I am is simply a spirited human being living in nature. That's it. And my personality is just part of the package."

So stand back. Be an astronaut. Don't get too close to the trees. You'll get lost. Don't get too close to your pain. You'll get lost. If you want to get to know the trees, it's a paradox of life that if you stand too near, you can't see them. If you see something every day, in time you don't see it anymore. Become an astronaut inside your own mind. Bring history into view. Be a good archaeologist. Be a good anthropologist. Study. Allow distance to develop. Keep your drama out. And let time teach you. There is a time and a place to turn things around. So start now. Turn your life around.

WHAT CAN I TAKE WITH ME?

My mind,
My personality,
all my thoughts.
Everything I have learned
about a tree, a wall, the light of day.
The teachers, the students,
the policemen, the cars.
The firemen, the business people.
The mothers, the fathers.
Red. Blue. Yellow.
Dark days, good days.
It will burn.
All of that will burn.
It's within time.

For when I pass away,
I have to leave my memories behind.
Even my bones will be left behind.

What is it I can take with me
that will last longer
than any mountain or any statue?
What is it?

Will it be your face?
Will it be your kindness?
Will it be when you hurt or disappointed me?
Will it be our laughing together,
or what we have built together?
Is it a love that I'll never forget?

What can I take with me?
In my pocket,
into my dreams,
into my old age,
into my passing away.
No matter where I am,
what can always be with me?

To be alive within the heart.

It's the Quality of Our Lives that Matters

It is not how many breaths we take, but the quality of each breath that truly counts.

One morning a few years ago I got a phone call from a 46-year-old woman who had attended my last workshop and fire dance in Berlin. Two days before she called, the doctors had performed surgery to determine the condition of her stomach. They found that she had cancer that had spread throughout her whole body. Before she became ill, this woman had never thought much about life. In the beginning of the Berlin workshop, her eyes were glassy and dull, although she didn't know she had cancer at that time. There was no life in her eyes. But something in the fire dance stirred her heart. You could see her come back to life again.

Now this woman had a most wonderful gift. She was given an opportunity to genuinely connect with life, because her mind could not play games anymore. It knew that her situation was real. This was not a story. When we don't understand the paradox, we live only on one side of what we think life is. Now the paradox was becoming apparent to this woman. Even still, what her mind naturally continued to do was to want life. "I still want to live. I want more time." This is our habit. This is how we inherently think, and it's understandable.

I told her, "Staying alive is not the point at all. The point is that it's the quality of your life, and not the longevity, that is important. Learn to understand the value and quality of the life that you have left. Longevity is not what you think. It's how you live your life, not how long you live."

Time had been on her side, but now it was no longer a friend. Now that time had been taken away from this woman, it forced her to look at life very differently. "Is this really all there is to my life in this world?" she began to ask.

You see, it's just that her thinking and her way of living were locked up according to how the "chicken coop"—the physical world in which we live—has always addressed it, which is from a linear perspective. She was caught up in the time between her birth and her death. But what if she could learn something that transcends the linear, where there are no more walls of the chicken coop? What if she could feel and see what is past the coop? That takes real courage and strength. What is truly important here? This woman living out her life? No, not under the circumstances. Instead, what matters is to get that mind and heart of hers to awaken as much as possible. Who knows what could happen as a result? It's an entirely different way of looking at life than most of us are accustomed to.

As I mentioned earlier in the book, a most wonderful movie called *Braveheart* came out in recent years. If you did not see *Braveheart*, I recommend that you do so. Some people say there is too much violence in this film. Yes, there is a lot of violence, but the director was able to show how harsh life was for the people of 13th-century Scotland. He did an excellent job of portraying this reality. But the movie also has tremendous heart. It is a beautiful film that is based on a true story. The main character, William Wallace, was a man who actually lived and showed extraordinary courage in his life. Before their first big battle with the English, Wallace talked the Scottish soldiers into standing their ground and fighting instead of running away, even though the Scots were outnumbered by something like three to one. He convinced the soldiers to stay and fight for freedom.

His speech was something to this effect: "Yes, you can run and live, at least for a while. And yes, you will probably live until you are old men. But what are you going to wish you did as you lie dying in your beds? That you just lived out your lives? Or that you had the courage to stand your ground today—and tell our enemies that they may take our lives, but they'll never take our freedom?"

Everyone is going to die, but how do you die? How do you live your life? So take this same attitude into your own life. Look how long the story of William Wallace has lasted and will continue to last. You see, he never really died.

Does It Match the Space Between You and Me?

*I want life to teach me what it sees and what it thinks.
And this space gives me access to life's point of view.*

I know of a good reference point that helps me tell the difference between temporary and permanent realities. I call it "the space between you and me." If something doesn't match this space, it's not permanent. There isn't much reality there. If you have a question, if you have a problem, if you want to understand something — think about the space between you and me. Does it match this space? If it doesn't, it is temporal. If something doesn't match this space, it is of one's mind. It's a story, it's drama, or it's ignorance. The anger, the arguing, the pain, the causes, the conflict, and the confusion will end. Do you want to hang onto something that will always end? Or do you want something that you know will always be with you?

Questions, doubt, feelings, thoughts, words, memories — *anything* that you could possibly think, do, hear, or say — is going to fall into the category of not matching the space between you and me. That amounts to about 99.999 percent of our thinking. Yet the living elements I mentioned earlier — kindness, forgiveness, a genuine love of the heart — make it easier to connect with this space, because both these elements and the space have to do with permanent realities.

So my recommendation is to head toward this reference point. Does it match the space between you and me? Is it this peaceful? If not, it's only a phase — a temporary phase that will pass. Most people would say, "What do you mean, the space between you and me? There's nothing there." Oh yes, there is. "But, gee, it's boring. You can't do anything with it." Oh yes, you can.

You know, people say we have various subtle bodies that extend outside of us. People also say that we leave the body after we die. Many of us might say to that, "Where does that leave me? After I die, what do I do? Fade myself into the space? Into thin air?" Actually, yes.

If I have these subtle bodies, and they exist in the space between you and me, what does that mean? It means that, whether I'm here in this physical body or I have died and no longer have a body, I still exist. I'm still me. So if my subtle bodies extend into the space outside my physical body, I'm out here, too. I'm not just inside my body. So there's a connection between the space inside us and the space out here. There's essentially no difference.

If I exist outside of my physical body, that means that my space is meeting an external space out here. And if this external space is meeting another space, what is that space meeting? We know that as two people approach each other closely, they begin to affect one another. One space is meeting another. The closer I get to you, the more I'm going to affect you, and the more I'll touch the deeper aspects of you, if you let me.

Learn to be present in that space between you and me. This will help you to understand that you already *are* in this space. What is in this space? Consciousness itself. Consciousness is the space between you and me. It's already present. It doesn't need memories. When you die and your brain ceases to exist, you have no more memories. But when you begin to understand the space in between, you see that whether or not you have died, you already are this consciousness. That doesn't mean you have developed consciousness within your physical mind and body, but it is still right in front of you. You are in this space already. It doesn't require a brain for your subtle bodies and your spirit body to exist out here in the space beyond your body. They are already in existence.

You see, reason and logic will pull us into our brain, which is already conditioned. It's the personality that sees through this conditioned brain. When I understood this, I realized that I already know what *I* see. I already know what *I* think. I want life to teach me what *it* sees and what *it* thinks. And this space gives me access to life's point of view.

Here's another way to look at it. In 1977, Charles and Ray Eames made a film called *Powers of Ten*. The movie starts at the far edge of the universe, millions of light years away from Earth, and heads toward our planet in a series of pictures that take the viewer closer and closer as the camera moves ten times nearer to earth every ten seconds. Millions of galaxies are visible as the viewer travels through space. Finally, Earth approaches and all of a sudden we find ourselves in a Chicago park where we see a man basking in the sun on a blanket. As the camera zooms in on this man's hand, we dive into the skin, through the cells, and into the molecules, until finally we find ourselves in the subatomic world where there is nothing but space again. Suddenly it feels as though we are back in outer space once more where there are galaxies with vast spaces in between. Astonishing! Space inside, space outside. So what is really out there? And what is really in here — the person who's arguing, the person who's eating, the person who's dreaming, the person who's pumping the blood? Or something else that is residing in this space?

I once heard a story about a physicist who worked at the Los Alamos National Laboratory in New Mexico many years ago. This scientist delved into the subatomic structure of matter to the point that he realized, "My god, *everything* is made up of atoms, and in between the atoms there is just space. There is actually more space than there is matter." He didn't just intellectually understand this, he realized it. In fact, it became so real to him that he began to wear a special pair of custom-made shoes that were extremely wide, like duck feet, so he wouldn't fall through the atoms. Because he was able to see the world on a deeper level, he actually developed a fear of slipping through the floor, which, like everything in this world, consists of atoms separated by vast spaces. One could say that he got lost in the microscope. But his realization was real. What's in between the atoms? There is nothing but space. The world isn't as it appears. Life is not what we think.

I wish I had the intelligence to invent some special goggles that I could put over your eyes, which would allow you to see the subatomic world of matter. Now that you're wearing these goggles, what would you observe if you could see nothing but atoms? You wouldn't see your friend, you wouldn't see your neighbor, you wouldn't see your hand—you would see nothing but space and the atoms themselves. That's it. If you think about how you would perceive the world through these goggles, this will help you to understand "the space between you and me."

The space in front of you is something you can trust, but your mind has no conception of it because you look right through it. You don't pay any attention to this space. You can't sell it. There's no rhyme or reason to it. Yet within this small space in front of you—even though it may be only a foot—is infinity. Any little bit of space is the same bit of space anywhere. In time, after becoming more aware of this space, you will begin to sense something. You will sense a presence. You'll feel a peace.

So remember that if you follow this rule out, you'll do well. If you want a reality that is permanent, take the space that is about one foot in front of you and use it a reference point. If your dream doesn't match this space, it doesn't have much reality. If your concepts and feelings don't match this space, they don't have much reality. If your pictures don't match this space, then you know they are just pictures, and they will all pass in time.

It is like the moon and its reflection. When the moon is out, and you see the reflection of the moon in a pool of water, which is more real—the moon or its reflection? In reality, you could say that the moon is more its reflection than its physical form. The physical moon is less real than what is behind it. It is the same for the space between you and me. In this space are the strongest realities, the ones that have permanency. Everything else in the external world is like a reflection of these realities. This is also true of you. You are more your spirit than your physical body and personality, which always goes back to dust. Your spirit is more real. That is a permanent reality. Your personality is but a temporary reflection of your spirit. It is the same with everything in this world. In this sense, the world is upside down, once you start to understand it. The external reflections mimic our internal world, which you could call the heart or the soul, which in turn is a reflection of life itself.

The mind has no references for the space between you and me. It says, "But you can't get a cause out of it. You hit it and nothing happens. You can't grab it and put it in your pocket. What's in it for me?" The mind is always trying to get cause-effect out of this space, but it can't.

Look at it this way. Do you want reason and logic? Here is a different kind of reason and logic. If you want to understand this space even better, go watch someone pass away. But don't just observe the body. Sense the spirit of the person as it leaves the body. When life takes away all the causes and effects, what is the spirit going to do with reason and logic, now that it has no brain, no nervous system, no eyes, and no ears? Now the person is in the "space." Oh!

"Space logic," call it. More evolved logic. Future logic. Transcendent logic. Spirit logic. But there's no reward in this space. People keep wanting the reward, yet what is the reality of that door of passing away? We go back to the space. Life is always telling us this.

So you have to become very smart with life, in order to transcend cause and effect and head toward the reference point of this space, which will help lead you to those realities that are permanent. Use your reason and logic. It's just that your reason and logic have to elevate themselves to another kind of reason and logic. There is the reason and logic of an eight-year-old. There is the reason and logic of a sixteen-year-old. There is the reason and logic of a 10,262-year-old. And that's the reason and logic you need.

The Nature of Impermanent and Permanent

What I'm trying to do is lead you to a reality that is very, very potent — because where there are strong realities, there are massive amounts of energy.

Another key to help you tell where strong realities exist is to understand the difference between permanent and impermanent. Let's take anger. Anger is something that gives us a tremendous amount of fuel when it arises. As a result, we think we are correct in our anger because we have this apparent energy supporting our feelings and thoughts. That's why we can do what we do in our state of anger. We feel that life is supporting us.

But what happens? The support stops after a while. We can't hold onto it, can we? Where's all that wonderful fuel and energy? We don't have it any more. Now all of a sudden, we can see the destruction we caused or we can see what we have built with our anger. With anger we build a different house for ourselves, so to speak. We build our character, our personality, our relationships in a negative way, as we construct new perceptions, walls, ideas, and philosophies in our minds and in other people's minds. We're building not just with words, but energetically. When the anger goes away and we have this building we've just constructed, our feelings no longer match this building, which doesn't have a good foundation. When the support stops, this indicates that what we experienced is temporary and doesn't carry much reality. With anything that has a support in which you get great bursts of energy, there isn't much reality.

Well then, what is reality? It is when the energy is always present and steady. You could say it's when your emotions and thoughts do not keep fluctuating up and down. However, the mind has been accustomed to the highs and lows. It says, "Steady? But that's boring. And nobody's going to like me if I'm like that." You see, that's what I used to think, too. And that is why a lot of people stay away from receiving permanency or reality where there is a steady, harmonious flow. There's no spark, no pizazz, no drama.

What most people will respond to is the energy of what is in the "chicken coop"—our physical universe. Because everything is so impermanent in the chicken coop, we can only grab hold of something for how long? A year? Five years? Twenty years? A thought arises, then the next thought comes. What actually makes up the chicken coop? Immense amounts of energy. Look at this earth. It's not dead, it's alive. Is the wind and all the light that shines down just nothing? No, it's tremendous energy, very much alive. What is running inside our brain, up our spinal cord, through our nervous system? Massive energies. Whoom, whoom! Just one thought is immense energy. If you put a lot of thoughts together to form one picture, that is even more energy.

But we are not this energy. The problem is that, because we have been raised in the chicken coop, we assume we are this energy. We have associated ourselves with these temporary energies, believing this to the point that we think we *are* these energies, and this is how we get into trouble. This is why we take all this in the chicken coop so darn seriously.

Outside the chicken coop is Uncaused Light, but it's not energy. Consciousness is not energy. Our spirit is not energy. Nonetheless, these are extremely strong realities. Our spirit creates the energy and throws it out. Everything in this world reflects the intention of spirit itself. First there is spirit and *then* the energy is seen, shaped as a result of the intent of what is backing up that spirit.

You see, what I'm trying to do is lead you to a reality that is very, very potent—because where there are strong realities, there are massive amounts of energy. It is just that these kinds of realities are not quite understood by most of us. If you lead your mind to temporary realities, energy is present but it doesn't last. You can't rely on it. But if you have something that you can always rely on and tap into, you have a permanent reality.

Here is another way to think about permanent realities. The greater the reality, the more invisible it is and the harder it is to perceive. We can see our bodies here in the physical world, but when we pass away we perceive differently. When we go into our dreams at night we also see quite differently. What is behind the dream body and what is behind the spirit body? That is our soul, which is a living being, as alive as we are here.

Now if I were to give you special glasses so that you could see the soul, you would see that the soul is much subtler than the atomic structure of matter. It is even more subtle than the spirit. So to connect with a reality that has permanence is to learn to either feel, see, or acknowledge the presence of the soul within ourselves and in all human beings. If you cannot see it with your eyes, try to sense it or acknowledge it in some way.

Do you think the sun is powerful? It's nothing, really. This one sun is merely a small match, lit up. Scientists know that galaxies in the universe are clumped together in groups. Yet according to the way physics operates, they shouldn't be clumped together. They should be spreading out like marbles rolling away from each other. But they don't do this. Galaxies stay bunched together. Naturally the physicists wondered why these galaxies tend to cluster together, when the distribution of matter throughout the universe should be relatively uniform. They found that they are apparently held together by "cosmic strings" of energy that lasso the various galaxies and keep them bunched in certain groups, due to the massive gravitational or magnetic fields exerted by these strings. Although these ideas are considered to be theory at this point, the mounting evidence strongly suggests that they are true.

Stretching far out into space or possibly forming closed loops, cosmic strings are essentially invisible. They consist of extremely thin filaments that are narrower in width than a proton. Yet they're so packed with energy that they are worth billions of suns. Just one centimeter contains an astonishingly concentrated mass-energy of around ten billion tons. However, these thread-like strings are extremely subtle; it is as if these suns have condensed themselves into such small particles of matter that you cannot see them any more. Imagine the incredible density of these strings of energy! Yet you can physically travel right through them. They are quite soft. So again, it shows that the more subtle it is, the more powerful it is in life. That's a reality.

We're also finding that in our world the softer something becomes, the more powerful it is. What produces light? Do you know what makes a light bulb work? The filament. Is this filament made out of hard steel that is two feet thick? No. It's a thin, delicate piece of wire. The filament is very soft and tender. It's extremely fragile inside, encased in a strong, heavy light bulb. The filament breaks quite easily. But if you use it under certain conditions it can hold immense energy, softly. It can put out nice warm light. Where there is immense energy, everything becomes more and more subtle. More delicate. Finer and finer. *Extremely* soft. So we know that the more powerful something is, somehow the softer it has to be. The kinder it has to be. As it is for us inside. Genuine kindness is very soft yet one of the most powerful permanent realities.

You see, a person who is outside the chicken coop of this physical world sees the nature of these realities. Everything that is outside the coop is totally alive. The light, which is Uncaused Light, is extremely soft and very much alive. Within the chicken coop this light is also alive. We are as alive inside the coop as we are outside the coop. Whether we are inside or outside the coop, we will always exist in some place at some time. It is just a matter of waking up in the dream of life, as some have called it, and connecting with these permanent realities.

Seek What is Infinite
Will the sun last forever?

What so many human beings ultimately seek is not just an experience that lasts only a week or two, not just a thought or an idea that lasts but a month or a year, not just something that will wash away, like snow, with the next season. We yearn for something that has a permanence to it.

Who wants to die and fade away? No one. No spider, no ant, no goldfish, no soaring eagle or hawk wants to die. Yet the fact remains that, like all of life on earth, we are temporal. We can only last for a short time, whether it is merely a minute or one hundred and eight years.

If I am so temporal, lasting but a few moments in the vastness of time, then who in the world am I that only lasts for so long? I must be nothing but a reflection of my spirit inside. Am I a dream of my spirit? Yes. And yet I am no dream, sitting in this chair. Still, yesterday is all but memories and dreams that have faded away. A paradox.

Will the sun last forever? No. Will the moon always stay up in the sky? No. Will the earth one day cease to exist? Yes. Will all the stars eventually fade away? Yes. Will all our dreams vanish, too, evaporating like the oceans that will also disappear in time? Yes. Then what is it that is everlasting? It is the spirit deep within our chest. That is what we naturally seek. And helping us to find a way in are the filaments, you could call them, that are attached to our spirit and somehow picking up what is infinite inside, what is eternal.

Sit yourself on top of a mountain, and stay there for three hundred thousand years. From an astronaut's point of view, that's not a long time at all. Pack a lunch. And observe. Watch history unfold in the valleys. Watch the great rivers turn into small streams. Watch the settlements arise. Different cities come and go. Warfare takes place. Armies march in and out of the valleys. Civilizations decay. New ideas emerge and then fade away. Watch steel and aluminum fly through the sky. Watch bombs flying too. Watch babies being born—millions of them. Watch people growing and shrinking. New philosophies taking shape. Many different clubs and religions being born. Different colors and designs evolving. New Messiahs coming and going. And they all disappear in time. *All disappear in time.*

After the three hundred thousand years have gone by, climb down from your mountain top. Stretch and shake your legs. Get ready. Because now you have to go back down into that valley and do it, too. But this time you're going to do it differently.

Now you see life through different eyes. You care so much more. And your mind and heart have expanded to the point that no religion can bend you. No philosophy can touch you. No time can mark your skin.

And one day you turn into the mystic, as the clouds finally part and you can see the stars above, and quite easily you become a witness of what is infinite. You can sense it. You can see it. You can feel it running through your bones. It is of you. And now the day seems like a dream, for what is infinite does not go away. Infinity is not just a picture on a wall that has to be taken down, but a picture that lives inside you, and in the hearts of others, too.

Seek infinity. Don't ever stop. Let your thoughts be of infiniteness. And let your sight be, too. Let your search have the elements to seek out what is everlasting and not temporal. And your compass in time will align itself to what is infinite, deep inside your chest: the traveler, the sailor, the voyager. Your own spirit.

CHAPTER 10

THE PRECIOUSNESS OF LIFE

Many people want to experience just one external vision because it will change the rest of their lives. But what if life itself is the vision—twenty-four hours a day?

Imagine that your eyes are closing for the last time and you will never again see this light of earth as you see it now. You will no longer breathe this air. You will no longer see the friends you've made. Try to imagine what that would actually be like for you. How would it affect your heart and your mind never to see the light of the sun or breathe with these wonderful lungs life has given you that last only a few decades? Then how precious this life would seem. My god, what a gift. But most of us have numbed ourselves to the preciousness of life.

When people have near-death experiences, what happens? They're out. The impact is enough to force them out of their mind and down into their heart, and now they see and understand life *very* differently. Sometimes it takes war, or it takes a tremendous illness to break down all those defenses and all that fancy thinking to the point where a surrender takes place, and the value of one's life becomes apparent.

Watch babies being born and notice how they look at this light with amazement. They have never seen the light of the sun. A newborn has come from a totally different space and time. To see this light is amazing. Whether it is the light of twilight, dawn, or day, our planet has a most unique light. It's one in a trillion.

How precious is the chance to witness this light—an artificial light, one could call it. To witness the wind and rain. To witness heartache. To witness how vulnerable we are. To witness tears and disappointment. To witness hunger. To witness what it is to have a job. What it is to be a father or a mother. What it is to be a grandfather. What it is to die young. What it is to die old. To witness what it is to walk on something that's solid. We can build walls here. We can plant trees. We can go surfing. We can take a ride in a car. What happens when we can't do this anymore?

A most difficult thing to do is to be a human being. It is rare. Do you know what it takes to be a human being, to have a birth and a lifetime? It is as though everyone in the world has a winning lottery ticket. What are your odds of being that lucky winner who is born? Yet it is not by chance or luck that you are living here as a human being. It is you — your will, your courage, your strength, your determination — that brought you here. It is because of who you are and how you have walked through life. It is the adventure within your blood, within your bones, that pulled you to be born as a human being. Life on earth is an extremely intense adventure. To have that ticket takes so much courage. Whether one is born into famine and ignorance, or into better conditions — to live here still takes great courage and strength. That is why we must hold the utmost respect and honor for all human beings and their conditions.

There are only so many mothers in any given century who can give birth. Not everyone can be born. What a wonderful gift. Take a look at how many mothers in this world struggle to survive or live under conditions of great ignorance or hardship. How many of their children will be caught in a predicament of war, famine, or misfortune? Millions. And in the past, life was even more difficult for women.

In comparison, how many mothers live under good circumstances? There are not many women who are healthy in mind and body, who have education and freedom. You see, we're fortunate here in the West. Very few people on this planet have the good graces to be born as Westerners. What are your chances next time? Yet how many of us are caught up in working every day, too busy to contemplate what it is to be alive?

The Buddhists have a story about how rare it is to be a human being. Imagine a world ten times the size of earth, but filled entirely with water.

The Preciousness of Life

No land or continents exist. There is nothing but a very deep sea. On this ocean there is no rest, for the entire planet is constantly battered by storms and the winds are blowing the water about in every direction all day and night. There is no peace or stillness anywhere.

Floating on the surface of the ocean is an oxen yoke that is being tossed about here and there. On the bottom of the ocean lives one tortoise. Once every hundred years, this tortoise swims up to the surface, puts its head through the oxen yoke, takes one gulp of air, and then descends back down to the ocean floor for the next hundred years. It is as rare to be a human being as it is for that tortoise to be at the right time and place to put its head through the oxen yoke to take that breath of air. You could say that it's practically impossible to have the opportunity to be born as a human being.

This is a difficult concept for most people to understand, because very few of us can contemplate vast numbers. To put it into perspective, there are as many zeros that can be counted in the numerical system—an infinite number that will continue forever—as there are spirits that can be born as human beings on earth. And for a particular spirit—one of those endless zeros—to be born on this planet as one of the 6.4 billion humans living today, what are the odds? The odds of being born as a human being are infinitesimal. You could say that such a birth would be a miracle.

In the past, if one considers the entire scope of human history, there were perhaps a total of only one or two billion people born on this planet before the population explosion of recent times. This reduced the odds of a human life even further. Yet whether there are two billion or twenty billion people on this planet, these numbers are still insignificant in comparison to the number of spirits that exist.

Although a human birth is extremely rare, so many of us spend our entire lifetime trying to get away from being human, from our feet. "I can hardly wait until I get to be spirit. To be free! So I don't have to brush my hair, drive to the store, go to work, look at television, talk with my friends, or even get sick! I can be free of all this." To be human is a most wonderful gift, yet it is so difficult at the same time. Believe me, we are all very fortunate. To be able to see a mountain, to walk down a city street, to read a book, to have warm houses, to have friends, to go to workshops — it is all so precious.

If you were to go into a space where you could see the "movie" of your entire life, as all human beings do after they pass away, you will see how tender your life really was. You will understand what it actually means to be alive as a human being — to be taken care of, to be cuddled, to be fed, to be clothed. How immense it is for another human being to be just a little kind. For a mother to show what is so ordinary: to touch you, wash you, cook food for you. A father to go to work for you. To have sunlight. To have friends to play with, to see many colors. To have pencils, pens, and paper. To have school teachers who care. To have food in the cupboard.

Suddenly the stream of consciousness will start to weave together all these moments, everything you touched, everything you couldn't see. You will see how it wove you from day to day, hour to hour, minute to minute — from the experiences that hurt you to the experiences that gave you joy. Then you will understand how valuable your life was, regardless of who disappointed you, what happened in the newspaper, or whether your dreams turned out or not. It was the entire experience, moment to moment, that mattered. All those times you washed your face, brushed your hair, and looked in the mirror. All the funny things that you heard. The cars going by. The sounds of the horns. The sound of feet on the sidewalk. Waiting to go home from work. All these tender little moments sewn together to make your movie.

Do you realize how rare it is for a human being to have an external vision? Many people want to experience just one external vision, because it will change the rest of their lives. But what if you were to use your intelligence to ask yourself, "What if life itself *is* the vision? What if it *is* the vision — twenty-four hours a day?" That makes you look at life completely differently. In essence, it's true — you could say that life really is the vision. So whether you call it a vision, enlightenment, or waking up, all these states show is that what you are searching for already exists and is always there.

Miracles Don't Work

The miracle of our birth no longer tantalizes us.

A most astonishing fact to realize is that it is impossible for life as we know it to exist. And yet it does exist. It is impossible to have a planet with water. Do you know what the possibilities are of living on a planet that has rivers and seas? Two-thirds of our world is filled with ocean. Our sun lies just the right distance away from this planet so that it doesn't bake us or freeze us. Do you know how impossible it is to have everything set up exactly the way it is? The oxygen content of this world is twenty-one percent and doesn't fluctuate. If the oxygen content were to rise to twenty-five percent and someone were to light one match, the whole world would go up in flames, for the atmosphere would be too flammable. And then to have a life form such as ours arise? We can live together. We have our problems, but we're doing all right. Sunlight comes in through beautiful stained glass windows. We can laugh, we can cry, we can invent, we can lie down, we can sleep. It's a miracle. To deny the miracle is to deny the obvious.

Go sit someplace where there is nothing but nature, with an intent of wondering about the water, the ocean, the sky, the sun, the rain, the oxygen, the earth, the fire underneath, the lava, and the molten nickel at the center of the earth. Imagine life and intelligence coming out of these elements. My god. How in the world can life come out of that? Whose hand grabbed the mud and the sticks and started rubbing them together to create the fire of life within?

It is literally impossible for life to happen, with just those elements. In essence, there is something going on here that is really much bigger than us. A miracle has happened. And miracles are everywhere. There are over six billion miracles — human beings. But the miracle of our birth no longer tantalizes us.

In nature, it is almost impossible to have a pencil. How long did it take to produce a pencil? A *very, very* long time — millions of years. We're extremely fortunate that we have pencils today. You see, miracles don't work. They are for people who love sugar. But if we want to see the real miracles — the ones that have substance, that sustain us — all we have to do is look around. We have glasses to help us see — that's a miracle. We don't eat each other—this is a real miracle. To live in any century, to have a name and to be amongst people, to live in a generation where there is relative peace — we are blessed.

WHAT GOOD ARE MIRACLES?

*If a human being cannot see
the phenomenon of the day
that brings on a ceiling of light
above our heads
and makes it blue,
and the phenomenon of the night,
where the stars and infinity
suddenly appear,
what good is a miracle?*

*If a human being cannot see
the worms and the ants
that are constantly working
beneath our feet,
creating vast networks
of tunnels and communications,
what good is a miracle?*

*If a human being cannot see
how we can take earth, air, fire and water,
a little idea, a little enthusiasm,
a little creativeness,
and make an airplane fly in the sky,
what good are miracles?*

*If a human being cannot see
that we have just barely come out of the jungles,
and we have risen up very fast,
and we're smart enough to grow food,
paint walls, wear shoes,
and even control fire
to cook up our meals in our kitchens,
what good are miracles?*

*If a human being cannot see
how difficult it is to work eight hours a day,
and then to go home, smile, and love your kids,
or love your friend or your lover,
and feel the warmth of your heart,
and have the courage to be kind and soft,
what good are miracles?*

*People, miracles don't work.
They really don't.*

The Beauty of Life on Earth

Here we can hold a rose and watch it wilt, and it does not disappear like a dream in our hand as it does in spirit.

Our body exists because of our heart, our soul, our spirit. That's the only reason it stays alive. The reason our muscles are taut enough to allow us to stand up is because of the spirit within us. As the body needs the spirit, the spirit also needs the body, for without the body, spirit cannot do as much, grow as much, or learn as much, which I will explain later. By putting the atoms of our bodies together in a world of matter, you could say that we are able to put ourselves in front of ourselves. We can play with these atoms and learn what life is. We can wake up within the life. A student of mine once remarked that the body and the physical world are like "legos" for spirit. Well said. In essence, that's true. For those of you who haven't heard of legos, they are toys made of different plastic pieces that children use to build whatever they wish.

It is the slowing down of energy that allows matter to be visible and solid. Yet within the body, we still run at a faster frequency. Inside we are the same as we were long before we were conceived: immense amounts of energy worth the fire of billions of suns. What keeps the molecular body together is like a massive forest fire, but we've learned to slow down this energy and contain it as a campfire, so we don't burn our skin, so to speak. We have water and wind to keep us cool. We have air to nourish our lungs. We've learned a powerful balancing act. Now we need to wake up in it.

Once you think about it, the nature of this earth is really quite wonderful. Where else can we find a place where we can ride in a boat or swim in an ocean? A place where we can breathe in this world, go to sleep in another world, and get our spirit to see through both worlds. We can sit. We can stand. We can run. We can eat. We can walk. It's remarkable. Look what children do with it. They want to keep their eyes open all the time because it's so wonderful here. We are living in worlds within worlds. What better design could there be? What more can you ask for? This world is ingenious. But how many times have we thought, "Ah, gee, it's just another day."

You see, life loves life so much. Life is love, and creativity is love. The creativity of life exists all around us. All we have to do is open up our eyes and see it: to have so many different kinds of human beings, to have another day arising—how amazing! Cars going down the streets. Rain dripping down. We can put on different clothes. We can dance. We can do all kinds of things with our faces. We can be sad or happy. We can draw all sorts of pictures. We can put on glasses that help us to see better. What a wonderful opportunity to have electricity to light our world at night when it's too dark to see. And then to have the experience of growing up. "Hey, I'm getting taller. I'm not even doing anything. Wow, look at this. What a miracle!"

We have an opportunity to walk into a wonderful microscopic world here on earth. It's like a microscopic world because matter is extremely condensed. Only through the eyes of a human being can we see the earth from our unique perspective. What spirit can see the earth like a human being sees it? No animal, no insect, no god can perceive as a human can. Not even an angel can see the earth as a human does. An angel sees the earth differently. This is one reason why the crossover communication between spirit and human can be difficult. It is like one species trying to explain something to another species from a totally different perspective. This is also why people have often found it confusing when the saints or various sages have tried to describe life as they see it. These individuals transcended human sight and developed a more spiritual sight.

All perceptions are different. A bear can only perceive the earth through the eyes of a bear. A fish can only perceive the earth through the eyes of a fish. So the earth is viewed from many different perspectives, depending on the development of one's brain, nervous system, wiring, and knowledge. All those who are not human cannot see the ocean as we see it. They cannot see the mountains as we see them. They cannot walk up the stairs in buildings as we do. They cannot draw as we can draw with pencils and paper. Only human beings can do these things. Something to think about.

※ ※ ※

It is much easier to understand the nature of life as a human being than as a spirit. This is because once you pass away, the life after is very potent. The realm of spirit is far more vivid and alive, and you can find yourself going from one dream to the next, one illusion to the next, without even knowing it. In spirit, it is but a dream — a lucid dream — coming and going. One's existence is fluid, transitory, and smoke-like, and it is extremely difficult to wake up. It's hard to hold on to anything in spirit, because everything is so elusive. Whatever your whim or your wish is inside, it becomes real. And then another wish and another whim manifests. Your emotions come and go like the ocean tides that rise and fall or a storm that builds and then dissipates.

When you are in a dream, first you're in one place, then you're in another. Then the scene shifts and you find yourself involved in yet another experience. In spirit it is similar. You cannot hold on to anything, so you move from one picture to the next, from one feeling to another. In the dream state and in the spirit, it is like going to a Broadway play that is very vibrant and real, with the actors and actresses totally involved in the play. Then all of a sudden the lights go off and there is a whole new play. Whoom! You're involved in the action again. Three minutes later, the lights go off once more. Ten seconds later, the lights go on again and there is an entirely different play, with new actors, new customs, and a new story. In spirit it is that captivating.

The paradox is that in spirit it is *so* clear that you are completely immersed in the reality before you. Your spirit radiates Uncaused Light in all directions, and you are simply present with it. What else is there? It is like being underwater in the ocean. You cannot help but be immersed in the water. You cannot help but feel the presence of the water because it's all around you. Now imagine that the water is light, except that the effect of being immersed in this light is much stronger than what you would experience if you were immersed in the water. That is what it's like in spirit.

In our physical world, it is very different. Our opportunities are *immense* because of time. As human beings, we can see what we place on a table and develop trust that it will stay where we put it. We need the kitchen table to stay there and not just walk away. That's the beauty of stability. Have you ever tried to sit in a chair for six straight hours in a dream? It's very, very difficult. Here we can do that. We can hold things and study them. We can stand and talk. We can work things out. We can learn what real love is. We can hold a rose and watch it wilt, and it does not disappear like a dream in our hand as it does in spirit.

In essence, we can see the results of our actions much faster. We are able to witness the effects we have created in front of us. Whether or not the effects are good, the results are there for us to see and to learn from. We also have time to contemplate these results.

If we build a house somewhere, we can trust that it will be there for some time. The mountain stays put. It doesn't just disappear when we wake up in the morning. We're pretty lucky it doesn't. When it does, we know we're dreaming. It's important that we don't suddenly change from one day to the next. Our mothers would go nuts. That is what is so wonderful about this world: there is a reasonable amount of time for us to get it, to wake up, or to accomplish whatever our ultimate agendas are.

In this world of linear time, because things stay in front of us much longer, time is now helping us, not working against us. When I realized this, I befriended time and took advantage of it because I knew it would not last. If we were to suddenly find ourselves in a nonlinear dimension, it would be extremely difficult to change anything about ourselves. We wouldn't have much of a chance. But here on earth where life is linear, it is much easier to change. And that's the blessing of time.

Every second we spend contemplating and utilizing the gift of being alive in this world of time, we are developing a deeper sense of reality. Time is valuable. So we're turning linear time into medicine to help us with this entire process of waking up because time goes with the package of being born here.

Although time is what makes human life so valuable, it is also why there aren't many of us and why it is so difficult to live here. We have to stay and deal with life. But in spirit we can hide, like a loose leaf that is whisked away by a fast breeze. Here on the earth, it is much more difficult to hide. It takes so much courage to constantly deal with the day, with other people, with the bills, with the sunlight exposing everything. Yet by doing so, how much better we become. This is our gift.

* * *

Here is something else to consider. We absorb—learn, grow, experience, and understand life—at an extremely fast rate here in the physical world in comparison to spirit. Why? Life here is impermanent. With anything under the context of impermanence, there is only so much time available. So the day ends, the birthday parties end, the doorbell doesn't continuously ring. Everything has its time and we sense this. All that we do, think, hear, say, and contemplate has its moment and can't last because we go on to the next moment. As a result, all of our processes here burn at a very fast rate, and we learn and grow accordingly.

In this world, we're under an external pressure cooker, so to speak, in relation to survival and our daily lives: our businesses and jobs, our families, our relationships, and so forth. But this is what helps us to learn. Without stress and pressure, we don't learn much. We need exterior motivations besides our own internal motivations to help us grow, accomplish, and see things in a different light.

We're also under an internal pressure cooker. In any given moment, there is so much activity taking place within the body: the constant chemical reactions, the carbohydrates getting eaten up, the manufacturing of hormones, the strategies of the immune system. These internal processes don't stand still. Nothing stands still, just as nothing in this universe stands still. Because our mind is within the body, it is feeling all this simultaneous activity. Our mind is very much at the mercy of how our body is conducting itself, which is reflected in our moods and feelings. As a result, the thought processes of our mind are affected by this time pressure and constant activity within the body.

So within these two environments — internal and external — we are always under two different time pressures. When you consider the vast amount of activity occurring within the body, and combine that with our thought processes as well as the tremendous amount of external activity of a person living life within a twenty-four-hour day, you can see that we take in, feel, see, and experience an immense amount in that period of time.

On the other hand, in spirit, as in dreams, the element of time does not exist. Without a time sequence, the pressure we find ourselves under in the physical world disappears. In spirit, you could think of a twenty-four-hour day as equivalent to a fraction of a second here. As a result, in spirit one is absorbing much less than a second within a twenty-four-hour period, in comparison to someone who is alive in the body and actually absorbing the full twenty-four hours. So the rate of absorbing is very slow for those who exist only in spirit. Even if one isn't involved in any kind of process of waking up, the time here on earth is always precious, for one is still absorbing, learning, and growing.

Keep in mind that I'm just trying to give you a relative idea about the value of linear time, because it's complicated to compare the two dimensions. I can't provide a fixed comparison of what a second in spirit is worth on earth. Why? Because it's always in fluctuation according to one's state of mind, as well as the level of development of one's mind, in each environment — the physical world and the spirit. Time is relative here depending on one's perspective, as it is in spirit.

Still, there is no doubt that every minute I live as a human I grow thousands of times more than I ever can in spirit. A minute on earth is like a thousand years in spirit. Every minute here is worth that much — and even more. I would rather be a human being any day than to be of spirit and not have a human body.

Here we have a chance for our spirit to learn what real spirit is. It's as difficult to realize spirit as it is for a human being to realize life. But the opportunities in our physical world are far greater than in spirit. Life on earth is a most ingenious device, and whoever put this together — I simply call it life — is a genius, compassionate and kind.

Why Am I on Earth?

You have plenty of time to be spirit after your life has ended, but now be here on earth.

So many people today don't want to be human beings, they just want to be "spiritual." But let's use our common sense to reflect on this attitude. We know we were born on this earth. We may live as long as eighty-five or ninety years. That's an extremely short lifetime relative to the billions of years the universe has existed. But after enough time has passed and we've lived on the earth for three or four decades, many of us just want to head toward something better, whether that is spirit, the heavens, nirvana, or bliss. That's where we think the value lies. For most people, the grass always seems to be greener on the other side. They don't like the material world. The material is not good. Many of the world's religions even encourage this way of thinking. But after our lives are over, what are we going to be? A human being or spirit?

If you take away one thing from this book, please remember this: you will die soon enough. We all have to die. And after you die, you can be spirit all you want. You will be spirit for a very, very long time, trust me. And you'll do a much better job of being spirit there than you will here. But you will not understand what it is to be awake in spirit if you play this game of wanting to be spirit while you are a human being. Why? Because you will be dreaming after you die. You will be a dreamer there because you are a dreamer here. Don't you think you already spend enough time dreaming at night? The more you come to terms with the reality of this world, the better you can come to terms with the reality of the world of spirit when you go there. Then you will not be asleep in your own dream, but see spirit for what it is. Now that you are a human being, be a human being first, and you will do well wherever you go next.

It is relatively easy to have one's head in the clouds but difficult to be in one's feet. You have to ask yourself: *"Why in the world was I born as a human being? Why am I here on earth?"* The storms. The clouds and rain. The cold. People yelling. People saying 'no.' People saying 'yes.' Taking my land. Selling my land. Planting. Looking around. Traveling. This to do. That to do. Why am I here, living under the sun, on a planet with gravity that constantly holds me down on the earth twenty-four hours a day? Life must have a good reason to hold me down and keep my feet on the ground. Why am I on earth?" In essence, it is to learn what it is to be a human being, and to get the spirit that you are into your skin.

What if you were to keep your feet on the ground and learn your world very well? You would come to terms with your environment and see it for what it is, whether you like it or not. This is your world. You were born into this world. Look at it. Touch it. Feel it. Be with it. You may not like it, but learn to understand it and make it better. It may be difficult to help others, but try anyway. Put more effort into caring for this world.

How easy it is to die and be spirit. Yet it's so very difficult to be born and to be a human being—to be of spirit and then, because of the strength of our spirit and the fire in our hearts, to be a falling star that dives into the earth, mixes with the waters, the earth, the salt, the silver, copper and nickel, the sticks and stones—and makes the earth stand up. Here we are, the walking earth, with spirit inside. And then to fight the heat, the cold, the dampness. To deal with the tigers and the lions and the demons. To experience loneliness. Nobody calling you. No one knocking on your door. Getting the bills. Having to eat, sweep the floor, and wash the windows. Yet despite all this, to be kind, to love life, to have courage. That's asking a lot.

It is not at all hard to give in to gravity and lie down. Gravity is always working against us, holding us down to the earth. It takes a great deal of courage to stand up against gravity all day long, and even to build in opposition to it with our buildings and skyscrapers. At night we have to succumb to gravity and sleep. But in the morning we get up and do it again. I've learned how difficult it is to be a real human being — to be a body whose bones will tire and whose excitement will come and go.

You know, people think it's a most wonderful thing to channel the spirits. I think it would be a most astonishing thing for a spirit to channel a human being. That would be a real trick. If you were to look through the eyes of a spirit, they would have a field day: "Oh my god, we channeled a human being today!" Really, in most cases it's of little consequence to channel spirit. Besides, discarnate spirits have their own problems, and they don't necessarily have any more clarity than we do here.

Yet the practice of channeling disembodied spiritual beings has become quite a phenomenon among New Age communities. The idea is quite appealing to people. In Santa Cruz, California, where I used to live, channeling is so widespread that among a population of about 200,000, there must be 100,000 channelers! It's phenomenal. Pretty soon a lot of us will be channeling Saint Michael, Saint Francis, and pulling in Mother Teresa. "Wow, I've got purple light running around my feet!" Wonderful. "Hey, I see spirits all day long!" Great. Good for you. "My god, I can channel Jesus!" That's nice. "I have lived in Atlantis dozens of times and I've been the high priestess!" Great, nice for you.

What is interesting is that most of the channeling actually involves people who are just channeling themselves. They've simply allowed something to come through. "So-and-so said it. I just listen. I just speak it." Ah! A little trick of the mind. Yet there are people who actually can channel other spirited beings. But my advice is to be extremely careful if you dive into it.

Years ago I had an encounter with a young woman who claimed that she was the best channeler in northern California. She contacted me and asked for my help because she had been feeling disturbed lately and she wondered if it could be related to her channeling work. She wanted me to "check out her channel," an expression that means, "I want to see if my channel is clear, to see if these beings are really speaking through me."

So I called in a couple of people as witnesses. We all sat down in her room and I said, "Go ahead. Let's do it. Bring in your channel." As the woman went into her trance state, these out-of-the-ordinary streams of colored light started to come down, which indicated that she was a real channel. Then various beings began to come — not just one, but quite a few. I already knew the story that she was channeling a group of individuals. So it was true.

They began to speak. I proceeded to ask questions of these spirits, gradually applying more pressure. This group of spirits had claimed that they were love from the heart. So I asked them to come into my heart. But they wouldn't come. At that point, I said to myself, "Something's wrong."

Then I tried to corner them with some questions, and one of the beings became angry. All of a sudden I heard a voice say, "But she belongs to us!"

"Got you!" I said to myself. Yet right before this, I heard nothing but lovely, benevolent, beautiful words. Because they are not human, they thought that they had gotten away with it, that I didn't hear it. But it was obvious to me.

So I cornered the beings once more and they became angry again. "But she belongs to us!" Ah, got you twice. Then the spirits started talking about love and goodness and the heart. So I told the beings to go away and explained to the woman what had happened.

What was so interesting was that this young woman did not want to hear it. Her investment was too strong, because her reputation made her a "somebody" and her personality did not want to give this up.

"It cannot be like that," she said. "They probably meant something else."

There is one thing to remember. It is extremely easy to be a disembodied spiritual being. And we all will be, sooner or later. It's not a big deal. But to be a human being — *that* is a very big deal. If you could see how precious it is to have a life as a human being, you would start kissing your hands and feet every day.

And whose life is it, anyway? Whose life are you giving up? You're giving up your own life. A lifetime is very precious. It is your life. It's not your mother's, not your father's, it's not Jesus's, not Saint Michael's. *It is your life.*

Watch the children and let them teach you, for they want to touch and see and do everything. There are so many mountains to climb, so many interesting books to read and beautiful places to see. Remember this and don't let your life be ruled by hurt and disappointment or even guilt, because a life is a tremendously valuable thing. Just understand what hurt does. It's all right to get hurt. It's okay to be disappointed. You have to make it all right. Why? Because we are on earth, living as spirited human beings in nature.

In realizing this, you see that problems are just problems, drama is just drama — it goes with the package of being born. Some of us are fortunate and some of us are not. It's all right. But *you're alive.* An opportunity is here for you, because new days come. There is always another hour. Don't let anyone take your life away from you.

Because of hurt and disappointment, we think that the big spiritual aspiration is to get out of this lifetime, *and not to come back.* We think that the goal is to come out of our misery here, our problems on earth, but that isn't it. We come in. We leave. We come in. We leave. A lot of people like to imagine, "Once I die, all suffering will stop. I'll go to heaven and

I'll get my 'badge.' I did it. And I won't have to eat anymore. I won't have to sweep the floor. I won't have to do anything, just live in bliss."

In reality, it's not quite this simple. Just because people have passed away doesn't mean they are continuously immersed in bliss. Some will even continue to sweep the floor. It depends on their dream. It's as if they live out an entire lifetime in this dream until they realize that they have actually passed away and they're not holding a broom as they thought. Then they go into a space where they see more of what the actual spirit is.

You have this lifetime for a very good reason: to be a human being. If you want to detach, you can teach yourself to become light in your feet, let your mind fly way up in the clouds and feel quite detached. In fact, many people have a complete misunderstanding about this. They think that when they practice meditation, or go through a process of waking up, they're going to become more and more "blissed out," go away, and become separated from others.

But what happens when you go into bliss and separate yourself from others? You start to "levitate." You can't work. You can't be responsible for your kids. You can't communicate with ordinary people on the streets. You can easily get yourself into many different kinds of blissful states. But after you die, you'll realize that you missed the point while you were alive as a human being. To learn to be present in one's life is the hardest thing to do, because it can hurt. It is not easy here.

There are very few lamas who have genuine wisdom and a real understanding of life. Most do not. One of the lamas who had it died a few years ago in the south of France. When I met this lama, he said to me, *"Run around the earth as much as you can before you no longer can."* I believe that this lama spent almost forty years in solitude. He did not belong to a particular lineage so he was not recognized by the traditional Buddhist organizations. A lama must belong to a certain "club" to be recognized. But when you met this man, you could see that lineage didn't matter. "Clubs" didn't matter. He understood the nature of what it is to be a human being.

Passing away will come soon enough. But while you are in your feet, the mountains are there for a reason. Your country is there for a reason. Your neighbors are there for a reason. People are there for a reason. Your buildings are there for a reason. Be human as much as possible. Cry as much as possible. Laugh as much as possible. Dance and run as much as possible. Be all the aspects that you can and become rich with as much variety as possible.

When you eventually have to leave, it is your own "sailboat" that will take you into another time and place. Then what have you learned that will help you to be a better sailor? What are you rich with? Have you learned to lay bricks? Have you learned to paint? Have you learned computers? Have you learned to draw? Did you dance well?

It is relatively easy to have intelligence and it's also easy to judge. To develop a wall around us, it doesn't take much hurt. But it does take a lot of courage to understand and to forgive. It takes an awful lot of courage to have mercy. It takes a tremendous amount of courage to embrace fear and ignorance. And what we have learned of courage or forgiveness as a human being — this we can take with us.

Remember that if we follow the nature of life itself, we'll see that everything is in constant movement. Our hearts are pumping blood through our veins, while our nervous systems are sending impulses that move from head to toe in an instant. Massive activity is taking place in the brain. Thoughts are moving at tremendous speeds. Our bodies are fighting bacteria, viruses, and diseases every moment. Constant warfare is taking place inside us.

Is the earth standing still? No. It is moving at great velocities through space. This planet spins around its axis at speeds of almost 1,700 kilometers (km) per hour and revolves around the sun at over 100,000 km per hour. That is about 120 times faster than the speed of a 747 commercial jet airliner. Our solar system rotates around the Milky Way Galaxy at nearly 800,000 km per hour, while our entire galaxy, along with the Local Group of galaxies, is traveling through space at even faster speeds. When you take all these velocities into account, the earth is traveling at speeds of over two million km per hour — 2,333 times faster than a jet! It never stops.

The land beneath our feet is not solid. It is always shifting. The atoms are in constant motion within the subatomic structure of all nature. The sun does not sit still. Our thoughts do not sit still. Not even our children can sit still. Yet we can sit down, relax, and have a cup of coffee while we read the newspaper. It's quite a world, isn't it?

That is why it is important to embrace the culture of the Western world. Embrace the times in which you live. Embrace your work. Embrace your creativity. Embrace your tiredness. Embrace your silence. No matter how fast we go, we are all very still. The beauty of speed, the beauty of silence — all within the same nature. Life is action and life is rest. Life is movement and life is stillness. Life is building homes. Life is sitting down. Life is working at the office. Life is walking home. Take in all of it. Receive as much as you can. Absorb what you can absorb. Embrace your whole life as much as you can all day long, for one day you will have to leave.

Condensing Time

When you find yourself in your heart, condense that moment.

As Westerners, we have a problem. And the problem is that, for most of us, there isn't enough time in the day to even begin to contemplate life, to realize the value of our lives, or the opportunities we have here. We're too busy living. Westerners are a very active people. We're not passive. We have learned to work at a fast pace in our culture. Our brains are traveling hundreds of miles per hour faster than those of the people in the East. If we were in India, I would teach very differently. But we have invested our lives into being active, and that's good. We don't want to get passive all of a sudden. We don't want the phones to stop ringing.

But the fact remains that we really do not have much time for ourselves. We have things to do. The phone is ringing. Someone's at the door. Distractions. We have to be very attentive in this world. We have to pay attention when we're driving cars, to make sure we don't run into people in the streets and cause an accident. We have to pay attention when we're buying bread and milk. We have to keep our flats clean. It takes so much energy just to live. And then once we start having families, our busyness seems to multiply by the thousands.

In fact, there really isn't much time to live an entire life, for most of our time is spent working and striving and arguing and eating and sleeping. Sleeping especially takes up a big chunk of our time. If we spend one-third of our lives sleeping, we will sleep away about twenty-six years, provided that we live to be seventy-eight years old, an average lifespan in Western countries. That leaves fifty-four years of waking time.

Our days are consumed with grocery shopping. Our taxes. The current political arena. What we want. The chores we have yet to do. Our appointments and errands. That little ache in our backs. Sore feet. Have we even thought about how much time we spend paying the bills, cooking, washing the dishes, talking on the phone, and so forth? On the other hand, how much time have we spent with ourselves, reflecting on our lives or trying to understand our mind?

Researchers have actually done surveys on how many minutes, hours, and days we spend waiting in line and doing various activities. If we spend just twenty minutes each day brushing our hair, that amounts over one year of our lives. If we watch television for two hours each day, that totals nearly seven years out of our lives, nearly nine percent of seventy-eight years. All this takes so much time out of our lives — our precious lives.

And what about all the time we invest in our various moods, emotional states, and dramas? "Well, let's see, I've spent at least 2,446 days being angry — over six years of my life. I've devoted 8,712 days — nearly 24 years of my life — to being sad or worrying or just being complacent. What is left?" How many days do we have when everything is fine, like those wonderful Sundays when the sun is out and everything seems to work? We only seem to have a few days of our entire lives to look up into the sky and see infinity and wonder what life is. Most of the time we are too busy looking down at the ground.

What does this mean? It means that we have to take what time we do have and turn it into good, quality time. We have to take our Saturdays and Sundays and condense them, so the weekends become full. We can do that, can't we? Most of us have become very good at it, out of necessity. We've found that the faster we go, the more important our time becomes.

We need to use our intelligence, our intent, and our will to concentrate the little time we do have and compress it, like homeopathic medicine. One of the most beautiful inventions that has come into this world is the science of homeopathy, which involves a very sophisticated and subtle system of healing, designed with a goodness of heart and an intelligence of mind. Homeopathic medicine condenses substances into extremely minute doses to treat various ailments. Throughout our day, we must use an internal homeopathic medicine to concentrate our time so that it becomes more potent.

But what is the price to do this? We can't live out our dramas for hours and hours, like we used to do. We can't hold on to our hatred for weeks, days, or even hours. We can't hold on to our anger or our hurt for months on end. We can't even hold on to our confusion anymore. We can't do this if we are going to concentrate our time. We don't have that luxury. "But wait a minute, I worked so hard to be neurotic!" It's not easy to constantly let go of all these things. But it is worth making the effort in order to concentrate our time and extract more value out of our lives.

When you find yourself in your heart, condense that moment. Any chance you get to understand yourself better—concentrate it. But realize that the phone could ring. Your child could come up and ask a question. You have to condense that moment quickly. And that's all right.

Because time is an illusion: all it takes for a human mind or a human heart to awaken is but a moment — just one quality moment. It's only our perception that makes us think, "No, I need an hour. I need at least twenty minutes."

So in between your aches and pains, in between your wonderful insights, in between the times that you punch in at work, in between answering questions — any chance that you get — speak to life. Connect. Take this quality time that you have just for you, and start to speak into your heart. Remember to speak as if to a good friend. And in time, your voice goes away from speaking only from your mind, and little by little, it begins to speak from your heart. Start to personalize your life in this way. You'd be surprised how personal you are to life. We have been made to feel isolated and alone. My god, I wish I could show you what I see. Life is so full. And your life is just for you. What a precious gift. Don't let your life be ruled by busyness and complacency. Condense time. And respect the gift.

THE GIFT OF LIFE

Life is precious,
too precious to hate,
too precious to be confused,
too precious to be naive,
too precious to be ignorant.

When you lay down your head each night,
realize that every word you speak is precious,
for it could be your last.
Every day is precious.
For after that you have to dream.
Do not devalue your life or your time.

Life is a gift.
It is nothing but a gift.
It is not a right.
How many full moons
do you have left in your life
to learn to use and understand
what the gift is?

THE WINDS OF YOUR HEART

CHAPTER 11

BECOMING A BETTER SAILOR

In essence, I care where you go. And I care how you go.

We all arrived here on some shore. We each came in our own sailboat. Every one of us is a traveler, voyaging from life to life. We love to travel. But some sailboats have many holes in them. Some people are terrible sailors. Some become lost while sailing and don't know where they are going. Their boats are pulled by gravitational-like forces called "karma" and "fate." They think that the winds are free. But they're not free. These individuals don't have a chance to land on a good shore unless they become better sailors.

Wouldn't you like to become a better sailor? A better driver to navigate your way through life? If you look around, you will see so many people who don't have a prayer to become better sailors. But if you learn to be a better sailor in life, this is how you can help others.

The reason we are here is not to experience constant joy and happiness and have everything work out for us. We won't gain anything. It is to temper our own selves. We are here to temper and strengthen our spirits. In doing so, we become better sailors.

As we arrive in our own sailboat, we are tempered by disappointment and hurt and diseases and failures, in addition to the joys and the laughter and all the wonderful things that happen to us. It takes both kinds of experiences on this planet to help us become more. We gain strength by feeling discord and disharmony, and by getting bumped here and there. We need all the difficult times, too, for this is what makes us rich.

We already have all the goodness and wonderful joy that we are. We don't have to worry about that. We *are* this. It is what we *don't* see and what we *don't* understand that can hinder us from becoming better sailors. All the lines on our faces, our hands, and our feet — that is our story. And if our story has brought us to this point in time, which it has, you could say that whatever is inside us is something most wonderful. It is something so divine. We can put our complete trust into this.

You can't stay here long. None of us can. So while you are here, get as much as you possibly can from this life before you are forced out of it. That means allowing yourself to experience all the scars, and when an illness comes, using it to grow and change, if you can. If you lose your money or your business, try to take it well. For it is not how much or how little you have. That is not the point. It is how you stand back up after the setbacks and how you handle the successes that helps you to become a better human being inside.

From a personal point of view, my purpose is not necessarily to make people happier or more successful in their lives. There are already too many good workshops out there that will teach you how to make more money, how to be more positive, or how to polish your personality. My intention isn't to change people, because I understand the predicament: it is so difficult to change anybody. Why? Because you are who you are.

My main emphasis is on your far future, because your future will always come. To realize this is to think as an astronaut. I am not as concerned about your life today or tomorrow, because you are probably going to do what *you* want to do anyway. That's the way we are. So in most cases, there's no use in trying to tell you what to do, because the conditioning has got you by your throat, whether you realize it or not. There really isn't much you can do about it. Besides, *nobody* likes to be told what to do.

What I care about is how you leave. Because that's what is really going to change your life. My main concern is your sailboat, your ship, your little canoe, your rubber raft, or your ocean liner — whatever it is that reflects your spirit — and in what direction it heads. My hope is that you learn to build a better ship, that you become a better sailor, that you have a compass and a map, and that you know where you are going. My concern is also that you become well connected, because so many spirited beings have no connections, no friends to help them along the way.

And when the time comes, I want you to go where *you* want to go. I don't want to tell you where to go. But to be a good sailor, you need a good boat. You need a good, strong wind — not a wind that will deplete you, but a wind that will carry you with joy.

You see, this generation will go by. And where will your sailboat take you? The last generation really did go by. The great-great-grandfathers are gone. Whether it is the year 2,642 BC or 80,208 AD, I invariably find myself in some time, in some place—always alive. It is just a play of numbers, a change of time. If I can find myself alive in a moment of infinity out of the fifteen billion years the universe has existed, I exist on a line of linear and nonlinear time. This moment of existence is almost like a nanosecond — a billionth of a second we exist out of time. Yet each moment resides in infinity.

So in essence, I care where you go. And I care how you go. I care about your future because I have realized that other people in the past cared about my future, even though they didn't know me. There have always been people throughout history who have cared — not just for their own families, but for humanity. They cared that people would have greater freedom, less ignorance, more understanding, and better lives that offered more than a constant struggle for survival. They hoped that others would have more heat in their villages and homes. They looked far ahead into future generations and cared. And just because most people do not care is not the point. If just one person cares, that's what matters. Then there's hope.

I care about you and your future because everybody has the same feelings that I do. We all want to live, to eat, to have friends, to communicate, to seek attention. We all have the same feelings of wanting to be loved and cared for, at times. Wanting to see what is on the other side of the mountain, at times. Not wanting to be hurt, at times. Not wanting not to move from our position, at times. Wanting to yell and scream, at times. Wanting to be understood, at times. Wanting to build or destroy, at times. And because we all have these same feelings, I care. I'm no different than anybody else. Besides, someday you may come across my sons or my great-grandchildren, and I may cross your path one day in the distant future.

In this world, try to become smart as quickly as possible. That does not mean just living out this life with intelligence. One of the most beautiful gifts the Western world has brought to this planet is to learn to respect the future, for your future is important. A life insurance policy for your children, your wife, or your husband is important, so when you do leave, your family will be secure. Their lives will be better. And if you can do that for them, you can do that for yourself, with the big life. Essentially, it's a matter of injecting a different kind of "life insurance policy" into your life.

Dying Alive

Hold it in your heart, make it your intention that if you have to die, you will die alive.

When you lay your head down on your pillow at the end of the day, it's over. There's nothing you can do to turn back the clock. That's a reality. And if that is true for the day, it is also true for your life. When you pass away, it's over. And what did you do with your life? Personally, I make my choices based on the future, not the past. I always ask myself, "When I take my last breath, what am I going to wish I had done?"

Most of us don't realize that we have to pass away. Perhaps a better term would be "to relocate." Intellectually we know it. But it is almost impossible for any human being to realize it. And because it eventually happens, my intent is to give you enough of an education to become a good boy scout or a good girl scout. It is to teach you to pick up pertinent knowledge and information along the way, and to contemplate your life enough so when this event happens—probably the most important event in your life—you are prepared. The time of passing away is a major crossroad in your life. This is the time when you can literally change the direction in which you are naturally headed. My hope is to give you better options at this time.

At the moment of passing away, you have reached another environment where you are no longer bound by gravity. You're no longer bound by your bills, by your job, by what you need to do. And if you are prepared, you have trained yourself to the point that you realize you have total freedom to make a decision about what to do and where to go, instead of just continuing on as you were yesterday, locked up by your emotions, your relationships, or your guilt. It's the transition, the moment before traveling, more than death itself, that gives you this moment of freedom.

To learn to be a good sailor requires the same kind of dedication it takes to become a professor. It's difficult to get around our tendency to live from moment to moment, with our conditioning and our habits. As a result, you need to spend enough time contemplating this. You don't train to be an astronaut in a weekend or a month. It takes years to learn what it will be like to live in a totally different environment. You cannot imagine what it means to be in space unless you actually go up into orbit. But with plenty of training, you can adjust to the new environment as quickly as possible.

You really do not know when the moment of passing away is going to happen, unless you receive a death sentence due to an illness. In this case, you are actually much better off because you know. You can prepare. But most people will never know, and they get caught off guard. They have not prepared for this moment. Always remember that what brought you into your circumstances in this given life is a result of something that happened somewhere deep in the past.

So my intent is to give you a little nudge, a good push, a better sail, a better rudder, a better engine. To give you, in essence, some sense of direction so you become a good sailor when you do pass away. This is the time and place when I know I can capture your attention, because it is going to mean so much to you at this point in your life. I care more for your future than for you at this present moment. And you are going to care more for your future, when the time of death comes, than for yourself at this immediate moment. It's a harsh reality, but that's the way it is.

The future is more important than most people's current lives because the majority of people are not very present or awake in their lives. But when a process of passing away is happening, you become more awake. The "guru" has come. The mind has opened up. When death is taking place, whether it is your own death or someone else is passing away next to you, you become more of a mystic than you ever were in your life. This is a gift to all human beings.

The dying process actually encompasses both the person passing away and the other people in the room. To what extent this process has the potential to affect others varies a great deal according to the consciousness, awareness, and state of the individual passing away—whether he or she is asleep, full of drugs, fully present, and so forth. But the "guru" still comes. When a person is dying, it opens up the channel, and others are affected by it. When someone passes away, it actually alters the light, and it also opens up the crown of everyone's head to some degree, although the one who is passing away opens up the most and has the greatest potential to become more awake. So take advantage of this crossroad, whether it is a friend, a lover, or yourself who has reached it.

When you become a student of life, you will find that to cheat the system is to wake up prior to a bodily death. That's cheating the system. When this happens, you know you will die alive. To cheat the system is the death that all the great sages and mystics talk about. And what do you find? An Uncause. A Saint Francis. A love. A reason that cannot be understood using logic and analysis. You cannot sell it. You cannot stick it in your pocket. You can hardly even speak of it.

Do not be fooled by time. Do not be fooled by situations. For time will come and go as quickly as you have reached the age that you are at this moment. How fast it came. Do not be deceived or let yourself be blind. Realize how short this lifetime is. Prepare.

When most people in this world pass away, they're not only unprepared for this crossroad, but they pass away dead. Too many human beings die dead. Very few human beings die alive. My aim is also to teach people how to die alive, for those who do are very fortunate.

Dying alive is not an easy concept to understand. To die alive, you must work very hard to be more at peace with yourself, with your environment, and with the people around you. When you die alive, you do not rely only on experiences or memories. Instead, you have established a vivid relationship with yourself as well as with this planet. There's a feeling of passion for this relationship that easily lives within you. You have developed some form of consciousness in which you know that you are in a world where there is something more to life than just your life. No matter how you pass away, whether it's by means of a car accident, a bullet, or old age, you still naturally carry this feeling for your relationship with life, this sense that life exists outside of your own life.

The more consciousness you have and the more awake you are, the more alive you are in your passing away. To be in love also helps one to die alive. You can be in love but not have consciousness. Or you can have consciousness and not be in love. But if you have both, it's even better. The highlight of passing away is when you do have both: the consciousness to see, and the love to be the wind. It's rare to have this combination. As the end draws near, most people find that they do not have much passion for life. Most do not even try to hunt for something more to life than what they know or have been taught.

You can be in love not only with a wife, a husband, a lover — but in love with your garden, your home, your town, your grandchildren, the rain, or with life itself. It is not easy to find yourself dying of old age, having lost many of the people you love. But it's often the reality. And if that is the case, it is not the sorrow that becomes the focal point. It is the reality of all those who have passed away, leaving you at the very end of the string. It is the mystery of it all. Yet you had your time when you were with your loved ones. And what did you do with that time? This also reminds you of how precious this life is.

So hold it in your heart, make it your intention that if you have to die, you will die alive. If you have to go to sleep, you will wake up alive. If you have to wake up, you will live your day being alive. For if you can learn to be alive in your own shoes today, you will surely be alive in the next life.

WHAT DO YOU WANT?

Sailors,
with the wind at your back.
Sailors,
know your winds.
For the winds of passion
will take you to a certain place and time,
to find certain people, certain lands, certain parents,
to be raised under a certain environment.
Sailors,
know the winds at your back.
The winds of confusion
will lead you to the lands of confusion.
The winds of hope
will lead you to the lands where there is hope.
The winds of care
will lead your sail to the lands where there is care.
Sailors,
you want war?
The winds of war
will lead you to the lands of war.

Sailors,
what do you want?
Just give it time.
The great farmer,
which is life,
is tilling the soil
for your tomorrows
and for your tomorrows
and for your tomorrows.
Just for you.

The Winds

You created the winds of your heart and your mind that have brought you here.

For one to find this tiny water planet in such a vast universe, one is a good sailor. Yet after finding this world, there are so many people who go into their dreams at night, and they're lost. There are so many people on this planet who pass away, and they're also lost. There are oppressive places and difficult families to be born into on this earth. There are centuries when one can be born in war, in poverty, or in famine. Yet there are many wonderful centuries and beautiful places to be born in, too.

For you see, life is very much like a magnet. All thoughts, all feelings, all actions turn into a particular kind of a metal. And the winds of magnetism at a given time will pull you into a certain direction, although you probably won't even know it. If you found yourself in a good country, with good parents, you're very fortunate. But can you do it again? It's not easy to get reborn in your own land. Some people do. But many don't. It depends on your winds.

If you want to understand these winds better, ask yourself this question: "Once I pass away, what is my means of transportation?" There's always a means of transportation in all realms. Are you going to drive away in a brand new Ford? In a BMW? Does a hawk come down and take you on its wings? Does an airplane come around and pick you up? A UFO? You have to ask yourself these questions. They're very practical, common-sense questions, if you really think about it.

"Well, I have to leave the keys to my car behind. I can't take those. My driver's license is no good. I don't think an airplane or a UFO is going to come by and pick me up. And I'm not going to have my legs anymore. I'm not going to be able to use my mouth to call out to somebody, 'Come pick me up!' So what is my means of transportation?" It is the winds.

Your spirit is somewhat like smoke, as it rises up. You become very light and susceptible to the winds. What are these winds like? Are they the same kind of winds that push the clouds around? The same winds that brush your face as you are walking outside during a storm? No. But they are winds, and as spirit, you are traveling somewhere, in some direction.

What creates these winds? Your feelings, your actions, your imagination, your goodness, your fear, your dreams, your hopes, your lack of hope, your aspirations, your passion, your lack of passion, and the development of your mind and heart. Your whole life is what constitutes the winds. Once the spirit completely leaves the body, the sailor is at the mercy of one's winds.

How have you consciously *lived* your experiences, lived your day? Did you put value into your life? Were you a dreamer or a person whose feet were firmly planted on the earth? Were you a person who was a little touched? How did you look at your friends, your town, or your fellow human beings: was it with good common sense, with good hope — without hatred, malice, or fear? It's how you walked out your life, consciously, that determines the winds, although the moment of passing away has an especially great influence on where the winds take you.

You have to ask yourself, "Will I be in a small rowboat? Will I walk on water? Will I be in a sophisticated sailboat, or a sailboat with holes in it? Will I have a rudder that works or a rudder that's half broken?" You could say that your petrol is also the winds. How much petrol do you have and how far will it take you? Is your boat clean or is it infested with rats? All this is determined by your life.

Remember that you can always change your boat. Everything counts so much. How you live your life, how you take care of your room, take care of your teeth, take care of your thoughts, take care of your feelings, take care of your automobile, take care of your backyard — all of it matters. And it's this maintenance that helps you to become a better sailor. Then how to sail well becomes more natural. This is the training and the preparation.

That is why I'm always trying to teach you: learn to be a human being first. Then when you get on the other side, you will *know* that you are spirit, because you have spent the time knowing what it is to be human. As a result, you will have a surefootedness, something solid beneath your feet, with a strong wind pushing you: your own breath, from your own lungs.

Pay attention to the winds you have created. And if you find yourself in a storm, just know it, and ride out the storm as well as you can. Get to know yourself and your winds. Your mother didn't create them. Your father didn't create them. You created the winds of your heart and your mind that have brought you here. And when one awakens, the winds stop. When one awakens, the storms stop. Life just is.

Your Plan

Learn to love and respect your future. And in time, those winds will start to support you, and you will be guided very differently.

Here's a question for you. We all know we're going to pass away eventually. What are you going to do once you get on the other side? What is your plan? This is how I'm asking you to think. Don't stop your life when the door closes. There's always a future. *What are you going to do?* Carry on, from one day to the next, one life to the next. Carry on.

We know that there are certain people in the world who just fell right into their niche. They found what they came down to do and they took off with it. But most people have no idea what they're doing, where they're going, what their plan is, or why they're here.

So think about this and hold it in your heart: what are you going to do after you leave here? What is good to do? It's like asking yourself as a child, "What do I want to be when I grow up?" Have something inside — a knowingness, a plan, an idea to ignite those winds. What would be good for the environment? What would be good for humanity? What would be good for you? You could have a passion to design a broom, to invent a vacuum, to create a new medicine, to discover electricity — anything to get your plan started. Your plan could simply be to love somebody. Caring for someone is just as good as inventing something. It could be to see the beauty of life. Or to realize that you're alive.

No doubt, your plan will affect the winds at your back that determine where you're going to go. The winds of your intent, as well as the winds of your emotions, your thoughts, your behavior, your attitudes, all slowly start to create a storm behind you. When you get into your sailboat and leave — no matter how big or small your boat — these winds created from your past will come and take you.

What are you going to do? Love life? That's good. Be lost? I don't know about that. Stay lost? Those winds will not be so favorable. Be confused? I don't know if I would do that. Lose hope? It's not so nice when there's no hope, when there are no winds of hope. Give up? When the winds give up, what will fill your sails?

What are you going to do? You don't need to be a great inventor. Just get that sparkle back into your eyes. Live. Life does not ask anything of us at all. All it does is give and give and give to those of us in the sandbox — the earth. What are you going to do in the sandbox? And after you leave the sandbox, what do you want to do?

Don't live just for the day. As a young boy, I remember hearing the story of the grasshopper and the ant — I believe it was one of Aesop's fables. The grasshopper lived just for today. But the ants worked all summer long.

"Why are you working so hard every day?" said the grasshopper. "I mean, just take it easy. Come and chat with me. It's a great day."

"I am helping my family to store up food for the winter," said the ant. "And I recommend that you do the same."

"Why bother about the winter?" said the grasshopper. "We have plenty of food right now." But the ant went on its way and continued its work.

When the winter came, the grasshopper had no food, and found itself dying of hunger, while it watched the ants eating corn and grain from the stores they had collected in the summer. Then the grasshopper knew: It is best to prepare for the days of necessity. It took me a long time to understand the meaning behind that story — about twenty years! Care for your future.

Most people get up in the morning and just live their lives, without thinking much about the future, especially a future that encompasses more than just this life. This future is something that they can't see. They can only speculate about it. Many of us even have a hard time planning for the next year or two. So people basically just let the future go, because they don't think they can do much about it. When it comes to the past, you can't do much except put lotion over your scars, or go to a therapist and talk about it. But your future? That you can change.

But first you need to give your mind as much solid evidence as possible that the past really does affect your future, and that your future really does affect your life. You have the knowledge of who you are today and the memory of what made you who you are: your past. All you have to do is go back into your past and remember everything that happened. Now you can see how a certain mentality or behavior affected your future, and how the future affected you.

"Oh, that's right," your mind will say. "It really did affect my life. If I had known this before or done this differently, my life most likely would be very different today. So how I think today is going to affect the next day and all my tomorrows." That's all the evidence you need.

And this takes you back to your winds. "Why did you take me here? Why did you drop me off here, winds?" They're your own feet. Learn to love and respect your future. And in time, those winds will start to support you, and you will be guided very differently.

As you are looking for the "formula" to become a better sailor, looking for that magic key to unlock those favorable winds, remember this: in reality, you were born with it. We were all born with it. But we have been taught otherwise. We have been taught to feel badly about ourselves. We have been taught that other people are bad, that this world is bad, that life is suffering. We have been taught that we are nothing but sinners. We have been taught to look at life with no hope and no future. We have been taught to embrace defeat. We have been taught to lie. We have been taught to enjoy hurting others. We have been taught to get what we can get. We have been taught "survival of the fittest."

But if you think deeply enough about all these "commandments" that we have been taught, what do they do to help you build your sailboat? Do they help you when you sail away into your dreams at night, into your nightmares, into your confusion, into your beauty, into your fascination, or into nowhereland?

Have the courage not to believe these commandments. They don't work. You have a future. After this life you still have a future. You must fight for your future and have the courage to go against the commandments and philosophies that tear down your self-esteem and this planet. Have the courage to leave this planet with a better future and more hope. You will find your own sailboat getting better, with more hope, which is the wind behind you. And do not only care for yourself. You do have to feed your stomach to survive another day, but slowly, slowly begin to care that everyone becomes a better sailor and has a brighter future with more hope, too.

THE WINDS OF YOUR HEART

YOUR WINDS

In what world, sailor,
in your own sailboat will you go?
What world?
And the sailor says,
"What is my guide? A compass?"
And the sailor says,
"Who's going to blow my sails?
What winds?"

The winds do come eventually to all.
And what has created the winds
that blow into your sail,
is your life.
Your dreams.
Your hopes.
Your clarity.
Your insanity.
Your anger.
Your hatred.
Your joys.
Your quiet moments.
All of it.

And your compass?
You.

THE WAITING

*To show you more of my heart,
more of what I feel inside:
I love life so much.
I love the sun rays hitting the leaves.
I love the wind blowing the flies around.
I love the little pebbles moving in the sand,
washed around by the waters.
I love the clouds, merging and throwing water onto the earth.
I love the light that life has given.*

*For I live in the grace of God.
I can do no more.
I love life,
for life is a miracle,
that gives and gives and gives,
and does not ask for anything.
Life waits and gives.
Whatever you ask in time comes.*

*Life gives the reflections of light
that shine from our foreheads.
Life cushions our feet,
comforts our lives,
soothes our throats,
touches our cheeks with its breath.
Gives us another word, another tool,
to help us with what we wish.
This I love of life.*

*To come down into our hearts a little more,
what would we do?
To touch our hearts
with the fires that life has given us,
what would we do?*

*Life loves us so much.
It provides all the time in the world for us.
Life loves us so much,
for life loves itself,
with grace, with compassion, with understanding
...and waits.*